# Storefront Revolution

# STOREFRONT REVOLUTION

## Food Co-ops and the Counterculture

## CRAIG COX

RUTGERS UNIVERSITY PRESS

New Brunswick, New Jersey

*Library of Congress Cataloging-in-Publication Data*

Cox, Craig.
   Storefront revolution : food co-ops and the counterculture / by
Craig Cox.
      p.   cm. — (Perspectives on the sixties)
   Includes bibliographical references and index.
   ISBN 0-8135-2101-7 (cloth) — ISBN 0-8135-2102-5 (pbk.)
   1. Cooperative societies—Middle West.   2.  Food industry and
trade—Middle West.   3.  Subculture—Middle West.   4.  Social
movements—Middle West.   I. Title.   II. Series.
   HD3446.A3A143   1994
   334'.68413'00978—dc20                                       93-45522
                                                                    CIP

British Cataloging-in-Publication information available

*To Sharon, Nora, and Martin*

# CONTENTS

# PREFACE

Writing a history of something so ephemeral as a "movement" is not a task one takes up eagerly. A movement, after all, is simply a collection of people, ideas, dreams, and practices knit together by circumstances largely beyond anyone's control. Trying to chronicle the activities of such a convulsing collection of emotions and consequences—much less analyze or interpret it—is a bit like drawing a picture of a thundercloud. Not only are there hundreds of ways to picture it, but it's constantly changing shapes, and you've got a good chance of getting rained on while you do it.

Compiling a history of the co-op movement is especially daunting. Though there were some fundamental theories that defined it and a few leaders whose personalities and influence provided the sorts of clues necessary for a writer to get a grasp on the movement's purpose and direction, the co-op community that evolved here did its best to confound any observer who attempted to place it in some well-worn political or countercultural box. People came and went almost as regularly as customers at the till, leaders bloomed and wilted like dandelions in spring, and the mission behind the movement varied widely, depending upon who was talking at any given moment.

Although much of what I cover here involves the food co-op network that sprouted so successfully in the Twin Cities, the movement encompassed much more than these ragtag community-owned grocery stores. It embraced every alternative enterprise promising "revolutionary" change, from worker-owned restaurants and rural communes to tenant-owned housing co-ops and a wide range of "collectively" run businesses. What held them all together was a fervent belief in sustainable, community-based economics, and a desire on the part of workers and consumers alike to wrest control of their lives from the forces of capitalism, imperialism, and materialism.

Those motivations certainly helped to define the movement—as it developed both here and elsewhere across the country in the 1970s. But they seemed so self-evident to those of us active in the movement that I never intended to commit much energy to analyzing them. In fact, when I began my research in 1978, my intention was simply to unravel some of the mysteries behind the much-discussed "Co-op War" that had crippled the co-op network three years earlier. Though I had worked for a student housing co-op and had been active in NASCO (the North American Student Cooperative Organization) since 1975, I'd followed the Co-op War from afar. Only upon joining the collective that published the local co-op newspaper, the *Scoop*, had I begun to learn of that conflict's intricacies—and the mysteries that surrounded it. Everyone I talked with about the war wanted to know who was really behind the reformist faction that had stormed the beloved Peoples' Warehouse, attacked several stores, and allegedly threatened the lives of co-op leaders. Who were these Stalinist yahoos who were messing up a perfectly lovely countercultural economic system that seemed capable of carrying its devotees comfortably into a politically correct old age?

It took nearly fifteen years before I discovered any credible information about the organization instigating the reform movement and the man who ran it. Much earlier, though, it became clear that the war itself was only part of the story that needed to be told.

The war ripped apart much of what the movement's leaders had built and resulted in a dramatic reevaluation of the ideas and motivations upon which the movement had depended for its development, but when the smoke cleared, not much had changed. The community's values remained pretty much the same as they had been all along. Its mission continued to be centered internally (on personal growth) rather than externally (on social and political revolution). For this observer, at least, the question that remained to be answered centered less on who prosecuted the war than on why such a struggle (and the ones that followed) was inevitable. Why are such self-centered social and political movements fated to collapse?

Although much of this history focuses on the events and people that characterized the war over the Peoples' Warehouse, its chief mission is to paint the sort of movement portrait that will give outsiders some sense of what it was like to be a part of its swirling, cacophonous growth, and bittersweet demise. In the process, I hope to describe how that movement borrowed from earlier movements for social change and how it affected revolutionaries beyond the Twin Cities co-op community.

I can't profess objectivity in this exercise, but I can say with some certainty that whatever biases are evident here come from an evolution in my own thinking about the co-ops, the political left, and my onetime devotion

to both. While mired in the inconsistencies and hyperbole of these movements in the mid-1970s, I believed fervently that the concept of cooperation, as embodied in worker- and consumer-owned enterprises, would
eventually have a small impact on the way our society functioned. The Co-
op War, to my mind, had been an unfortunate interruption in what many of
us saw as a slow but ultimately successful campaign to bring cooperatives
into the American mainstream in a way that hadn't happened since the
1930s and 1940s.

From my perspective outside the food co-op network in 1975, the war
seemed mostly bizarre. Revolutionaries, after all, were supposed to be
united against the forces of mainstream society. Few of us neophytes understood that the Left was riddled with factional disputes at the time. Indeed, at a time when the "Movement" (a slightly ostentatious label that
served as a catchall for every fringe idea traveling the revolutionary turn-
pike of the times) had become more accessible than ever before, young
radicals like myself had a good deal of difficulty figuring out the political
ground rules. Was communism still considered the best hope of an oppressed working class? Was Marxism relevant to an army of radicals pos-
sessed by a blissful love affair with the counterculture? I considered myself
fortunate, under the circumstances, to have encountered the co-op movement as a journalist. My work with the network's newspaper, the *Scoop*, allowed me to taste its many flavors and assemble my own opinions in what I
thought at the time was a thoughtful manner.

Unfortunately, by the time I eased myself into this journalistic exercise,
most of those who had played important roles in the conflict had disappeared. Those who remained active—Dave Gutknecht (with whom I
worked on the *Scoop*), Annie Young, Susan Shroyer, Kris Olsen, Chuck
Phenix, and others—represented only one side of the argument. As a result, the portrait of the Co-op War that emerged in the *Scoop* was hardly
kind to those who fought to steer the movement away from its mission of
personal liberation and alternative economics toward one with revolutionary political goals.

The more I learned about the war and the longer I stayed in the food co-
op movement, however, the more I came to understand why the conflict
was inevitable and why the movement now no longer exists. Where I once
looked on the movement's critics as misguided, power-crazed dogmatists, I
gradually began to see them in a more favorable light. Many of them had

helped to build the network in the first place, and in their love for that creation strove to keep it pure. Their actions, of course, were inexcusable when they weren't ludicrous, and the hate and fear they inspired will always stain their legacy, but the lessons they taught about the real Left woke a lot of us up to a more realistic view of the world.

Eventually, I found myself editing the newspaper and working for the All Cooperating Assembly, the federation created after the demise of the Peoples' Warehouse. There, the biases and narrow-mindedness that had come to characterize the movement became ever more obvious, and the motivations of those who fought to transform the co-ops seemed to me to become less and less purely evil.

If asked to cast my vote with one camp or the other, though, I'm afraid I'll always feel more akin to the anarchistic co-op pioneers with whom the reformers fought so fiercely. Their humor, creativity, resiliency, and spunk shaped me in ways I still haven't completely grasped during the decade since I left the movement. The values they taught allowed me to enter the real world without worrying about being swallowed whole.

Indeed, for all the cold political theory and nasty sectarianism that formed the basis for this book, writing it has been mostly a labor of love. That's not meant to defuse criticism, for I suspect there is plenty to criticize here; it's simply meant to remind myself as well as the reader that, for all its flaws, the co-op movement taught me lessons I will use the rest of my life. The eight years I spent in the movement's embrace were golden ones, and no matter what indictments seem to issue from these pages, they are indictments of minor offenses when compared to the greater good most of us derived from our participation in this peculiar campaign.

More than anything else, that's really why I wrote this book. I figured that, after giving so much to so many over the years, the co-op movement and its accompanying alternative culture needed to be acknowledged, to be remembered for what it once was.

*—Minneapolis*
*June 1993*

# ACKNOWLEDGMENTS

I need to extend my thanks to several people without whose assistance and encouragement this project never would have been completed. My wife, Sharon Parker, whose devotion to historical research made her a much more qualified candidate for this project than I, spent more than a dozen years quietly cheering me on. My former co-op colleague Kris Olsen, for whom the co-op idea remains alive, if not always healthy, provided greatly needed assistance and cooperation throughout the course of my writing. Co-op veterans Dean Zimmerman, Terry Hokanson, Annie Young, Evelyn Roehl, and others provided invaluable assistance by entrusting me with their bales of co-op meeting minutes, fliers, newsletters, and other sources of information. The story could not have been told without them.

To the dozens of reporters, editors, and production and distribution volunteers who somehow got the *Scoop* newspaper out the door every six weeks or so throughout its brief but noble life, I extend my heartfelt gratitude. Nowhere else was the co-op movement so faithfully chronicled during its heyday than in those pages, and its contribution to this history—indeed to my own journalistic career—cannot be overemphasized.

Finally, a word of thanks to all of you who dared dive into the co-ops during the past two decades. History, after all, is composed of people—in this case an army of wildly idealistic, naive, excitable, dogmatic, bizarre, refreshing, exasperating, thoughtful, visionary, and, most of all, pleasantly revolutionary individuals whose actions over the course of my own life in the movement never failed to generate some electricity. Thanks for the spark.

# Storefront Revolution

# CHAPTER ONE

## Dancing on Dogma

Of the myriad social and political crusades given birth during the era we've come to call the sixties, it's hard to imagine events, ideas, and characters more outwardly pragmatic than those that comprised the cooperative movement. Yet, having traveled inside the movement for several years myself, I can at the same time imagine no other cause more utopian.

Planted with hybrid seeds from what was known to many as simply the Movement, the co-op idea sprouted in fertile pockets from coast to coast in the late 1960s and early 1970s. Ostensibly, these new-wave co-ops—like their old-wave predecessors of the 1920s and 1930s—were economic entities, consumer-, or in some cases, worker-owned businesses designed to provide goods and services. They looked a little different maybe than the basic mom-and-pop grocery store or neighborhood bakery or bookstore, but they were, in many ways, simply an extension of the reliable supply-and-demand concept so central to our free enterprise system. What set the co-ops apart from every other radical and pseudoradical enterprise of the times was the remarkable notion that these stores could sustain a revolutionary network that would outlast the Vietnam war, the draft, and bell-bottomed jeans.

Plenty of movements promising radical change leaped from this era, including campaigns on behalf of women, gays and lesbians, Native Americans, consumers, and the environment. Some of these continue to labor against the forces of intolerance and injustice even today. None provided much in the way of sustenance to its devotees, however, insofar as success in these movements could be measured by legislation, electoral politics, lawsuits, and other mostly administrative standards. All had glorious visions of a world unalterably changed for the better, but even their dreams

1

fell short somehow when put up against the graceful concept of the "cooperative commonwealth," an idea that to one degree or another drove every cooperator happily to and from work each day.

The co-op commonwealth was a rather quaint nineteenth-century vision borrowed from any of a number of pioneers who themselves used it to build the original cooperative movement during the early days of the Industrial Revolution. Only the most dedicated of these new-wave co-opers bothered to peruse the works of co-op gurus James Peter Warbasse, or Robert Owen. Indeed, few were aware that the principles of consumer cooperatives—democratic control and the return of profit to its members—did not emerge from the writings of Karl Marx, but were established in 1844 by twenty-eight weavers in Rochdale, England.[1]

Nevertheless, the commonwealth idea—the notion of a self-sufficient network of cooperatively owned enterprises serving the common good—was pervasive. It was manifested in various ways, of course, but just about every co-op organizer in the 1960s and 1970s entertained some variation of this utopian vision. For some, it may have involved nothing more daunting than creating a sort of alternative chamber of commerce in their city—a clearinghouse for information on local social and economic experiments. For others, the commonwealth had no limits, incorporating organic farms, grocery stores, distribution systems, homebuilders, natural healers, and hippie lawyers—all connected by a spiritual, cultural, and economic fabric woven from shared experiences and beliefs.

These days such a concept may seem quixotic, but anyone swept away by the sixties can tell you that, for a while, just about anything seemed possible—or at least worth trying. Many of the new-wave co-op pioneers had already compiled healthy résumés from earlier political or social movements, campaigns for civil rights or against the Vietnam War, for instance, that had met with enough short-term success to keep their adrenaline pumping, but promised no long-term nourishment. It was the long-term prospects that eventually attracted them and so many others to the co-ops.

For all of their excitement and cultural transcendentalism, the sixties were hard on people. By the time of the Kent State murders and U.S. incursions into Cambodia in May of 1970, many Movement veterans wondered whether another mass demonstration really would be worth the effort. Prospects for radical political reform had died with Bobby Kennedy and had been further squashed by Mayor Daley's police force at the 1968 Democratic National Convention. If you couldn't change American society via the ballot box or one more giant demonstration, then why not retreat and create an alternative of your own? If the world was so out of control, why not do everything possible to take control of your own life?

Dropping out of society, of course, was a popular notion long before the first contemporary food cooperatives opened their doors in the late 1960s. The entire countercultural experience that so spiced the era was essentially a material manifestation of the dream of ignoring the insanity perpetrated by the established culture. To some degree, escapism was as much a political statement as participating in an antiwar demonstration. The personal had become political long before Ho Chi Minh or Che Guevara became countercultural icons.

As early as 1962, Tom Hayden and the founders of Students for a Democratic Society (SDS) were expressing the view that what you did with your life had political connotations. The Port Huron Statement, written by Hayden and considered the manifesto of the New Left, called explicitly for an end to the "depersonalization that reduces human beings to the status of things." Implicit in its challenge was an understanding that the new radical should not simply chase political reform but rather pursue a complete social metamorphosis.[2]

The manifesto, Sara Evans explained in her ground-breaking work on the feminist movement "represented a fusion of the personal and moral optimism of the southern civil rights movement with the cultural alienation of educated middle-class youth."[3] It was another five years before the "personal is political" assertion emerged as a central focus of the new women's movement, but it clearly informed much of the development of the counterculture and New Left political activity throughout the decade.

Intimately entwined with that notion was a desire—especially after the end of Vietnam War—to deal with what Theodore Roszak called the "intelligent compromise" that radicals were forced to make as they looked to their own futures.

How do people who have refused to buy into mainstream American attitudes and values "grow up?" he asked.[4] "SDS offers no long-term livelihood, nor does SNCC [Student Nonviolent Coordinating Committee], nor CORE [Congress of Racial Equality]. And damned if you'll make that intelligent compromise! But you are 25 and there are 40 or 50 years ahead (if the bomb doesn't fall) and they must be shared with home and family, and be buoyed up by dependable subsistence or that future will be a gray waste and the consciousness of life you want to expand will shrink and become bleak. So how do you grow up? Where is the life-sustaining receptacle that can nourish good citizenship?"

The answer, Roszak argued, lies in building communities and enduring friendships, to make your living through "honorable and enjoyable labor" and make ends meet through "mutual aid." Unfortunately, he also admitted, there weren't any models.

"The old radicals are no help: They talk about socializing whole economies, or launching third parties, or strengthening the unions, but not about building communities," he wrote, adding that perhaps we need to look toward Native Americans, utopian precedents, Israeli kibbutzim, or the Hutterites. "Maybe none of them will work. But where else is there to turn?"

 By the 1970s, thousands would turn to the co-op movement, which embraced that notion of community and personal politics with astounding vigor and extended it just about as far as was economically, socially, and politically feasible. The co-op stores were created, first of all, as a perfectly logical response to the demand among young radicals for the goods and services necessary for living a life outside the established economic system. In a network such as the one that evolved in Minneapolis and St. Paul, for instance, the well-connected revolutionary would have purchased groceries at the neighborhood food cooperative, set up digs in a tenant-owned housing co-op or informal commune, and earned a living as part of a worker-owned or worker-managed business. The kids played at parent-run child-care centers while Mom and Dad were at work. If somebody got sick, the community clinic provided health care for free or on a sliding fee scale. For recreation, there was a movement-wide softball league, lectures and workshops on the issues of the day, concerts and films organized by brothers and sisters in the community of radicals, and plenty of opportunities for informal chatter at the local worker-owned coffeehouse/restaurant.

It was, at its peak, an extraordinary network of life-sustaining options for the revolutionary determined to survive and prosper (spiritually, at least) outside the mainstream society. It enabled thousands of people to make the personal political statement that Hayden and other SDS founders had envisioned years before.

That the co-op movement lacked political cohesiveness and ideological discipline is well documented. Some critics argued that the proliferation of food co-ops could not even be called a movement, since the goals and strategies varied widely from store to store and region to region. Some wanted simply to sell good food cheaply; others wanted to challenge the supermarket industry; still others wanted to mobilize and empower neighborhoods to take control of their destinies.

In a 1975 study of food co-ops, Daniel Zwerdling argued that the co-ops were too independent, too loose politically to constitute what we normally think of a movement. "While most food co-ops agree on what they are declaring their independence from—the oligipolistic supermarket industry—they sharply disagree on precisely what kind of food system they want to establish and what kinds of goals they want to pursue instead," he noted.[5]

What Zwerdling overlooked in this analysis was the fact that the co-op movement was not built on food policy or even on economic issues—the foundation of this movement was constructed from an almost religious belief in the value of personal and community empowerment. Nearly every food co-op in the Twin Cities hosted debates about what the store should sell, how the profits should be divided, and what the network should do to make the world a better place. What was never questioned was the value of mutual aid, the notion that people working together would strengthen the community as well as the individual. "We can do it better," was the rallying cry.

The movement also was explicitly nonviolent in its strategies for liberation, a direction that diverged sharply from the path most revolutionaries had chosen to follow in the post–SDS years. While police repression and political disasters sent the most serious activists in search of new, more militant tactics in the early 1970s, many other, similarly serious, radicals concluded no amount of gunfire or bomb-throwing would bring down the system. They would simply have to build a system of their own.

During its seven tumultuous years, SDS managed to link radical political activists with members of the counterculture around issues of war and peace, and around the general insanity of technocratic society, but its campaigns always attracted a strong ideological component from among the New Left. By 1966, members of the Progressive Labor party, a Maoist-oriented faction of the American Communist party, had become an influential block in SDS.[6] They were joined by Black Panther party sympathizers, feminists, GI organizers, as well as the ubiquitous hippies, represented by Abbie Hoffman's Youth International party (Yippies) and a Detroit-based group called the White Panthers.

Eventually, disagreements over ideology, direction, and constituency tore the organization apart, and by 1969 the larger youth movement SDS had so eagerly sought to represent had fractured into a collection of wayward fringe groups dedicated either to the violent overthrow of the United States or to the building of a working-class party. Each had its own constituency, or perceived constituency: Progressive Labor sought to organize the industrial working class, the Black Panthers the black proletariat, the Yippies and White Panthers looked to the hippies, and the Revolutionary Youth Movement (RYM)/Weatherman faction saw the counterculture and young white working class as the key to revolutionary mobilization.

According to Ronald Fraser, this move toward violence was a direct response to the 1968 Chicago debacle. The refusal of the Democratic Party to transform itself into an antiwar, progressive political force threw everything the New Left had represented into a fanatical mode, characterized by a commitment to a "regurgitation of the Marxist formulation of the working class."[7]

There are other explanations, as well. Young radicals in the late 1960s were almost universally convinced that the "system" was about to collapse and that revolutionary crusades best defined one's personal and political future. "Such beliefs solved the problem of personal choice by obliterating it," Jack Whalen and Richard Flacks explained.[8] This frame of reference defined commitment as total absorption in self-sacrificing collective action. "Do not worry about becoming an adult, the argument went, with all the moral ambiguities and problematic decisions that would entail—there would be no possibility of normal life in an apocalypse."

The apocalypse never quite arrived, of course, and as less committed radicals deserted the revolution for more satisfying pursuits, those who stayed behind increasingly required a strong, hard-line political discipline to sustain their own beliefs. After all, Whalen and Flacks note, "The party promised explanations for past failure, and assurances about history's course, that helped members cope with political frustration and uncertainty. Its hierarchical structure offered the promise of a political leadership capable of special wisdom that could effectively distill collective experience. In addition to political stability and direction, such parties implicitly promised personal solutions. All provided members a chance to embark on stable—and even conventional—everyday lives, while simultaneously assuring them that their activity, however mundane it might appear, had revolutionary historical significance."[9]

Ronald Fraser argues, however, that most of the more peacefully radical of the New Left's ideas were trashed in the revolutionary process. "The American student movement had long prided itself on its combination of ends and means, participatory democracy as a goal and form of organization. The demands of revolution, however, seemed to dictate a different structure and different principles."[10]

For most of the thousands of devoted radicals nationwide, violent revolution made for scintillating coffeehouse discussion, but it never really represented a viable path to the political promised land. There were plenty of reasons to be disgusted about America, but there was little to justify taking up arms and putting one's life in peril—especially in light of the beating revolutionaries were taking at the hands of police and soldiers all over the country. To be part of the armed insurrection required a courage and discipline few leisurely revolutionaries could muster. To do so meant leaving behind the successes the larger movement had already gained—a new sense of community, a life style that transcended the blandness of established culture—and replacing it with a life entirely devoted to the futile pursuit of a Marxist-Leninist (or Maoist) working-class revolution.

The reality of that life was not particularly attractive. Weatherman members, Fraser notes, were subjected to "an intense process of self-transformation in which every aspect of personal life, from eating habits to family relationships, was subjected to intense scrutiny."[11]

Such scrutiny took place inside the new co-op movement as well. Converts were generally expected to eschew the trappings of the prevailing materialist culture and to defer, at least publicly, to the vegetarian leanings of movement leaders. There were plenty of people with narrow-minded political and countercultural biases operating in the co-ops, but none of them required the total personal transformation demanded by a cadre organization such as Weatherman. It was revolution made easy.

Though the co-op movement would take its share of jabs from allegedly more principled revolutionaries in the first decade of its growth, those in the middle of the movement could argue just as persuasively for their particular brand of revolt as could any rifle-waving Weatherman. Indeed, by the time SDS disintegrated there were great masses of self-proclaimed revolutionaries across the country (one million on college campuses alone in 1970, according to a *Fortune* magazine survey) who believed armed insurrection was madness and for whom co-ops represented a middle road to liberation.

Sit-ins and mass demonstrations made great headlines and radicalized thousands of people in the 1960s, but street fighting never held much allure. Weatherman's much-ballyhooed "Days of Rage" in October 1969 drew only six hundred people to Chicago—not the "tens of thousands of youth they hoped to rally to tear apart Pig City."[12] As much as the Movement needed to be redirected away from political reform tactics after Chicago, there was certainly no consensus to move toward guerrilla fighting.

Where was the principled leftist to turn? The traditional left-wing political groups had withered and died by the time this new army of revolutionaries was ready for action, and there were no well-established networks for activists looking for jobs. They had to create their own roles, their own organizations, their own futures.

Many of these wayward revolutionaries directed their attention toward community development, neighborhood organizing, and mutual aid efforts. The Black Panthers had already demonstrated their effectiveness in operating food drives and other neighborhood services in Oakland, California, and elsewhere. In Minneapolis and St. Paul, and in other major metropolitan areas, neighborhood groups came together to draft pragmatic, long-range development plans. Not surprisingly, co-ops began to sprout as well.

The proliferation of the movement in Minneapolis–St. Paul and throughout the Upper Midwest was not particularly surprising. The state had proven to be fertile ground for co-op organizing since the turn of the century, when Finnish miners on the Iron Range came together to create their own stores.[13] Dairy farmers were organizing cooperative creameries around the same time. By the 1930s, co-ops had become a fixture on the rural scene throughout the Upper Midwest. The region also was home to a long tradition of progressive politics.

In the sixties, the Twin Cities already boasted a strong radical community from which the new co-ops could draw energy and support. Antiwar/antidraft organizing was flourishing both on and off the various college campuses that dotted the landscape, and patches of countercultural activities were sprouting as well. Once the co-op idea caught hold, it spread with remarkable speed.

There was, however, never a strong consensus on the Left about the movement's role in the larger crusade for a new society. Advocates of the hard-line Marxism that characterized the remnants of the New Left after SDS split certainly had little interest in co-op organizing. Historically, socialists have had some enthusiasm for the co-op model, but Marx had argued that "restricted to the dwarfish forms into which individual wage-slaves can elaborate it by their private efforts, the cooperative system will never transform capitalistic society."[14]

Still, local Marxists-Leninists did devote an inordinate amount of attention to the Minneapolis-based movement. The co-ops, after all, represented a vehicle by which a segment of the working class could be reached—but only if the escapist, anarchistic enclaves were reshaped into disciplined neighborhood stores designed to promote a political program. From 1974 to 1976, the anarchists who dominated the movement sparred with Marxists over the mission and strategies of the co-ops. Skirmishes that began with a flurry of contesting political position papers and formal debates escalated eventually into a full-blown Co-op War that featured the occupation of the central warehouse and various co-op stores, as well as life-threatening displays of violence between people who, only a few months earlier, had been comrades in the struggle to transform American society.

On the surface at least, the issues fueling the Co-op War involved questions of the movement's purpose. The stores, many of which were located in poor, inner-city neighborhoods, should be selling products regular folks used rather than catering to a health-conscious elite. Bring the working class into the stores, reformers argued, educate them about the capitalist system, and build a working-class revolution. Without that mission, they claimed, co-op leaders were just playing store.

Beneath the surface were larger issues, questions about the future of the Left in America. The co-op movement, like SDS before it, had successfully linked political and countercultural elements and was attempting in its own inarticulate way to maintain that alliance through an economic, rather than political, entity. Society would be changed, co-op leaders argued, individual by individual, neighborhood by neighborhood, through cooperative empowerment. It would be a revolution without guns, without dogma; a revolution that always valued the individual over political parties, people over profit, peace over provocation.

This anarchist-versus-Marxist debate is as old as *Das Kapital* and the *Communist Manifesto*, but its reemergence as an issue in the co-op movement illustrated more than anything else the failure of Old Left ideology to adapt to New Age demands. For all their political fuzziness, the anarchists who pioneered the new-wave co-op movement in the Twin Cities still wanted to create a revolution. Simply because they eschewed traditional Marxist dogma and rhetoric, this didn't mean they were unimpressed by its ideology.

The notion of subordinating oneself to any political party—or, indeed, to any political ideology—made no sense to a generation of radicals who had spent the past two decades watching heroes and heroines of the civil rights and antiwar movements risk their lives in defiance of what they had come to believe was illegitimate authority. Illegitimate or not, authority of any kind was looked upon with great suspicion by most of those radicalized during the sixties—most certainly by those anarchists who built the co-op network in the Twin Cities. The failure of the co-op reformers to grasp this fundamental characteristic of the movement served only to further demonstrate the inadequacies of the American Left since the demise of SDS.

Such developments as the rise of a new communist movement and the beginnings of a democratic-socialist political alternative (chiefly through the New American Movement, which was founded and based in Minneapolis) never really meshed very well with the post–SDS realities that nurtured the co-op movement. It wasn't that the new co-ops weren't politically motivated—they were; but the politics were defined differently. Co-op organizers weren't trying to build a working-class movement (though they wouldn't have discouraged such a result), nor were they much interested in changing the system through electoral politics (though that wouldn't be such a bad thing, either). The politics of the new cooperative movement borrowed more from the counterculture than from Weatherman. They were the politics of personal choice and freedom, spiritual awakening and liberation. Everything else—electoral politics, distribution of wealth, class warfare—was secondary.

Cooperators still talked of revolution, and marched when necessary against the enemies of the people, but they believed the real revolution was to be played out internally: a battle to overcome the conformity, apathy, and powerlessness the system instills in each of us and to transform oneself into a free, empowered individual.

The external revolution, then, became more of an evolutionary process. The system would only be toppled when enough citizens liberated themselves from its bankrupt values and reshaped society. It would be incorrect to call this a strategy, because there was no such thing as an orchestrated co-op strategy, but the emergence of co-op food stores and the network that supported them is convincing evidence of an evolutionary—not revolutionary—program.

The neighborhood food co-op would never foment a working-class uprising, but it could serve as a haven for veteran radicals, provide a liberating experience for neophyte revolutionaries, and even introduce the notion of community-based economics to otherwise unempowered citizens.

To do so, however, these co-op pioneers were forced to confront not simply the political contradictions noted by their cousins on the Marxist-Leninist left, but also the tensions inherent in the counterculture that so shaped their own values. Though celebrated by its members as an avenue to liberation, the counterculture by the late 1960s was neither easily defined nor particularly accessible. For some, entrance was gained through shared pseudocriminal experiences (illegal drugs) or through other conscious lifestyle choices (communal living, vagrancy, sexual promiscuity). As a result, the Movement's more noble values, those characteristics that motivated early co-op organizers, did not develop in the majority of those who lived the alternative life-style.

Indeed, one of the difficulties SDS encountered in organizing its counterculture constituency was its members' waywardness and lack of initiative, focus, and direction; character flaws that were abundantly evident among cooperative pioneers, as well. Though many put in long hours and remarkable energy to create and maintain the stores, volunteers and paid staff came and went with alarming frequency. Like any countercultural trend of the time, co-ops attracted an army of self-obsessed troops, eager to do battle with the established way of doing things—so long as their curiosity held out.

Drawing as they did from this pool of footloose cultural revolutionaries, the co-ops could hardly be expected to exhibit anything but a fuzzy sense of direction. After all, the counterculture was all about experiencing life in ways that freed people from the oppressive chains of convention. How do you run a business when freedom and personal expression are the chief goals?

The answer, of course, is that you cannot—unless you confine the opportunities for such liberating pursuits to areas that have no bearing on the bottom line: community meetings, lax or nonexistent work rules, consensus decision-making, an antimaterialist philosophy, and a happy-go-lucky workplace in which no one is in charge. These sorts of features helped the early co-ops capture wide support from those who considered themselves part of the counterculture.

Behind those liberating features in each co-op, though, stood a small core of players who, notwithstanding their belief in community empowerment, maneuvered their store around the daily obstacles every business encounters. They paid the bills, ordered the products, counted the money, kept the books, and generally made sure the doors opened every morning. Theirs was still a revolutionary experience, inasmuch as they brought to work with them a sense that they were part of a major social transformation, but their sense of mission was more focused than that of the countercultural troops who arrived at their co-op's doorstep looking for a brief transcendental experience.

Nevertheless, the co-ops couldn't have been born without their countercultural allies. They provided eager workers, a major source of customers, and instant credibility within the larger movement. Still, their participation presented a daunting challenge to the radical entrepreneurs who built the co-op network.

It was its alliance with the counterculture, in fact, that made the movement so odd. It was escapist, naive, flighty, at times inane. Its love of economic experimentation—turning the cash registers around to have customers check themselves out; proposing a co-op monetary system—seemed to know no bounds. Its self-conscious political posturing was remarkably pretentious. Such blemishes were part and parcel of the era, however. All the movements that emerged in the 1960s were guilty to some degree of overindulgence. The paths they were following, after all, had few signposts, and the directions they were given mostly were ignored.

The alternatives offered by Marxist-Leninist and Maoist fringe groups, the recycling of nineteenth-century political dogma and self-destructive visions of armed insurrection were no less naive, no less indulgent. Worse, they had already been tried and proven unsuccessful.

More than anything else, the sixties taught those in its grasp that the old solutions weren't relevant anymore. Something new was needed. For the new co-op pioneers, that meant reinventing culture, economics, relationships—everything that had been soiled by the prevailing powers. Old Left theories and strategies were almost as much a part of that stifling power structure as television and the military-industrial complex.

The cooperative movement would be built from scratch, without an instruction book. It would be pieced together with different-sized nails and boards that didn't match. It would be a movement without party lines or dogma, in which the pursuit of individual liberation ruled supreme. You can bring your manifestos and your Little Red Books to the dance, the cooperators said, but you'd better be prepared to hear a brand-new tune.

# CHAPTER TWO

---

# Reconstructing the World

More than four hundred thousand people gathered in New York's Central Park on April 15, 1967, to march in opposition to U.S. military involvement in Vietnam. Among the faithful was Don Olson, a lanky, quiet graduate student from the University of Minnesota. Olson was there for a couple of conflicting reasons: Like many of his peers, he was irritated by the war in Vietnam, and displaying that irritation as part of a massive demonstration helped soothe his anger. Spending a day marching in the rain and shouting antiwar slogans seemed as good a way as any to pass some of that irritation along to the warmongers in the government.

He was also there because those warmongers had paid his way out east to see if he had what it took to join them. On the Monday following the rally, he strode somewhat halfheartedly into the personnel offices of the U.S. State Department in Washington to be interviewed for a job. Olson, after all, was a fine candidate for government service. An international relations student at the U of M, he had come of age during a time when public service seemed like a perfectly acceptable career choice for an idealistic young academic.

The interview went all right. They voiced some concern about Olson's activities in a Minneapolis antiwar organization (he had chaired a rather passive group called Conservative and Liberal Americans Against the War in Vietnam during the past year), but all in all, the brief foray into government offices was not particularly unpleasant. Returning home, Olson knew he'd crossed a line. It was a bit as if he had met the enemy for the first time and escaped with his life.

There was plenty to do at home now, anyway.

The university community to which Olson returned certainly lacked the dynamism and vitality of Berkeley and New York, the centers of antiwar activity in the country, but it was quite clearly beginning to change. The West Bank, a soiled neighborhood on the fringe of downtown Minneapolis, was emerging as the cultural and political hub of the local counterculture, and it was there that Olson was drawn more and more. Flanked by the University of Minnesota's giant campus, the neighborhood attracted curious students, bohemians, serious artists, and hip intellectuals, blending a new hippie street scene with the slowly decaying businesses that had operated there since the 1930s and 1940s.

One observer recalled the scene there in 1967 as "two extremes of transition." Holtzerman's, a general store of long standing, displayed goods from the Depression era while, a block away, hippies clogged the sidewalk in front of Richter's Pharmacy, procuring various types of recreational pharmaceuticals. Down the street, the Electric Lunch served sandwiches at all hours. The juxtaposition was less severe elsewhere in the neighborhood, but the sense of change, of drifting into a new era, was pervasive.

Olson himself was adrift in more ways than one. He wasn't living anywhere, for one thing. As he crashed at friends' homes or sleeping in his car, his life had taken on a bohemian air, and a certain hippie consciousness was setting in. He'd been set adrift politically as well. The liberal philosophies that had guided him so effortlessly toward Washington and public service had been cast aside in New York. He would spend the Summer of Love looking for alternatives.

He was looking for something beyond the old solutions—ideas that would fall into place for him, filling the cracks between the old ideologies and the new idealism. Like others awash in this sea of change, Olson was searching for a political direction that would not feed on the self, something like the "magic politics" Allen Ginsberg preached—part theater, part poetry, with a sprinkling of political theory and moral righteousness, politics of the spirit and soul that would encourage rather than blunt personal growth while transforming society.[1]

The urgency with which Olson and his like-minded brethren pursued such a far-flung cause could be attributed to a few obvious factors: First, several thousand young men of college age had already returned from Vietnam in body bags, and the meat grinder President Johnson and the Pentagon were intent on turning seemed to have an unlimited capacity; second, draft call-ups had increased by 1967 to a level that threatened even the heretofore shielded graduate student; and finally, hard on the heels of tremendous political gains scored by the civil rights movement in the early to mid-1960s, the antiwar movement had pushed so many young activists so fast and far to the left that absolutely anything seemed possible politically, socially, and culturally.

It was all moving a little too fast for the old social democrats, socialists, and communists who had occupied the dusty left wing of the American political establishment. Sociologist C. Wright Mills had observed early on that there was no political future in trying to mobilize the working class for social change. "Such a labor metaphysic is a legacy from Victorian Marxism that is now quite unrealistic," he wrote.[2] Nobody was quite sure what to do with the young radical intelligentsia like Don Olson, who were making all the waves.

For example, national movement leaders were typically split on the strategy needed to stop the war. Most of the Old Left continued to advocate the mobilization of the working class against the war, while New Left groups looked to their natural campus constituency for support and energy. A compromise of sorts emerged from the April 15 New York rally. It was called Vietnam Summer, and sought to tap the seasonal energy of students for a campaign aimed at so-called Middle America.

The national organizers, mostly old-guard members of SDS and a group of Boston antiwar activists, proposed to hire students for $25 to $50 a week to canvas university neighborhoods with the antiwar doctrine. The goal was to establish a solid block of support in opposition to the war and to translate that support into electoral clout for the 1968 elections.

The results on the national level were hardly noteworthy; the Movement was no more defined in the fall of 1967 than it had been in the spring. Nevertheless, Vietnam Summer did bring antiwar activity to virgin territory around the country and helped to spur some ongoing activity in and around campuses.

Olson was only peripherally involved in the campaign that summer, but he did attend an evaluation session following the summer door-knocking effort and there met Dave Gutknecht, who was to lend some direction to Olson's meandering political journey. Gutknecht had moved to Minneapolis three years earlier from his hometown of Winthrop, Minnesota, to attend Augsburg College. Politically sophisticated even as a teenager, he had spent a couple of unsatisfying years as a full-time student before abandoning academic life and throwing himself into the antiwar movement. It was through his fight against the draft and the war that Gutknecht abandoned his own liberal predilections and embraced anarchism.

Contrary to its nasty reputation, fostered by history books that seem to include some bomb-throwing or revolver-firing anarchist in every chapter, the political theory of anarchism actually is less than ferocious. As practiced by Gutknecht and a growing number of devotees in the Twin Cities during the late 1960s, it had much more to do with decentralism, libertarianism, and a sort of rural romanticism than with lethal weapons. Anarchist theory informed much of the countercultural direction of the times, but Gutknecht and others would bring it to bear on the local movement to such a degree that it affected almost every piece of strategy the local movement devised during the next decade.

It certainly had an effect on Don Olson. In one discussion with Gutknecht, he began to see his beliefs fall into place within a new political framework. In theory, at least, anarchism made sense. It suited his distrust of political dogma and party discipline, blended nicely with his ideas of community-building and local control. Perhaps most importantly, it helped clarify his opposition to the war and the draft.

The antidraft sentiment that had been spreading on campuses across the country since the New York march presented a significant conflict within the political left. Old Left groups, particularly the Socialist Workers party (SWP), differed sharply with New Left sentiment on the draft issue.[3] The SWP and its youth affiliate, the Young Socialist Alliance, advocated a "proletarian military policy." The draft was not a primary issue, party members believed, and they urged revolutionaries to accept the military call if it came, thereby encouraging the productive class mingling so central to the party's mission. Two years in the army speaking against the war and capitalism to other GIs was more effective, they reasoned, than spending two years in prison or an indefinite period in political exile.

The New Left saw things a bit differently, as one might expect of a political movement fueled by campus activists. The draft was a big deal to students of all political stripes. It represented a major disruption of goals and aspirations, at the very least. At worst, it meant a state-sponsored push into a morally repugnant conflict, not to mention a distinct threat of bodily harm.

Despite the distaste most students felt for conscription, resistance had not by 1967 become a palatable alternative for many. The draft was certainly despicable, but the consequences of evasion or resistance were dire.

Boston antiwar activist David Miller had been prosecuted in 1966 for burning his draft card—the first man convicted in the Vietnam era—and was sentenced to two and a half years in federal prison. This conviction set a precedent of sorts that would haunt all potential resisters.

Precedent or no precedent, five hundred men burned their draft cards at the New York rally Olson attended. It was a gutsy move, a gesture of defiance Olson himself was not yet ready to make. But it did mark a turning point in his life and in the movement. In *The War at Home*, Thomas Powers wrote that the action "marked the beginning of an entirely new stage in the opposition to the war. They did not simply protest official policy, but disassociated themselves entirely from the government, and if need be, the country that sanctioned its policy."[4]

For Olson, draft resistance meant more than a clear stand against the war; it reflected part of a pragmatic anarchist program, a morally consistent stance against state-sponsored coercion. It made sense.

In the wake of the Vietnam Summer campaign, some Twin Cities antiwar activists began thinking about the need for an ongoing organization. Reflecting the beliefs of the most influential among them—Dave and his brother Doug Gutknecht, Sandy Wilkinson, and Don Olson—the resulting organization focused on the draft and maintained a style and tone consistent with their anarchist beliefs.

This is not to suggest that any consistent or clearly identifiable anarchist theory was evident or was about to emerge from resistance leaders in the Twin Cities or from the New Left generally. Nothing had been very clearly defined; everything was evolving. "There was a feeling that the old ideologies won't do, that we're kind of in a new situation and we have to feel our way through this," Dave Gutknecht recalled. "The situation seemed to grow more complex by the year. I think the awareness of the roots of the war, the roots of social evils that were destroying the environment and for centuries had kept women in a secondary place and issues of race—all of those things sort of compounded one another and there didn't seem to be, and there still doesn't seem to be any analysis that ties all that together. But as far as social organization and social power and the roles of authority, I feel like the anarchist vision inspired many people in this area and probably, aside from the liberal democratic ideas which led people to reform the Democratic-Farmer-Labor activities and the like, I would say probably it was the strongest alternative radical political vision going on."[5]

Paul Goodman, writing in the journal *Anarchy* in 1969, argued that what he believed to be the roots of student rebellion emerged as a hybrid of anarchist theories and practices. "They believe in local power, community development, rural reconstruction, decentralist organization. They prefer a simpler standard of living. They do not trust the due process of administrators and are quick to resort to direct action and civil disobedience. All this adds up to the community anarchism of Kropotkin, the resistance anarchism of Malatesta, the agitational anarchism of Bakunin."[6]

Goodman was well respected, almost revered, among young radicals at the time. His work, like the writings of Thoreau, Norman O. Brown, and the philosopher Herbert Marcuse, were standard reading for many New Left intellectuals. Gutknecht devoured everything of Goodman's he could find and came to believe in the virtues of Goodman's particular view of an anarchist or libertarian program: a demand for work that "realizes our human powers, cooperative jobs themselves worth doing, with the worker's full understanding of the machines and processes; a reassessment of the standard of living; the encouragement of childhood and adolescent sexuality; direct political initiative in housing, community planning, education, etc.; more human naturalistic ethics; and abstention from whatever is connected to the war."[7]

So when the Twin Cities Draft Information Center (TCDIC) opened in September 1967, it was with variations of these fundamentals that it operated. Of the four or five people initially involved in the project, Dave Gutknecht was by all accounts the most influential. Indeed, it was to some extent a Gutknecht family enterprise, with sister Ruth, brother Doug, and their mother, Ronelda, all actively involved.

The draft resistance movement operated without much national support or coordination.[8] A Philadelphia-based organization published and distributed a national newsletter for the various resistance groups around the country and coordinated national conferences. Beyond that, local anti-draft centers suffered or prospered on their own. Most of these groups had no political program or planned daily organizing work, and often resembled informal committees more than anything else. The act of resistance to the draft, itself a highly emotional, often irrational act, did not often contribute a sense of well-being, continuity, and security to the individual or the organization. In many cases, those most involved and vital to the organization's continued operation were the most likely candidates for prison.

Dave Gutknecht was himself in trouble with the local draft board in the fall of 1967, carrying a classification of 1–A Delinquent he had received earlier in the year. He was appealing the denial of his conscientious objector application and he knew then that he was going to test the Selective Service in court if the call came. Nevertheless, work at TCDIC was not much hampered by whatever uncertainty the draft injected into the scene. The operation actually may have been enhanced by it. In their book *The Resistance*, Staughton Lynd and Michael Ferber characterized the center as one of the most smoothly run in the country.

There was a work ethic at TCDIC that Lynd and Ferber found seldom displayed at other resistance centers. Long hours, solid execution, and precise division of labor characterized the organization, they said, and though they neglected to mention the forces behind the center's success, other observers pointed to Dave Gutknecht as the most potent influence. He was, according to Martha Roth, one of the "adult" supporters of the organization, something of a "benevolent dictator" at the center, a person who led, if not with rhetoric or charisma, then by setting an admirable example toward which others could strive. He was then, and remains today, a tireless worker, impatient with those who lack his drive and resolve. It is not surprising that the organization under his influence operated with a good deal of energy and efficiency.

Gutknecht was the first to admit that he was only one of many people who contributed to the success of TCDIC, however, and his role notwithstanding, other factors existed that did much to aid the center's development. Chief among these was the unity of purpose engendered by what in retrospect was an undeniable form of hero worship. There's something about defying immoral authority despite the threat of prison that brings out the oohs and aahs of righteous observers. This sort of reverence, if not always spoken, was at least quietly acknowledged among the people who participated in TCDIC activities.

At TCDIC, as elsewhere around the antiwar movement, it was the men, particularly those who had spurned the draft, who most influenced the priorities and strategies of the organization. The women who were at all active in the center's operation were generally friends and lovers of the men. "It didn't make a lot of sense for women to do draft counseling," said Ellen Hawley, a supporter at the time who, like other women, was reluctant to push against the sexism that was becoming more and more apparent in the movement.

Martha Roth recalled "a lot of sexual struggling" among the men and women at TCDIC, especially after feminist consciousness-raising became more prevalent in the area. "But any opposition looked divisive," she added. "If you pursued a sidetrack you looked mean."

Issues of sexism and heroism were not shunned, however. On the contrary, an entire new sense of politics—a personalization of the political—encouraged such struggling. "Deprivatization" was the term thrown around TCDIC and elsewhere in the movement. It meant simply that you put your feelings out there on the table with your political actions and opinions. Strategies and options could no longer be dehumanized. "At times Resistance meetings resembled group therapy," Lynd and Ferber reported. "Resisters, or those on the verge of resisting, stayed up all night talking, 'getting their heads out'—probing themselves and each other in a very personal way."

Barely six months after the New York march and only a few weeks after TCDIC opened its doors, another major demonstration brought Olson, Gutknecht, and a contingent of local activists east again, this time to Washington, for what was billed as a march on the Pentagon. The demonstration followed by a week the First National Day of Resistance, and from all across the country, resisters carried bags and boxes of draft cards to be presented to the U.S. Justice Department on the day before the march. Dave Gutknecht, David Pence, and a few other local activists turned in their cards during ceremonies on October 16, and the Twin Cities crew proudly delivered the collection to Yale Chaplain William Sloane Coffin upon their arrival in the nation's capital.

Don Olson's card was not among those turned over to the chaplain. "I was too afraid at the time," he said. His attendance at the Pentagon, however, would push him over the edge.

The rally featured the first appearance on the national scene of Jerry Rubin, a twenty-eight-year-old former journalist who had been invited by Dave Dellinger of the National Mobilization Committee to help in the organizing. Already acknowledged as the "master of the theater of dissent" for his work with the Berkeley Vietnam Day Committee, Rubin came to organization headquarters in New York with a reputation for the bizarre.[9]

In New York, Rubin met Abbie Hoffman, then a well-known CORE activist on the Lower East Side, and the two of them became fast friends. They shared a certain flair for political organizing and a vision of revolution as fun. Rubin was, by all accounts, clearly inspired by Hoffman's peculiar brand of radicalism, a perspective that transcended even New Left strategies and mixed anarchism with street theater. In Hoffman's view, it was more important to burn dollar bills than draft cards.

National organizers had envisioned the October 21 rally in the traditional mold: a peaceful gathering on Capitol Hill with speakers and some quiet display of indignation. Rubin quickly vetoed the plan in favor of a militant march on the Pentagon across the Potomac. This angered and worried some of the old-line rally organizers but pleased SDS militants who wanted to attack and occupy the building. That wasn't what Rubin and Hoffman had in mind. In prerally meetings Hoffman spoke of exorcising the evils in the Pentagon and levitating it three hundred feet in the air. He also vowed to release clouds of LACE, inflicting participants with uncontrollable sexual urges. All this was circulated in prerally press releases that confused the media and absolutely befuddled Movement leaders.

As a project coordinator, Rubin had to try to satisfy the disparate factions. As a result, the rally was actually organized in two parts: a peaceful demonstration at the Capitol followed by a march on the Pentagon. Participants could leave after the Capitol gathering if they didn't wish to confront the troops surrounding the Pentagon.

"Parade Permit Granted, Paratroopers Flown In" read the Friday morning headline. Participants were edgy; police were edgy. No one quite knew what to expect, how the government would react to a mass confrontation at the Pentagon. As it turned out, the rally and march were dominated by SDS militants, according to some observers, but the coordination was loose, and the many factions more or less governed themselves as they saw fit.

Approaching the Pentagon, the marchers broke ranks. "We got to this one area where the troops were," Don Olson recalled, "and I was part of this group that broke through the lines and ran up to the doors and just sat down and started the siege of the Pentagon."

It was a strange scene. The troops, their lines penetrated, quickly regrouped to repel any further advances and stood nervously, their backs to the rabble on the steps, facing a few thousand jeering protesters on the mall. Reporters and television cameras clustered at the top of the steps surveyed the scene and created instant analysis for Olson and the others on the steps. "Here we're sitting right by the Pentagon and we could look up and see these reporters commenting on what was going on. Some people had radios down here and you could hear what they were saying."

Olson burned his draft card there in the gathering dusk on the steps of the Pentagon. "Everyone else was doing it; it felt good," he remembered. Meanwhile, below, Hoffman's hippie deputies were walking down the line of soldiers sticking flowers in their gun barrels. Although he managed to avoid the head-bashing dished out by frustrated troopers after midnight, Olson missed the bus leaving Washington and had to hitchhike back to the Twin Cities. Along the way he noticed the numbers reported at the rally gradually diminishing in newspaper and radio stories. "This later affected me; I couldn't believe there could be such lying," he said. "Later on when I was smoking hashish, I realized I had this big gap coming back from this demonstration. I realized how corrupt and how distorted the newspapers were, and I kind of had this big mind-searching thing, going through all the things that had bothered me all my life. I kind of relived them as they raced through the corridors of my mind. I had this whole cathartic effect. Every time I'd be thinking about it I'd start shaking, like I was exorcising them out of my body."

All the long-held assumptions about country, society, politics, and goals were falling away quickly for Olson. They'd been suspect before, but after the Pentagon experience, they were clearly illusory, worthless, even deceitful. His commitment to the resistance grew accordingly.

A bomb blast destroyed the TCDIC office shortly after the Pentagon march, but nobody was injured, the center relocated, and soon antiwar activity was on the upswing. By April 1968, TCDIC was firmly established in south Minneapolis, with a branch office in the university neighborhood and an affiliated organization on campus, Students Against Selective Service, which Olson directed. "I was working full-time on it," he said. "I had stopped going to classes, I hadn't registered for school in a while. I don't know, maybe forty, fity hours a week. People did it. They worked full-time and the most they ever got was eighty dollars a month. At a high point we had like fourteen or fifteen people who were drawing money, who were working on it full-time."

January had brought induction notices to Dave Gutknecht and David Pence. Refusing the call, they were indicted and arrested. Their cases brought draft resistance into the public eye for the first time in the Twin Cities. There were demonstrations and rallies, with TCDIC acting as the central organizer. The two resisters were tried and convicted in July. Pence was sentenced to three years; Gutknecht, owing to his disrespectful courtroom manner, was to spend four years in federal prison. They appealed and were released on bond.

During the next eighteen months or so, TCDIC was in high gear. Besides counseling one hundred to two hundred young men a week, the center produced literature, leafleted daily at the downtown induction center, and sent speakers to high schools, churches—anywhere people wanted to hear about the draft and the war. The money to support the work came from monthly pledges, donations, and fund-raisers. At its peak, TCDIC operated on a monthly budget of about $3,000. The level of support—both financial and personal—was impressive, considering the political climate. The majority of Americans still supported the war.

"To a certain extent there was just a feeling that we have to do this, that the system is so outrageous that all we can do is, as Mario Savio [leader of the Berkeley Free Speech Movement in the mid-1960s] said, throw yourself against the machine, you know, try to stop the gears," Dave Gutknecht recalled. "There was definitely a strong moralistic tone to the Left—there still is—and the feeling that one can make a difference and should change one's own life, personally contribute to a movement."

The massive infusion of energy, love, and indignation that characterized the halcyon days of the Movement seemed to carry us all—activists and observers alike—from one event to another in a whirling, cacophonous display of emotion. Even those of us on the sidelines had trouble keeping up in the three years after 1967: the Tet Offensive, LBJ's early retirement, the student takeover at Columbia, the police riots at the Democratic National Convention in Chicago, Nixon-Agnew, the Days of Rage, Kent State, Jackson State, all of it flashing by like some prolonged surrealistic documentary. Faces, names, celebrities, fools—politics mixed with cultural revolution—a moralistic theater of the absurd.

In the Twin Cities there were trials, trials, and more trials. Nowhere in the country did the legal system deal so determinedly with draft resisters, war tax resisters, and other voices of dissent. By the end of the sixties over half of all federal court cases in the Twin Cities involved draft refusal, and these cases, of course, invited the outrageous. The trial of George Crocker, who would later distinguish himself in central Minnesota's power line protests in the mid-1970s, was a case in point.

"George is up there being convicted and he was going to be sentenced by Judge Mill," Gutknecht recalled, "but this one woman in the community stood up in court to protest what was going on . . . and then somebody else stood up to say the same thing. This was completely out of order. Then the third person stood up and starting saying something. By this time things were just completely breaking down, we were kind of taking over the courtroom, and the judge, after failing to silence us, beat a retreat, stepped down and out the door. So there we were. We started singing, taking over the courtroom. They turned off the lights, so we started lighting matches in the courtroom. Then we left the courtroom, went downstairs singing."

Because Crocker had been convicted prior to the outburst, his lawyer eventually convinced the protesters to return to the courtroom and allow the process to commence in order to ensure his client would be released on bail. "Sort of put a damper on things," Gutknecht said.

Between the trials, lending more spice to the often grueling work at TCDIC, were demonstrations, large and small gatherings of the faithful: twenty thousand on October 15, 1969, marking Vietnam Moratorium Day; fifty thousand on May 9, 1970, following the killings at Kent State. The local movement blossomed, but more importantly, a community was forming to carry its faithful beyond the war.

Lynd and Ferber noted that communities of resisters quickly developed in various areas across the country and led to a broader vision of alternatives. "It was natural," they wrote, "that resisters asserting at once their individual humanity against an impersonal machine and their sense of world community in general, would turn to alternative ways of living, like work cooperatives and intentional communities."[10]

Players outside the somewhat heroic resistance drama were also being pulled together, attracted to various political and social alternatives. "The social aspects were definitely important," Gutknecht said. "Making new friends, getting more of a sense of empowerment in the neighborhood. It definitely created some bonds that weren't there before." That desire to exercise more control over one's life, so clearly evident in the struggle against the draft, slowly began to be felt in other areas, around issues of sexism, the environment, health and nutrition, and life-styles. When combined with the perceived success of civil rights and antiwar movements, this "empowerment" consciousness gave birth to new movements. In the Twin Cities the new decade saw a proliferation of new social and political groups: a resurgent feminist movement, the American Indian Movement, organizations working for gay rights, an environmental movement, and the shaky beginnings of a "new wave" of consumer and worker cooperatives.

"The basic rule seemed to be that anyone could play," wrote George Bloom in the TCDIC newsletter, *Changes*. "Behind the familiar refrain of 'What can I do?' lay the supposition that every individual could do something. This included not only modifying one's personal behavior, but also implied that the average citizen could participate in the formulation of public policy."[11]

There was something about the sixties that told us we could all be meaningful. We could all, if we dared, play at the sport of social change. Nothing stood in our way but complacency. It was more than political, more than civil rights and the war and the draft and radical feminism, more than anarcho-marx-lenin-maoism. It was possible now to be different, a changed person, without necessarily incurring much pain.

"The great changes of the war's decade," noted Morris Dickstein, "were ones of sensibility, awareness, and attitude, not of institutions."[12] We were not going to exorcise the Pentagon; the government stood fast as ever against our rhetoric and the war economy rolled onward, but we could take our visions and fashion what we wanted for our own lives. We could move away as much as possible from those institutions we could not change and seek to control that which was controllable.

Cooperatives made sense in 1970. The concept of consumer- or worker-owned business may have been foreign to most of those who looked to the new model in the Twin Cities and elsewhere, but it was a feasible plan for the long term. You could grow there, settle in, commune. Your could run a business as it was run in your dreams—"people's wages," no bosses, no dress codes, no profit—political, but cozy. A stopping place.

The war was not over by a long shot as the sixties rolled into a new decade and revolutionary fervor still dominated life on the West Bank and elsewhere around the Twin Cities, but there was a growing inclination toward escape now, a need among radicals to construct a community within which they could nurture themselves and thus continue the revolution.

As Jack Whalen and Richard Flacks have noted, many young radicals were entering a new phase in their development by the end of the decade. Having been convinced that the social order was on the brink of collapse, they'd postponed all the decisions about their personal futures and thrown themselves entirely into movement work.[13] With the apocalypse fading, these young people were suddenly faced with the challenge of building "principled lives" for the long haul.

The cooperative movement they spawned wouldn't completely solve that problem nor generate much social or political change, but it would ultimately serve to insulate from outside diversions the counter-cultural values they had embraced and would provide a peculiarly institutionalized structure for the self-proclaimed radical life-style they all hoped to lead in the postwar years.

# CHAPTER THREE

---

# Revolutionary Food

The commune that beckoned Debbie Shroyer in the summer of 1969 occupied a renovated train depot in the tiny hamlet of Georgeville, Minnesota. Twenty people lived there together on the prairie, working the garden behind the building and crafting hippie artifacts. They were living the revolution, so to speak.

The building stood a couple of blocks off the highway, about ninety miles due west of Minneapolis, and was owned by a reformed real estate speculator named Larry Johnson. Also known as Ernest Mann, Johnson spent much of his time in the city producing the *Little Free Press*, infrequent pamphlets explaining the benefits of a moneyless society. He sometimes distributed his message on downtown street corners dressed as a robot, a mindless slave to wages.

Johnson intended to develop the Georgeville property into some sort of alternative rural shopping mall, a place where commune members could sell their pottery, clothing, bead jewelry, and smoking paraphernalia to eager tourists. The commune was just about all there was to Georgeville besides the requisite bar and gas station, but each weekend during the summer, curious city dwellers encircled the place, hoping to observe the hippie life-style at close range.

Debbie Shroyer came to know about Georgeville through two of her sisters, Susan and Jeannie, who lived and worked there. Susan, at twenty-four, the eldest daughter of the Shroyer clan, operated a head shop on the main floor of the old depot; Jeannie made clothing to sell there. Both had lived for a time on the West Bank in Minneapolis before casting their destinies with the communal life. Both could feel a part of the cultural revolution their youngest sister could only fantasize about.

Like many of her peers in the high-school class of 1969, Debbie

Shroyer looked out at the cultural revolution from her comfortable middle-class Iowa world and wondered why she couldn't play too. The music, the clothing, the drugs, the sex, the politics were all filtering slowly into the mainstream, and it hardly seemed a risk to dive in and live a little.

Unlike most of her classmates, Debbie had already tasted a bit of this life, vicariously enjoying the revolution through the stories her sisters told of California and the commune. Her appetite sufficiently whetted, Debbie "hooked up with a carny" she met at a local fair and, barely a month out of high school, prepared to skip town for this Eden in central Minnesota. She phoned Susan in Georgeville to alert her to the plan. Susan told her to sit tight until she could get down there to pick her up. A few days later, Susan and her friend Keith Ruona arrived to liberate her little sister from the long, dusty Iowa summer. On the Fourth of July—"My personal independence day," Debbie recalled—the trio made tracks toward the future.

Susan and Keith had taken up residence at Georgeville six months earlier, after they and their thirteen housemates had been evicted from a house on the West Bank. A city ordinance prohibited more than ten unrelated people from sharing the same domicile. Susan was running a little shop on Cedar Avenue; Ruona did odd jobs to make ends meet. Both had jumped at the chance to make it in the country.

The commune was characterized by one observer as "a leaderless group of organized, productive people."[1] Among the residents there were draft resisters, SDSers, artists, and mothers and children. They shared household tasks and child care and aspired toward self-sufficiency. In the garden behind the main building they grew their vegetables. They cut their own wood to heat the two-story building. The atmosphere was political, funky and rustic: a hallway cluttered with hundred-pound bags of grain, an expansive kitchen with earthenware pots and wooden utensils, huge pickle jars, astrological charts, Thoreau quotes on the wall. Sleeping areas with tentlike compartments littered one large floor, separated by India print bedspreads and a tree house platform for the children. A living area featured couches in a circle, books stacked on one side, sewing on the other, and a study area with an island for cluttered desks.

For the residents, this was a place to begin anew, a chance to build something with their own hands and their own visions, a way to survive legitimately in what they considered an illegitimate society.

They weren't alone. Some ten thousand hippies nationwide, weary of life in the city, had drifted to the country by 1968 and had come together to form an estimated five hundred rural communes. "Many of the young," wrote Loren Baritz in *The Good Life*, "thought of themselves as a distinct social reality, a separate nation, or, in moments of high enthusiasm, a separate race."[2]

For Debbie Shroyer, the journey to Georgeville carried few political ramifications. If the place tasted of utopia, she wasn't biting. The commune, she soon discovered, lacked the luster of her imagined New Age. The work was rarely enjoyable: a garden to weed, a meal to prepare, a bathroom to clean. The quality of life seldom extended beyond a sort of elemental tedium. Shortly after her arrival there, reporters from the Minneapolis papers came out to the commune to see what it was all about. One of them asked her, the most impressionable of the group, what she thought of the scene. "It was all kind of straight," she told him.

It's not fair to say Debbie floated through the commune scene without picking up some new ideas. The experience brought her a vague appreciation of the power of collective action. She discovered something else too: a new way of eating. Because the Georgeville pioneers had a lot more energy than money (they lived off income tax refunds and food stamps and whatever they could make selling their wares), they were forced to eat very cheaply. Those who had made the pilgrimage to San Francisco returned with stories of a group of food scavengers called the Diggers. These hippie anarchists were famous for sifting through the dumpsters behind grocery stores in the Bay Area, scooping up discarded but edible food and offering it regularly to the burgeoning population of hungry vagrants around Haight-Ashbury.[3] The Georgeville crew did no scavenging but did discover that they could feed themselves nicely by growing some of their own food and by buying in bulk quantities grains, beans, honey, molasses, dried fruits, and nuts. Behind the economics of such a dietary regimen was what they considered a very logical withdrawal from the capitalist food system.

If nutritional awareness had anything to do with the Georgeville menu, it was well hidden by economic and political considerations and the desire to escape from the mainstream insanity these communards found outside their loosely constructed environment. Ironically, Debbie soon found herself wanting to escape—to flee to the West. She had heard stories about San Francisco by now, and was eager to see it for herself. In September she got her chance. Hitching a ride with a vanful of pilgrims from Massachusetts, Debbie set out for the promised land.

Nothing about the sixties was quite so romanticized as life on the road. A certain fraternity was said to exist out there on the highway. People could get from coast to coast on their thumbs, the story went, and find a friend with every ride. Debbie believed it, so when the Massachusetts van ran out of gas and money in the Tetons, she didn't hesitate to stick out her thumb and hitch to San Francisco on her own. She caught a ride with a truck driver who said he was going straight on through to Oakland. What he didn't let on was that he was going to expect something in return from this hippie girl. "It was," Debbie recalled sadly, "my first experience with rape."

She had some phone numbers Susan had given her—comrades in the Bay Area encountered during an earlier, more magical time—and was able to find temporary quarters while she checked out the scene. She found that the Summer of Love had two years later become the autumn of greed. The hippie life-style had become a marketable commodity, and all around the Haight, merchants were cashing in. They were hawking mainstream America's version of hippieness—stereos, records, clothes, drug paraphernalia—to an eager army of tourists. On the street, where Debbie panhandled for spending money, life was getting rougher. The drug culture had lost its innocence, the huge market brought big-time dealers on the scene. Hippies were seen with guns, protecting themselves and their transactions.

Still, she stuck it out, and by the time Susan and Keith visited in December she was settled, living with a man she'd met shortly after her arrival in the city. She had a decent job by then, too, rolling coins with "the other minorities" in the vault of the Bank of America. Her sister was eight months pregnant, so she and Keith hung out awhile after the Rolling Stones Altamont concert—the main reason for their visit. Their son Leif was born in January, and the three of them returned to Georgeville.

Debbie had no intention of returning to the rustic life on the prairie, however. She was saving money to go to Europe. By March, with $1,000 in her pocket, she took off for New York.

Meanwhile, the commune had soured for Susan and Keith. Personality conflicts and financial difficulties tipped the delicate balance between joyful experimentation and insufferable inconvenience and sent some of the original pioneers back to the West Bank. When Debbie returned from New York after failing to get on a standby flight, she found her sister Susan settled once again into the hippie life, sewing for people and taking care of young Leif. Debbie also found her sister Stephanie and her husband in jail, busted for possession of marijuana and in need of bail money. She put up $500 of her remaining cash to get them out. Now, for the first time, all five of the Shroyer sisters found themselves together on the West Bank—all at loose ends, to be sure, but the reunion, if it could be called that, would send four of them in a new direction.

Pseudoreligious food purists were beginning to appear here and there on the hippie scene, and although the Shroyers would not have included themselves among that group, they did miss the economical meals from the Georgeville kitchen. None of them was holding down regular jobs. Like many of their peers on the West Bank, they were getting by on whatever they could earn outside of the system. Nobody was starving, but there was a general frustration about having to come down from the mountain every once in a while to get their beans and rice from the corner capitalist grocer.

One night in May 1970, while sitting around at Jeannie's house, the Shroyers hit upon a new idea. They would open a store to sell the kinds of food they'd eaten at the commune. Debbie had some money left from her San Francisco savings. Susan knew the bakery supply house downtown would still sell stuff in bulk. They even knew where they might be able to set up shop—on the back porch of a friend's house. "In a way it started out just as a way to get food cheap, good food cheap, as opposed to being very much about co-ops," Susan said. "We just decided to go out and get the food and do it."

Susan was no stranger to the business world—at least the hippie business world—having operated shops on the West Bank and in Georgeville. She knew the ins and outs of organization, if not the specifics of financial management. Debbie could supply some expertise in that area. At the time she was working as financial manager of the local underground weekly, *Hundred Flowers*. Vickie and Jeannie had time and energy to contribute. Together they mustered their forces for the project. Borrowing a truck the next day from a friend, the foursome traveled down to the Devorax Bakery Supply House and bought $100 worth of food: cracked wheat, whole wheat, honey molasses, oil, sesame seeds, sunflower seeds, Spanish peanuts, soybeans, raisins, and powdered milk. Susan had earlier arranged to sell the goods off the back porch of Diane and Alvin Oderman's house on 20th Avenue, and after the cargo was dropped there in the afternoon, the company of new grocers drew up some posters and fliers to spread throughout the neighborhood. The next day, Peoples' Pantry opened for business. "We didn't set it up as a co-op or anything because I was really tired," Susan explained. "To me it was a reaction against all the communal living back then. I was more interested, oddly enough, in not living like Georgeville. I wanted it to be organized."

*Hundred Flowers* announced the birth of the new store in its May 15, 1970, issue: "NOW—GOOD FOOD FOR STRONG REVOLUTIONARY BODIES AT PEOPLES' PANTRY 616 S. 20th Avenue (rear)." Debbie, who was storekeeper that first day of business, wondered if it was going to work. "I remember sitting out there alone on the porch that first day thinking maybe this was a bad idea," she recalled.

Neither Debbie nor any of her sisters expected to make any money from the Pantry. Indeed, in the beginning at least, there was little thought as to how the store would even sustain itself, inasmuch as the organizers refused to mark up the goods from the wholesale price. Profit was a dirty word in this crowd—if the service was worth continuing, the Shroyers believed, the community would somehow ensure that it would. Like the Diggers in San Francisco, the Shroyers wanted to provide food and a model, in hopes that collective action would spread.

At the same time there was, certainly in Susan's mind, a desire to "do a store" again, to advance some kind of radical entrepreneurship on the West Bank. Marxist critics saw in this attitude escapist tendencies, an unwillingness to confront the contradictions of business in the real world, but the prevailing opinion on the avenue was clearly one of approval. Dave Gutknecht, who was heavily involved in his own draft case and in the operation of the local draft information center when the Pantry opened, saw the project less in class terms than as an exercise in cooperation. "There was definitely a certain entrepreneur attitude on the part of some of the people doing it, and that's still the case today," he said. "You know, it's kind of fun to get your own shop going. But the mass of people using the pantry were just in it because they were cooperatively minded. They had no stake in it in any ownership sense except insofar as—and this is the sense that was cultivated—that we all own it."

The Pantry was open eight hours a week—Tuesday afternoons and Thursday evenings—but its patrons had little use for schedules and often came to shop at odd hours, leaving what they figured was fair payment for the goods they carried away. Though the late-night shopping sprees ultimately forced the Odermans to evict their popular tenant, it probably accounted for the $500 profit the Pantry earned by the time it was ready to take up new digs.

That such a radical food distribution system would thrive in the neighborhood was no surprise. Radical action was occurring all over the West Bank in the summer of 1970. Antiwar fervor was perhaps stronger than ever before. In May, fifty thousand marched in Minneapolis to protest against the killings at Kent State. In July, Don Olson and seven other protesters were arrested for attempting to destroy draft records at three draft board offices outstate (the Twin Cities word meaning "outside the Twin Cities but still inside Minnesota"). "They were almost apocalyptic times and at a certain point people realized it was just a death society," Olson recalled. "People were willing to do things. There was a song we sang about 'You got to go down there by yourself,' you have to be strong enough to live through it, that you're going to have to do the time but that also you're part of this movement."

Despite the outpouring of indignation that summer, Dave Gutknecht noticed, the Movement was experiencing growing pains. "It reached a point where mass demonstrations didn't seem to be as useful or as interesting anymore and people started going into more other issues: neighborhood organizing, women's issues, environmental issues and so on," he explained. "The nature of the developing movement was of expanding awareness, of more than one issue."

The central focus of West Bank organizing became in July the newly opened Cedar Riverside Peoples' Cooperative Center. It housed a health clinic and offices of the West Bank Community Union, and offered space to any community enterprise. The Shroyers and Keith Ruona (whose skepticism about the Pantry idea had been proved misplaced) needed a new home for the Pantry and approached the board of the Peoples' Center with a proposal for establishing an expanded store there.

Dean Zimmerman, a charter member of the board and charismatic neighborhood activist with roots in rural North Dakota, helped Susan secure a space in the center and encouraged her to match the Pantry's hours of operation with those of the clinic down the hall. The arrangement proved extremely successful. "All these bored people waiting for the doctor would go over and check to see what this was all about," he recalled.

With a new home, the Pantry polished its act somewhat. Susan,

Keith, and Vickie became regular storekeepers (they were paid in food) and they began charging a 10 percent markup on all their goods. The inventory was expanding, and monthly business had risen to about $5,000 by the end of the year, when the operation was discovered by the Minneapolis Health Department and was immediately forced to shut down. The Pantry crew, as disdainful of government as it was of capitalist business practices, had ignored the local licensing procedures when they had gone into business.

Though forced underground in January 1971 (they operated for a time in Liberty House, a sort of alternative office building/retail center that also housed TCDIC and required that shoppers know the proper password for entrance), the Shroyers and Ruona were not discouraged. Long before their eviction from the Peoples' Center they had begun thinking about expanding the Pantry into a storefront.

Two other hippie entrepreneurs, Tom Quinn and Roman (he used no last name), had opened a grocery store in August near Loring Park in downtown Minneapolis. The store, called True Grits, was mildly successful, but Quinn wanted to turn it over to the neighborhood and open a new store on the West Bank. Ownership, in a political sense, was never an issue to these entrepreneurs. In some ways, the formation of a business was seen as similar to political organizing. Once the enterprise was operating smoothly, the organizers could discreetly step away from the project and move on to some new challenge.

The True Grits crew had set their sights on the old Larson's Grocery on 22nd and Riverside, in the heart of the West Bank. Larson had recently called it quits after many years in the neighborhood, and the abandoned storefront presented Quinn and Roman with the opportunity they were seeking to get a market going in the hippie community near Augsburg College and the University of Minnesota. No organizing was going to happen on the West Bank without dealing with the Pantry, however. The Shroyers and Ruona had by then established themselves in the neighborhood as the alternative grocers, so the new kids on the block were forced to integrate their plans with those of the Pantry.

The True Grits model, though created with the neighborhood in mind, differed from the Pantry in various ways. Quinn and Roman owned the place, and were responsible for running it. Notwithstanding their expressed desire to "give" the store to the neighborhood, they clearly called the shots. The Pantry, on the other hand, belonged to no one. Everyone knew that the Shroyers and Ruona took care of the store, but decisions were made by committee—gatherings of interested patrons. The appearance of participatory decision-making was important to the future of any radical enterprise at the time, and Ruona, who'd spent some time with the local SDS, was well aware of the benefits and liabilities of participatory organizations.

In addition to structural differences, the two models diverged operationally. Like many of the businesses that sought to attract (and exploit) the hippie population, True Grits looked rough about the edges, but was run with an eye toward some functional level of efficiency. This is not to say that financial statements reigned supreme, only that there was a certain level of traditional business going on amidst all the political and countercultural posturing, a sometimes vague expression that perhaps the enterprise should make an attempt to perpetuate itself. Pantry supporters certainly wanted the project to continue; the planned move to a storefront location was testimony enough to that dream. Implicit in its entire operation—from the lack of structure, its vague ownership, its lackadaisical management—was the notion that the Pantry existed solely for the purpose of bringing neighbors together to feed themselves. Now this is an attractive concept, and was to a great extent responsible for the outpouring of support the Pantry enjoyed, but as a reason for being it departed radically from the goal True Grits and other hippie businesses pursued.

Discussions between the two groups and the demands of the building landlord, Augsburg College, created something of a hybrid store model— neither as loose as the Pantry nor as rigid as True Grits. Ruona, committed to the "rural romantic" model of operation, argued that the store should be community-owned. The "people" should make the decisions and share in the benefits. Though concerned that Ruona's "people" included only the hippies in the neighborhood, Quinn and Roman nevertheless relented, perhaps hoping their experience would ultimately give them more leverage in the store's operation. More likely, though, they were simply seduced by Ruona into believing a community store would best serve the local masses. "Keith Ruona," Dean Zimmerman said later, "could talk paint off the side of a house."

The compromise that resulted from these exchanges in December and January 1971 allowed rental negotiations with the college to proceed slowly but steadily toward an agreement. After Larson vacated the property, the college said it wanted to use the site to expand its art department.

Administrators were not eager, for obvious reasons, to rent to this ragtag coalition of grocers, but with pressure from the West Bank Community Union, the local neighborhood group, they were forced to sit down and at least talk about it.

By the middle of January, the two parties were still locked in what was fast becoming a neighborhood struggle. Fearing a backlash of the type that was being visited on other institutions by disenchanted radicals, the college caved in. There would be no agreement with an ownerless business, however, so the organizers had to come up with some kind of business structure that would satisfy the establishment without compromising neighborhood integrity.

Interviewed in the February 13 *Hundred Flowers*, Tom Quinn announced the plan for a "cooperative food service" on the West Bank. "We want the power of self-determination in one area of our communal lives—the food we eat," he said. The new store would be a cooperative. At the first community meeting following the agreement, two hundred people showed up to buy two-dollar shares of stock in the store. Bylaws were adopted and articles of incorporation reviewed. North Country Co-op was born.

Food cooperatives were not unknown in the Twin Cities at the time. During the 1930s and 1940s, a number of consumer-owned food stores operated in the area, connected to the far-reaching network of farm marketing co-ops, such as CENEX, Midland, and Land O' Lakes, that had proliferated during the first national wave of co-op development. They were much more common in rural areas, but enjoyed some success in the cities. In 1969, black leaders on the north side of Minneapolis had organized the Peoples' Cooperative Union, a food co-op designed to meet the needs of their community during a boycott of white-owned grocery stores. The store and its organizers, however, were constantly harassed, and in December 1969 the co-op was shut down by a fire of unknown origin.

Susan Shroyer and the Pantry crew were vaguely aware of the co-op model; they just never were very enamored of it. Indeed, Selby Co-op in St. Paul had opened in mid-February and was buying goods from the Pantry—making it, not North Country, the Twin Cities' first modern food co-op. The decision to incorporate as a cooperative came not so much because they preferred the model as because it was the structure most easily adaptable to their particularly quirky political, social, and economic vision.

By the time North Country opened its doors for business in April

1971, the Pantry crew had won another battle with Quinn and Roman. If the new store was going to serve the whole neighborhood, the True Grits guys argued, the inventory would have to include the kinds of items carried at True Grits—canned goods, pop, cigarettes—an inventory that could attract a wider clientele than the one that had frequented the Pantry. There would be so-called whole foods as well, but the store shouldn't be limited to that, they argued.

Food had become political, one's diet a collection of choices between capitalism/imperialism and Third World solidarity. Karim and Janet Ahmet, organizers of Ecology Co-op, an organic foods buying club across the river in Dinkytown, wrote in the January 1971 issue of *Changes* magazine that the natural foods "cult" was nothing to be ashamed of.[4] "The words 'natural' or 'organic' foods still trigger a negative response in many of us—for it seems to connote the fringe movement of the hypochondriac food faddist. However, lately, mainly due to the ecology movement, there is a growing awareness of the intrinsic soundness of the natural foods cult." The whole foods question would rear its ugly head often in the next few years, but at North Country Co-op it was laid to rest early on, to the dismay of some and the surprise of nobody.

It wasn't simply the pure food aura, the spiritually and politically superior diet, that attracted people to whole foods. What appealed to them was the notion of control, a sort of "dissenting consumption" that could be practiced by the enemies of capitalism. The way Keith Ruona told it, the co-op had a duty to encourage this sort of dissent, a duty the co-ops of the past generation had failed to perform. "They don't care about the revolution and revolution is the main thing. It has to come from within us," he told a visiting journalist shortly after North Country had opened. "The old cooperatives are still trying to get people to consume more. We want people to consume less."[5]

That principle must have seemed at odds with the scene at North Country in its first months of operation. People were coming in from all over the metropolitan area, drawn by the bargains at the co-op, which radically undercut the prices at local health food stores. Sales in the first summer of operation approached $50,000 a month, and the small workers' collective strained to keep up with the demand. The store was dirty, the goods poorly labeled, and service nonexistent, but no amount of discouragement would keep the throngs away. One Saturday, Dean Zimmerman, then one of the workers, hit upon a new idea. "People were lined up at the till twenty deep," he recalled. "So I put up a sign that said: If the line is too long, start a co-op in your neighborhood."

The stage had been set for proliferation. Despite their "small is beautiful" philosophy, even the rural romantics at North Country, seeing the demand for their goods, couldn't doubt the possibilities for movement-building. Some of the elements were already in place. Peoples' Bakery, operating out of the Peoples' Center, supplied whole grain breads to the co-op and was prepared to expand its operation. The burgeoning network also had a regular dairy supplier in Dyck Curney, a self-styled poet with a milk truck. North Country had already begun wholesaling food to buying clubs and to Selby Co-op in St. Paul.

Most important, they had a built-in consensus in the local community, massive support for economic development and social progress along countercultural lines. "We had to start rebuilding," said Dave Gutknecht, "and this anarchist vision sort of fit—some locally controlled institutions, gain more control over our lives—that was the phrase that was very common to many phases of political activity at that time. And so co-ops were a very, not easy, but after a little while, obvious way to many people to regain some of that control."

Requiring little analysis, little political struggle, little investment or risk, the co-op was in the Twin Cities a place for the tired activist to begin anew. If war was hell, Gutknecht said, co-ops seemed a little bit like heaven. "I remember this conversation with a friend who had been very active in the draft resistance, antiwar movement," he recalled. "We were talking about the food co-ops which were developing in the city and a lot of our acquaintances and coworkers were getting involved in that. I was sort of questioning that because it seemed a diversion from more urgent, immediate issues, and my friend said something like, 'Well, I guess they just decided they had to build co-ops in order to stop the war.'"

# CHAPTER FOUR

## No Bosses Here

The anarchist attitudes at North Country, which encouraged shoppers to organize co-ops in their own neighborhoods, also discouraged empire-building on the West Bank. By September of its first year in business (after the Shroyers and Ruona and other organizers had fled once again to the country), North Country had jettisoned its wholesale arm, creating a food co-op warehouse controlled by its users.

The Peoples' Warehouse was run by the former wholesale collective from North Country with the help of volunteers dispatched there regularly by the bakery and food co-ops that relied on the service. Like the Pantry and a number of the early co-ops, the warehouse wasn't "owned" by anyone. There were no incorporation papers, bylaws, or structure. Somebody paid the bills, and others made sure the various tasks were accomplished, but there was no ultimate authority, no accountability beyond whatever individuals routinely placed on their brothers and sisters in the community.

Operating out of a rent-free space owned by the University of Minnesota two blocks down Riverside Avenue from North Country, the warehouse soon replaced the so-called Mother Co-op as the hub of the co-op network. The volunteers who regularly gathered there to load and unload trucks exchanged news and gossip and became liaisons from their local co-ops to the larger movement. The co-ops provided the wages, workers, and capital. The representative nature of the warehouse work force also gave the enterprise immediate credibility. There was no selling necessary—political or economic—to convince the co-ops to buy from the warehouse. It became almost instantly the movement's primary service, main meeting place, and most persuasive political statement.

The rise of the Peoples' Warehouse was fueled by a slow but steady proliferation of food co-ops in the Twin Cities. By October of 1971, it was supplying goods to North Country, Ecology Co-op, Whole Foods Co-op, the worker-owned Peoples' Bakery and New Riverside Cafe in Minneapolis, and to Selby Co-op in St. Paul. In pockets throughout the inner city, hippies and neighborhood activists were getting the co-op message—through direct discussions with emissaries from the movement, shopping at North Country or, as Dean Zimmerman recalled, not shopping at North Country. "We made a decision to close North Country for a week," Zimmerman said. "We needed to do some repairs. And we posted on the door names and addresses of all the other co-ops around town. Our business dropped appreciably and all these other co-ops just picked right up."

The co-op idea was catching on in other areas of the country, too, as young radicals began focusing their energies on the building of alternative institutions. The trend, according to Whalen and Flacks, "represented the clearest collective effort by New Left graduates to continue the political and cultural logic of the sixties in ways that would mesh with the personal needs of members for livelihood, and the political need of the movement to connect with the everyday concerns of the larger society. Alternative institutions were capitalized by the professional skills of recent college graduates who were motivated to contribute their skills because, through the organization, they could finally hope to fulfill, rather than reject, vocational aspiration that the earlier movement experience had often led them to question."[1]

In Madison, San Francisco, Austin, Ann Arbor, Seattle, and other cities, food and housing co-ops were being developed in much the same manner as in the Twin Cities, but nowhere did they proliferate as they did there. Part of the reason for that can be traced to the prevailing decentralist attitudes among co-op leaders. The anarchist flavor first exhibited in the local draft and antiwar organizations informed much of the later co-op organizing efforts. Indeed, the two movements overlapped a good deal, according to Dave Gutknecht. "It was definitely coming out of the same movement and a lot of the same people. Now, naturally it expanded very quickly because the cooperative is an economic institution, it's not a political issue like the draft or the war, which was good because it led to a broadening very quickly of the kinds of people that had to be dealt with," he explained. "Even though the co-ops were class-biased and all those things the political struggle later was all about, still it did expand the kinds of people that got involved in some kind of community empowerment effort."

That sense of community—alternative community—so vital to the creation and sustenance of social and political causes, and so instrumental in setting the agenda for the new co-op movement, was fostered partly through this anarchist consensus that dominated the Twin Cities Draft Information Center and the hippie counterculture. Almost as important, however, was the decision made by so many activists to stay in town rather than emigrate to the more celebrated life on either coast. "There was a real tendency for the coasts to drain off people during this time," said Don Olson. "But here people said, 'We're going to do it here.' So there was a real development of community."

There were other, less romantic, reasons for the co-op craze in 1971. For one thing, storefront space was readily available and inexpensive, owing to the accelerated demise of Mom-and-Pop stores around the Twin Cities. (There was no lack of co-op excitement in New York City at the time, for instance, but co-op storefronts were extremely rare because the rents were so high.) In addition, coolers and other necessary equipment were cheap and plentiful; and well-defined neighborhoods and strong, credible neighborhood organizations also contributed to the proliferation. St. Stephen's Church, a progressive force in the Whittier neighborhood of south Minneapolis, was instrumental in the creation of Whole Foods Co-op in July of 1971. The West Bank Community Union helped bring North Country through its difficult negotiations with Augsburg College.

Two markets—cheap labor and nutrition-conscious consumers—also played major roles. In the organizing and operation of the new food co-ops, radical entrepreneurs exploited the seemingly unlimited pool of students, hippies, and otherwise politically conscious volunteers. Prices at the stores could be kept down, substantially below those at health food stores and even supermarkets, not just because the wholesale prices were low but because they paid almost nothing to their workers. The prevailing "people's wage" for co-op workers was then $25 a week. Volunteer workers received a discount on their food purchases and often worked well over the required number of hours for the benefit. "I was living on $30 a month," Susan Shroyer recalled. "Most of the people involved lived on very little money."

The demand for natural foods, as witnessed in the early days of North Country, would clearly keep a number of small neighborhood stores in business for some time. In 1971, food consciousness had just barely begun to dawn on the masses. Demand would soar in the next few years; co-ops needed only to expand quickly enough to fill the orders. Another factor seemed to be working, at least subconsciously, to steer the sixties' dissident toward the food co-op. A woman from Chicago, who moved to Minneapolis in the late sixties and was active in the local antiwar movement, noticed something about the place and the people that led her to conclude, somewhat cryptically, that food co-ops would thrive here. "The karma of this place is food," she said. The Twin Cities, she explained, felt to her like a nurturing place, a place and a people that would take care of each other. Food and food co-ops, then, could provide physical as well as psychic sustenance.

It was no coincidence that the new movement was heavily influenced by women. Left on the fringe of antiwar/antidraft work, progressive-minded women were immediately drawn to the opportunities provided in the new co-ops, where egalitarian structures and decision-making processes facilitated their participation and cultivated their leadership skills.

Perhaps the most significant factor in the rise of the movement was the fact that the new food co-ops were "antibusiness" enterprises, community service experiments emphasizing people over profit. This ideology attracted a mighty following from those yearning for a new alternative economic system, a system that would deliver high-quality goods and services to the people at low prices while simultaneously sending a message—words and models to live by in the great struggle against capitalism, materialism, and imperialism.

It wasn't enough to just set up shop. Selling food may have been a nurturing gesture to inner-city neighborhoods, but the real action, the true measure of one's self-worth, was centered on the teaching of the alternative dogma: wholesome food, a simple life-style, community control of institutions, and the evils of profit. As an early worker at Mill City Co-op, Hans Elf, put it, the movement goes way beyond food. "Co-ops are not only a means of determining what foods we put in our stomachs. Food cooperatives are a means of taking economic control of our lives. The less money we give to Red Owl, Super Valu, etc., the more we recycle funds in our own community projects, and the less dependent we become on corporate capitalism. The 10 percent markup at the stores will be used to fund new projects and non-profit organizations and to expand our network of serving the people."[2]

The new co-ops benefited from this sort of utopian consensus found throughout the radical counterculture on the West Bank and in pockets of activity in south Minneapolis in 1971. Neighborhood clinics, drop-in counseling centers, alternative schools, child-care centers, alternative newspapers, tenants' unions, community centers, recycling centers—all these models of idealistic social vision lent moral and political support to the development of a new vision of community economics.

The social aspects of the movement, the need for strong bonds among individuals, were also important to its development. A nonhierarchical, no-bosses approach to business was certainly an attractive lure for those seeking employment during a time of such disdain for corporate America. Ken Meter, who helped organize a community garage, praised the humanizing workplace possible in alternative business. "There are more personal needs felt commonly: a need for alternative service that is interesting and humanizing, a need for occupations that eliminate rigid corporate hierarchies and don't fractionalize people, a need for contact with human beings rather than just nuts and bolts, a need to find a relaxed workplace."[3]

Christopher Lasch, in his *The Culture of Narcissism*, would later take the generation to task for producing an environment that placed a premium on relaxation and "actualization" while erasing the productive aspects of stress and competition from its landscape. Indeed, this particular mission of the new movement would come under sharp attack by critics from within, as well. As a response to a society that valued its workers solely as units of production and its young draftees as so much cannon fodder, the alternative workplace seemed particularly compelling at the time. It was a way of playing out philosopher Herbert Marcuse's "Grand Refusal," a way of saying "nuts" to the real world.

As Gerald Howard has written, all this came about as a logical reaction to an America that had lost its appeal. "The radicalism of the Sixties grew not so much out of ideology, economics or specific issues as from a disgust at being used, lied to, and ignored, and from a refusal to enter a society that appeared to offer nothing worthy of emulation."[4] Within this context, this atmosphere of idealism, activism, almost utopian vision, the notion of a "cooperative commonwealth" began to spread. In October of 1971, Ecology Co-op moved into a storefront in Dinkytown and became Southeast Co-op; in January, Mill City opened in the depressed Phillips neighborhood just south of downtown Minneapolis; in February, Seward Co-op was organized barely a half mile from North Country. In March, St. Anthony Park Co-op, (SAP) opened its doors near the St. Paul campus of the university. It was created by Maren Jenson, who had once owned her own grocery store.

People came to the co-op, she discovered, not just for the prices. "I don't think it's to save money," she said. "You see, our prices are about the same as Target [which was in the grocery business at the time]. I don't think people are coming in here to save those few cents; they really want to buy that whole wheat flour in bulk, because they can buy the quantity they want and they don't have to worry about freshness or all that packaging. I think that's the main thing."[5]

Just as the range of shoppers began to diversify as the co-ops multiplied, so too did the once stable "family" of co-op leaders begin to expand. From the comfortable social group that grew up around the Pantry and North Country on the West Bank, the co-op community had begun to include people from other neighborhoods: activists and radical entrepreneurs with similar perspectives, but with sometimes divergent ideas about what the co-ops should be doing, whom they should be serving, how they should be operated. These questions always had been a part of the informal discussions between warehouse volunteers and West Bank devotees of the co-op way, but with the community growing, it was important for these disciples of participatory democracy to encourage a more formal dialogue.

The issues here were many and varied: philosophical and political questions of the movement's purpose, sexism in the workplace, accountability, and economic independence. These questions alone, however, probably wouldn't have been sufficiently compelling to bring everyone together on a regular basis. Only warehouse matters were immediate enough to get that much attention. It was, after all, the clearest evidence anyone had encountered that the revolution was alive and well.

By the spring of 1972, warehouse operations were becoming, if not complex, at least more daunting. The boundary between work and play was becoming more distinct, and opportunities for socializing within the co-op community were becoming less frequent. Nobody was yet particularly concerned about the ownership question, or questions of structure or function;

the community still trusted that, with the right blend of vigilance and good vibes, the operation would work out the kinks by itself. Inventory and delivery, communications and accountability, though, were issues that needed to be discussed. The warehouse, responding to that need, called the first All Co-op Meeting in March.

These meetings, involving representatives from all of the "new-wave co-ops" (a term used to distinguish the countercultural generation of stores from the established, conservative "old-wave" business such as Land O' Lakes, CENEX, and Midland), the bakery, and the warehouse, occurred regularly through the spring and summer of 1972. They were informal gatherings, usually convened at the Peoples' Center and guided by an agenda constructed at the scene by participants. Discussions ranged from the visionary (a proposal in March to print and distribute "co-op money") to the basic questions of warehouse service.[6] (When are the chick-peas coming in?) However, the gatherings, because of their vague purpose and direction, were often characterized by shouting matches and lengthy philosophical debates, dominated by a few contentious individuals. Warehouse issues were always discussed in some form, but seldom did the group come to any consensus, and when it did, the warehouse collective inevitably implemented the decision in whatever way it saw fit.

The proliferation of the co-ops meant a new independence for the warehouse. The co-ops still sent workers there each week, but the volunteer system no longer served the operation as well as it had in simpler times. The lack of continuity and expertise was hindering the business' ability to keep up with the avalanche of new orders. When a particularly experienced coordinator resigned shortly after the warehouse moved to a larger space in April, the regular workers' collective assumed tighter control of the operation.

Still, the warehouse workers, purveyors of the community-control doctrine, believed the stores should be consulted on larger decisions and tried to encourage the individual co-ops to discuss major warehouse issues at their weekly meetings. This proved awkward, and the warehouse was forced to focus on the imperfect, yet plausible, All Co-op Meetings for the sounding board it needed for a politically correct enterprise.

The meetings turned out to be mostly futile sputterings between those who wanted a more informal structure and decision-making process and those who saw that as an excuse for maintaining an "entrenched elite" of co-op leaders. The warehouse operation turned ever inward, relying almost exclusively on worker initiatives for decision-making, implementation, and planning. That wasn't all bad, of course, because in the fall of 1972, warehouse workers couldn't exactly bank on the business acumen of the people running most of the co-ops. Whole Foods and Mill City both tried the grand experiment of turning around their cash registers and allowing customers to ring up their purchases themselves. "After about the second day, people noticed there wasn't very much money in the cash register," recalled Chuck Phenix, an original Mill City worker. Whole Foods reported that the gesture cost them "several hundred dollars."[7]

Elsewhere, the co-op way was similarly challenged by the realities of business. At Selby Co-op in St. Paul, recycling was all the rage until the health department visited. Inspectors told them they couldn't reuse egg cartons, sell yogurt without a license, operate a recycling center in the basement, or use old fruit wrapping tissue for toilet paper. Inspectors cracked down on Whole Foods as well, and generally made life miserable for the new ventures.

Financial affairs fluctuated wildly. Mill City was barely breaking even when it fell prey to burglars and neighborhood bandits shortly after it opened. The "elves" (organizers eschewed all trappings of the traditional workplace) went unpaid for a time, but "managed to get by through other means."

At Whole Foods, workers thought everything was rosy until someone tried to balance the books. Faced with the prospect of "tightening up," coordinator Jonathan Havens lamented the costs of doing business. "Perhaps what it comes down to is the ancient conflict between structure-dependent security and structure-denying freedom," he wrote. "Having come so near the latter, the former's present dominance is all the more obvious and depressing."[8]

Even at North Country, people were forced to recognize the limitations of their structureless organization. The founders and much of the original collective had fled the city for a communal farm in western Wisconsin the summer before, and the store was suffering. Jobs weren't getting done, there were no organized meetings or work schedules, and no one was attending to the finances. For a week in March 1972, the Mother Co-op closed its doors and reassessed itself. When it reopened it was as a "membership store" with differentiated markups for members (10 percent) and

nonmembers (20 percent). Members were asked to pay a three-dollar annual fee and volunteer two hours each month. Community meetings were
still held weekly, but the new co-op generated less enthusiasm than its predecessor. Although the store was reported to be as busy as ever, membership slumped. "Strangely enough," coordinators reported, "many people
would rather pay cost plus 20 percent rather than sharing in the operation
of the store."[9]

Despite all these difficulties, there was a keen sense of opportunity at
work among people in the new co-op community, a vague realization that
they had latched onto something big. Dean Zimmerman was talking and
writing about building a "self-sustaining food distribution network" in
preparation for the day when the so-called system comes a-tumbling
down. Dave Wood wondered whether co-ops couldn't someday feed the
entire Twin Cities. "There's no reason why sometime in the not-to-distant
future (five years?) most of the Twin Cities' food needs cannot be served by
peoples' co-ops," he wrote. "One thousand co-ops each providing 1,000
people with healthful and inexpensive food grown on nearby farms by non-
exploitive (and non-exploited) farmers is not just a pipe dream."[10]

The vision of self-sufficiency that informed the new co-op movement, like the one that guided the Georgeville commune, contained plenty
of escapist tendencies (the prevailing system offers no appealing choices, so
we'll simply create our own system), but there was a sense among some of
the early co-op leaders that the establishments they were creating would
play a role in reshaping their communities, and that eventually people
from outside the movement would find themselves transformed as well.
These co-op enthusiasts were, on the whole, committed to the notion of
community control, for instance. Yet their countercultural mores and political biases prevented any substantive dialogue with local residents who
may have been interested in the co-op but whose life-styles clashed with
that of the co-op's workers and volunteers. In 1972, it took a good bit of
chutzpah for any member of the "silent majority" (President Nixon's term
for regular folks) to check out the bargains at the local co-op. It was just too
weird. As a result, in most of the neighborhoods served by food co-ops, the
"democratic" community meetings held regularly to decide store policies
looked more like Woodstock reunions.

Ideological purity also dominated within the co-op community. To
the degree that leadership was acknowledged at all, it was bestowed largely

on the basis of radical charisma and personal and political correctness. Nearly all of the early visible co-op leaders—from Keith Ruona and Dean Zimmerman to Chuck Phenix and Susan Shroyer—displayed common traits: a well-informed radical viewpoint, personal charm, and political persuasiveness, and a life-style free of corporate and consumerist influences. Ruona had been a member of SDS, and Zimmerman was a veteran of civil rights demonstrations in the South. There was more required of leaders in the new co-op movement, however. Not only did they have to withdraw from the capitalist system and embrace the hippie culture, they had to take a vow of poverty and lay off the junk food as well.

Built on the backs of volunteers, the co-op movement preached the simple life and expected its workers to practice it faithfully. Coordinators worked for a dollar an hour or less. Volunteers earned a 10 percent discount on their food. The idea here was not so much to force the simple life on cooperators, but to encourage the blurring of work and play. From the New Left doctrine of "personal politics," the co-ops had adopted the ideal of the integrated life-style, in which the barriers between home and job were removed. The structureless workplace, the collective, "family" approach to business, and the liberal exploitation of volunteer labor all served this ideal, as did the de-emphasis on wages and bookkeeping. The co-op community viewed the workplace as a nurturing place, and demanded of its leaders the same purity of soul the outside world demanded of its teachers, preachers, and parents.

The co-op as nurturer also demanded of its leaders a diet consistent with the vegetarian spiritualist nature of the stores. Burgers were definitely off the menu at the regular potluck dinners around which co-op meetings were conducted. Though early leaders were not all strict vegetarians, food and diet, like one's dress and other antimaterialist trappings, very quickly became a factor in separating the good, the bad, and the ugly in the community.

Not surprisingly, this gave rise to a certain level of self-righteousness within the movement. Just as the "straight" consumer was discouraged from participating in the co-op, so were the neighborhood radicals whose life-styles exhibited a more than justifiable level of political and countercultural inconsistencies. Throughout the winter and spring of 1973, the co-op elite fostered by this ideological purity solidified and began to encounter increased criticisms from within its movement while, on the surface, the dream of a local "cooperative commonwealth" seemed ever more plausible.

Although it was still perceived as an extension of the co-ops, the Peoples' Warehouse in May of 1973 was becoming more and more under the control of the half dozen people who composed the regular workers' collective. Its operation was coming under increased scrutiny by the co-ops, which had begun to realize that the relationship was changing and wanted to maintain some influence on the organization. Warehouse workers at the time were earning $30 a week, $5 over the prevailing co-op wage. While its members were not exactly moving into the middle class, the collective, by its higher wages and visibility in the network, was set apart from the rest of the co-op community. This didn't sit well with the arbiters of local counterculture taste. If the warehouse crew was to be paid more than everybody else, they determined, they should work full-time. The collective, however, frowned upon full-time work, even to improve service to its customers. A five-day work week, it argued, would be "oppressive to brothers and sisters who are not as physically strong as others." Besides, it added, part-time work is "nonexistent" when "you care about your work and workplace."

Bakery workers were also coming under fire by their customers for their lack of accountability. For two years, their collective had refused to deliver to St. Paul stores and when finally persuaded in May of 1973, sent the truck east across the Mississippi only one day a week. While ignoring its St. Paul customers, the bakery struck up a deal with a local vegetarian restaurant, the Mudpie, selling bread to what its critics called a "profit-oriented capitalist institution devoted to ripping off the people."[11]

In a system built upon the desire for control, these worker-consumer conflicts confounded co-op leaders and previewed issues that would soon begin to threaten their dream. Whose fantasy should yield when worker control meets consumer demand? The dilemma, disturbing in the best circumstances, was made more perplexing by the new movement's lack of structure and coherent purpose and exacerbated further by its demand of moral and ideological purity.

The dogma of the co-op community, much of it unspoken, weighed most heavily on those groups, like the warehouse and bakery collectives, that saw themselves as visible community leaders, indispensable servants to the budding network. These collectives were the first to take seriously their role as businesses in a specific, if idyllic, sector of the real economy. They were among the first people in the counterculture to envision their businesses as a means for building and maintaining an alternative career.

Roman, who along with Tom Quinn and the Pantry crew had helped to create North Country, was an inveterate entrepreneur, a man who saw in the co-op movement an opportunity both to earn some bucks and to have some fun. After the warehouse split from North Country, he floated into organizing other ventures for the revolution—a soap business and a nut butter operation. Operating out of the warehouse, he and his colleagues sold a variety of nut butter products to the new food co-ops.

Never known for his ideological stature in the community, Roman was nonetheless an accepted member of the co-op network. He had, after all, been a part of the North Country creation, which in a very short time had become, to the uninitiated, an accomplishment of nearly mythical proportions. His standing slipped precipitously, however, when in June of 1973, he confessed to having sold five hundred pounds of "people's flour" to a local health food chain, Nutrition World. He and his three partners in crime each realized a $7 profit from the sale.

The movement was enraged. Incensed co-op leaders confronted the crew at the warehouse and "expelled" them from the community. Co-ops boycotted Roman's soap business, which he later shut down, and criticized him openly for his brazen profiteering. He twisted people's arms to sign checks, they claimed; he sold inferior soap products, he was uncooperative, and, worst of all, he "lived off the co-op movement." Responding to the charges in an open letter to the co-ops, Roman argued for a more merciful verdict. "I spent close to a year working in North Country for which I never received a cent," he wrote. "I located both Peoples' Bakeries, again no payment. On soap, I average $11 a week." John Adams, one of the four ostracized for his role in "Flourgate," wrote later: "I personally have lost much faith in the co-op movement."[12]

Roman and his nut butter crew were not the only ones feeling alienated from the movement. The moral strictures and righteous demands that sent them packing were also affecting others. Warren Hanson, who had helped create *Hundred Flowers* and actively supported the new co-ops as a legitimate radicalizing tool in neighborhood development, found the self-righteousness too much to take. The taboos were oppressive, he recalled. "You couldn't get a haircut without being looked down upon. A straight job set you apart, and your friends wouldn't talk to you if you were going out with a woman who wore makeup or dressed nicely." Hanson was so fed up with the limits imposed here by his peers, in fact, that in the summer of 1973 he split for Texas.

Michael Rachlin went south, too. A coordinator at Selby Co-op, she traveled to the Deep South in August, visiting with co-op leaders and political activists in Atlanta, before checking out the co-op scene in Bloomington, Indiana; Chicago; and Milwaukee. When she returned, she carried a new message to the community: It was time for criticism. "If we are in a position to do some business, then I think we should look carefully at what business we want to do and with whom," she wrote in *This Is About Us* in September.[13] "We could begin to forge some new and working alliances with people we politically need and want to be allied with . . . and in the process of building alliances, we might well learn to hear criticism we have not heard before: we may just become flexible enough (unculture-bound enough) to survive."

The alliances to which Rachlin referred were political connections to the working class, connections not only for business purposes but for political mobilization as well. The co-ops had become insulated from the real world, Rachlin argued, distanced from a constituency that could provide a political base for revolutionary organizing. Get the masses into the stores, she claimed, and you could exploit them for the important political work the co-ops were ignoring. In other words, it was time to get serious about the revolution.

Rachlin was not alone on the platform for a renewed revolutionary cause. North Country cofounder Keith Ruona and a friend, Bob Haugen, had been studying the situation for a couple of years from the rustic confines of Winding Road Farm in western Wisconsin, under the tutelage of a former SNCC organizer named Theo Smith. There, the two conspirators organized Marxist study groups, reread the classic works of Lenin and Marx, Stalin and Mao, and analyzed their relevance to the co-ops in the Twin Cities.

The renewed local interest in Marxism followed a national trend on the left that was sparked by increasingly repressive measures by police and federal agents against radical groups. Combined with the failure of political reform efforts inside the Democratic party, the violence perpetrated against dissenters nationwide was enough to send activists away from peaceful forms of dissent and toward wild-eyed dreams of armed insurrection or working-class revolution. There were other factors as well. For all its liberating rhetoric, Whalen and Flacks explained, the New Left lacked the sort of coherent doctrine, strong discipline, firm leadership and clear direction necessary to push the revolution beyond the stage of dreamy-eyed longing to a level of pragmatic action.[14] "Instead of a rather diffuse focus on reaching older people and regular Americans, the neocommunist activists were attracted to an orthodox, explicitly working-class, Marxist analysis," they wrote. "Radicals should abandon their futile strategy of creating liberated zones in places like Isla Vista [California]. They should ally themselves with the workers, reject the self-indulgent lifestyle of the counterculture, transcend their class position, and repudiate their privileged origins."

It was clearly an appealing message. After the split of SDS in 1969, two new revolutionary groups formed to forge an alliance with the masses against capitalism and imperialism. The Progressive Labor party sought to ally itself with the industrial working class; the Revolutionary Youth Movement (later to become Weatherman) "saw the way forward as building a revolutionary movement among white, and increasingly counter-cultural, working-class youth."[15]

The two groups may have had different constituencies, but they shared the view that the only course of action left for what remained of the New Left was to build a "vanguard Leninist party."[16]

Such a party would not only move the revolution to its next level, Whalen and Flacks noted. It would provide young radicals with excuses for past failures and a place to begin making decisions about life in "post-apocalyptic" society. "The revival of interest in the doctrinal, Leninist-style party revolved around the assumption that the disorientation of the post-apocalyptic period could be overcome through party structure, party discipline, and party line. The party promised explanations for past failure, and assurances about history's course, that helped members cope with political frustration and uncertainty. Its hierarchical structure offered the promise of a political leadership capable of special wisdom that could effectively distill collective experience. In addition to political stability and direction, such parties implicitly promised personal solutions. All provided members a chance to embark on stable—and even conventional—everyday lives, while simultaneously assuring them that their activity, however mundane it might appear, had revolutionary historical significance. For all of the new parties, despite their apparent differences, advocated as a high priority that members participate fully in the everyday world of the working class, preferably by becoming factory workers. To be effective in such a role depended, it was believed, on members' living conventionally, in normal households, and abandoning the petit-bourgeois bohemianism of the counterculture in favor of marriage, family, a tract house in an industrial suburb."[17]

As an organizing vehicle, the co-ops certainly bore little resemblance to the local auto plant or machine shop, but it's clear that the notion of party discipline, structure, and direction held some allure for disaffected cooperators in the Twin Cities. The strategies formulated at Winding Road Farm and through the various Marxist study groups operating in the Twin Cities were based on the assumption that the co-ops, transformed from hippie enclaves to traditional neighborhood grocery stores, would successfully promote a revolutionary movement through their role as a community service. If the co-ops were truly neighborhood focal points, then they should be used to focus attention on the class struggle.

Rachlin's criticisms presaged any concerted movement toward this co-op transformation and were greeted with some interest. Issues of food policy—whether or not to carry canned goods, white sugar, and other such capitalist fare—resurfaced in the fall of 1973 and seemed to indicate at least an acknowledgment of the movement's insularity. Nonetheless, working-class style remained antithetical to the movement, and any notion of mass political organizing, despite the professed radicalism of the enterprises and their leaders, would tend to pull the community outside its protective cocoon and thrust it into the harsh realities of Old Left political contradictions. Still, Susan Shroyer knew that sooner or later there was going to be a political slugfest. "As soon as we get big," she remembered thinking, "they're going to want to take this over."

The Marxist-Leninist left, as was the case with the Finnish cooperative movement on the Iron Range in the 1920s and 1930s, took little notice of co-ops in the 1970s until they grew to proportions large enough to be considered for mass organizing.[18] The study groups and criticisms from that militant revolutionary wing of the left did not descend only upon the co-op, however. There were campaigns in child-care organizations, women's groups, the Southside Garage, and in various fringe political groups. The co-ops only provided the most visible target.

Haugen, Ruona, and Shroyer had returned in the fall of 1973 to Minneapolis and settled for a time near Mill City Co-op. Shroyer renewed the sewing business she had begun on the farm (selling skirts and shoulder bags to North Country General Store, where sisters Jeannie and Vickie presided), and Haugen and Ruona tried to put some of their new ideas into practice at the local co-op. One of the most delightfully anarchist stores in the Twin Cities, Mill City seemed an odd place for a Marxist transformation, but its neighborhood was one of the poorest in the city, minority population was high, and the lack of structure in the co-op seemed to make it ripe for the picking.

The two Winding Road disciples began volunteering time at the store and attending community meetings, all the time pushing the leadership toward what they considered to be a more working-class analysis. Though they managed to sway some in the collective, the leaders, especially two staunch anarchists, Chuck Phenix and Nancy Evechild, were unmoved, and they challenged the newcomers strongly enough to force a retreat.

While Ruona and Haugen went back to the Marxist drawing board, events unfolding at the warehouse would set the stage for a new opportunity to remake the revolution.

# CHAPTER FIVE

---

# "Criticism, Discussion, Transformation"

eoples' Warehouse, which had been operating for a year and a half at Seven Corners near the West Bank, lost its lease in September 1973 and was forced to scramble to find a permanent home. The collective had invested a good deal of time and money in the space and, in seeking a new location, hoped to buy a building and avoid still another inconvenient move in the future. It found a place at 26th Street and First Avenue in south Minneapolis, near Whole Foods, that seemed to suit its needs, and it negotiated a contract for deed with the owner, a plumbing contractor.

The building was in an excellent location for food distribution to the co-op community and the terms of the contract were reasonable—$69,900 for the building at 8 percent interest. The first annual principal payment of $10,000 wasn't due until November of 1974, and the balloon payment didn't come due until four years later.

Business was booming at the warehouse; expansion was inevitable. Although questions about service and accountability were circulating, loyalty to the network and its central focal point remained strong. As a result, when the warehouse workers came to the All Co-op Meeting in January 1974 asking the group to coordinate and promote a warehouse building fund, the co-op community responded with a unity of purpose recalling the earlier, more romantic times of co-op building on the West Bank. Jars went up on every co-op's checkout counter, and workers, customers, and volunteers, many of whom had no idea where or what Peoples' Warehouse was, promoted the building fund, and contributed coins and cash. The dream of a co-op-owned warehouse building moved slowly toward fruition.

Even as the co-ops kicked in for the new building, it became apparent that there were holes in the argument for acquiring the real estate. The warehouse, by entering into the legal, contractual world of mortgage and finance, needed suddenly to clean up its act, reevaluate its structure, and take the first disagreeable steps beyond the utopian anarchist vision it had for so long followed.

The warehouse had never incorporated, had never officially hired or fired workers, or set pay scales. No structure or process existed for these basic necessities of business operation. The All Co-op Meetings ratified or questioned worker initiatives or made alternative recommendations that the collective ignored or implemented according to its mood, but, as Cy O'Neil observed later, nothing was in place that would prepare the co-op network for its warehouse's becoming a real live business. "This opened a frightening array of new decisions and legal responsibilities for which the All Co-op Meeting was decidedly malequipped, so the initiative passed to the warehouse collective, which invited in the spring of '74 its co-op customers from the Upper Midwest to come together and form a policy review board for the newly created Peoples' Warehouse Inc."[1]

In June, a month before representatives from the Upper Midwest co-ops gathered in River Falls, Wisconsin, four warehouse workers incorporated the business as a nonprofit corporation, whose articles stated that "the membership of this corporation shall consist solely of the members of the Board of Directors of the corporation from time to time constituted."

Why not a co-op? According to Susan Shroyer, who in the heat of the crisis a year later was shocked to discover the warehouse's legal status, local lawyers were unfamiliar with co-op law. It was, she said, the easiest course in view of fees and time. There were two problems with this form of business structure, though: Taxable net profits had to be returned to the co-ops or taxed by the government; no rebate process had been formulated or written into the bylaws. In any case, such a rebate could strap the warehouse for cash. Also, under this arrangement, if the corporation went under, assets and property would go to the government for distribution to a "public purpose." The co-ops would have no say in the matter.

The co-op representatives who gathered July 20 in River Falls to discuss these and other fundamentals arrived ill prepared for the task at hand. These were fledgling businesspeople, content with the slow life in the co-op lane and hardly qualified for the tensions and complexities of an enterprise serving a five-state area and approaching a million dollars in annual sales.

Although it was more organized than the All Co-op Meetings, during its inaugural weekend the new Policy Review Board (PRB) demonstrated the same sort of indecisiveness and lack of identity that had plagued its predecessor. The group, composed of two representatives from each co-op store that patronized the warehouse, discussed various issues during the two-day meeting: credit policies, warehouse salaries, financial reporting, funding for the pharmacist operating out of the warehouse, the building fund, imports, and co-op communications. By the time the group scattered on Sunday night, it had, according to Cy O'Neil, decided it would be the decision-making body for the warehouse. What it couldn't decide was precisely what issues it could act on and what it would leave up to the warehouse collective. This pattern of inaction, exacerbated by the three-month intervals between meetings and the general awkwardness of the proceedings (large agendas, mass participation, little time), was to keep the warehouse in limbo for much of the next year, and leave it vulnerable to the ideological transformation being planned behind the scenes.

"To some extent," O'Neil wrote later, "the initiative to bring some coherence and direction to goings-on at the warehouse, the very center of co-op activity throughout a five-state area, had been passed back out to the all-co-op level. And there it lay, untouched for nearly a year."[2] With the PRB struggling to assert itself as a legitimate governing body for the co-op community, reformers within the warehouse collective and some of the individual stores began to make their case for change. At the bakery, Mill City, Selby, the Beanery, and the new Green Grass Grocery, debates over food policy and political purpose were heating up.

Green Grass, the first co-op to open with a pledge to serve "ordinary" people, created a stink by declaring in November of 1973 a new, "more liberal" food policy. "Instead of being radical and waiting for the revolution," reported coordinator Dave Olmscheid, "Green Grass is becoming the focal point for community efforts to organize and fund other programs to meet more needs."[3] To do that, profit, sound management, and canned goods would be needed.

The Green Grass position, like that of Rachlin and others on the radical fringe of the local co-op movement, sought to address the question of elitism in the stores. Olmscheid's position, though, parted company with that of the new reformers on the question of political purpose and democratic process. The new store would cater to its blue-collar neighbors, but without playing the political tune advocated, however subtly, by

Rachlin and the rest. It would, in theory at least, answer to the demands of its members, encouraging rather than discouraging the participation of a broad-based membership.

The second and third PRB meetings, both convened in the Odd-fellows Hall above Green Grass in St. Paul, featured some lively discussion of these reformist measures. In bull sessions outside the formal proceedings, activists debated the pros and cons of canned goods, paid workers, and imported foods. Traditionalists argued for unpaid workers and the participatory benefits of volunteerism, while reformists cited the benefits that paid staff would provide in continuity and efficiency. Besides, they argued, the co-op should reward those most active. "People involved in the co-op should not have to make a living working in Red Owl," one conferee noted.

On the flip side of that particular argument was the question of worker motives. Volunteers, it could reasonably be assumed, would be putting in their time in support of the co-op dream. Paid workers would invite suspicions, some claimed. They might be doing the job only for the money. Careerism (to the extent that "people's wages" could support any long-term career goals) was not condoned. The good cooperator participated willingly, subordinating self-interest to the collective purpose.

On the canned goods front, the lines, as usual, were drawn between the desire to create "a learning experience" for customers unfamiliar with the evils of the capitalist diet and the store's responsibility to stock what the neighborhood really wanted to eat. On one side were co-ops such as Good Grits (the direct descendent of True Grits), whose leaders saw themselves as educators with a goal: "We should not indiscriminately pander to people's wants that we think are wrong," one coordinator explained. On the other side were co-ops like Green Grass that believed that "the primary purpose of the co-op is economic." Co-ops, Olmscheid said, should meet the needs of their members, and should not be "quasi-moral" agencies run by "elitists" who determine other people's needs.

Both of these issues illustrated the basic worker-consumer conflict that would come to plague the co-ops as they grew larger and more visible. Co-op workers, by nature activists and educators rather than grocers, worked in the stores in response to a need for socially and politically useful work. Suspicious of those they saw as using the co-ops for more pedestrian purposes—like a job—they erected barriers to discourage careerists (low pay, amorphous structure, complicated and distorted decision-making processes) and to maintain their control of the stores. Quite unintentionally, these obstacles also hampered customer service and discouraged meaningful member participation. This agenda and the priorities established by early co-op workers, regardless of their intentions, drove a wedge between workers and consumers that later would become an effective organizing tool in the hands of reformers.

Despite the conflicts brewing, the network, and hence the warehouse, was blossoming into a full-fledged wholesale business. By October of 1974 the warehouse was moving $68,000 worth of food every month. A year earlier, its monthly volume had barely topped $15,000. The building fund campaign had succeeded beyond all expectations, and a committee reported at the October PRB meeting that it had already raised $12,000— $2,000 more than was required for the first annual payment. The movement was flush with cash, and by the third PRB meeting members would have to decide what to do with all their good fortune.

The financial report at the February PRB meeting revealed a warehouse profit in 1974 of $58,000. To reduce the tax burden on the warehouse, co-op representatives debated various proposals: A rebate to co-ops, a retirement fund, and a contingency fund were among the most attractive of the options. The warehouse lawyer recommended a rebate plan for the co-ops, but, passive as ever, the governing body refused to approve or reject the plan, leaving the issue floating somewhere between committee investigation and collective whim.

Meanwhile, a grand experiment was under way at one of the weakest links in the new food co-op chain. Two former warehouse workers, Rebecca Comeau and the ubiquitous Bob Haugen, veterans of the Marxist study groups then in vogue among certain co-op reformists, had taken control of the Beanery Co-op in south Minneapolis with the intention of showing the community what the proper ideological practices could do for an ailing victim of the "hippie elite." Plagued by poor member participation and a structureless business operation, the store had been sinking slowly into oblivion when Comeau and Haugen came on the scene. The warehouse had stopped deliveries for lack of payment, volunteers had abandoned their work shifts, and the neighborhood was prepared to let the beast die. No strong leadership existed at the store when the two reformers marched in, so what little resistance there was to the radical changes proposed quickly succumbed to the transformation message. Comeau and Haugen closed the store for a week of reorganization. They cleaned it from top to bottom, called meetings to explain the new concept to the neighborhood, and led training sessions designed to promote efficient store operations and a unified political message. That message, and the substance behind the transformation of the Beanery, were made public in March of 1975, when Comeau and Haugen released a new manifesto for the co-op movement, a critical analysis and call to arms that became known as The Beanery Paper.

The paper, which borrowed much from the writings of former SNCC executive secretary James Forman and fused it with some basic Marxist and Stalinist rhetoric, sought to rewrite the history of the New Left and to explain the true motivations of the local co-op leadership.[4] Its authors asserted that the new co-ops had emerged from the latter days of the antiwar movement and the beginnings of what they termed the "antiimperialist" movement. The parting of the two movements, according to the paper, was based on class differences. The antiwar movement was a peace movement of people who saw their essentially happy and secure lives being threatened. The antiimperialist movement, on the other hand, was a struggle of oppressed and disenfranchised people. The black liberation movement, through SNCC, had linked the Third World liberation struggle to the black liberation movement, the paper noted. "Therefore it was SNCC that spearheaded the anti-imperialist movement which linked blacks' social oppression and economic exploitation with the Third World's peoples and encouraged young blacks to resist the imperialist war in Vietnam."

The white antiwar movement picked up on this black antiwar sentiment in 1967, but didn't "keep it in its proper context of anti-imperialism," the authors claimed. In fact, the white antiwar movement differed in significant ways from its black counterpart. It set up draft counseling and elicited "enormous" financial and material support from religious and charitable organizations. Rather than fight the imperialist system, the white movement opted to drop out of it. The path to Canada followed by thousands of draft resisters attested to the general escapism of white radicals.

The original co-op leaders couldn't make the leap from antiwar to antiimperialism, because their co-op movement could only gain legitimacy by building on a political conviction to overthrow monopoly capitalism, a plan that had to be carried out through working-class struggle. Because the co-ops were created by people "grounded in the colleges and universities," the paper continued, the community was essentially white.

The manifesto went on to criticize the present leadership of the local co-ops, borrowing from Forman's analysis of class control to assert that the lack of formal structure was, in fact, not a charming coincidence, but an intentional strategy to maintain a status quo that prevented working-class leadership.[5] "There are many forms of control," the paper argued. "But the most effective control that the bourgeois leadership has exercised is establishing its class ideology as supreme." This ideology was illustrated by the co-op's problem-solving approaches ("illusory community meetings") and by the establishment of its own priorities ("do your own thing and eat organically"). "Hence we must view its control as an attempt to prevent working-class attitudes and control from replacing theirs."

At the root of the Beanery paper lay six, mostly Marxist, principles:

1 Your social bearing determines your consciousness; your position in the social system (class) determines how you look at the world.

2 Everything is interconnected. Co-ops are part of the capitalist social system and cannot be isolated from its contradictions, nor can they be isolated from other movements and struggles.

3 Everything is in a state of continual renewal and development.

4 Development proceeds from a slow and hardly noticeable buildup of "quantitative" changes that lead to abrupt "qualitative" changes.

5 There are contradictions in all things, and the struggle between these opposing forces is what causes change and development (exploiter vs. exploited, privileged vs. underprivileged). In the co-ops, the struggle is between those who regard the co-ops as their property, allowing them to escape the struggles of the working class, and those who regard themselves as part of the struggle of all exploited and underprivileged.

6 The struggle is to overthrow capitalism, replacing it with a socialist system controlled by the workers.

The Beanery Paper touched a nerve in the co-op community and proved that the Old Left–New Left ideological conflict still smoldered beneath the utopian network's mostly tranquil exterior. Clearly, the role of the working class in the new cultural revolution had not been examined, and the reformers who authored the paper were playing on the extremely defensive sensitivity that college-educated radicals betrayed toward their own class identity.

On the other hand, the new analysis gave these early co-op leaders way too much credit when it accused them of "controlling" the co-ops. Early organizing efforts did result in community meetings, and, of course, ordinary working people were seldom attracted by the hippie cult that predominated, but there was not much evidence to suggest that the Pantry crew and the rest were doing anything consciously to ensure the alienation of the working class. That they were left out of the co-op vision was certainly true, but there seemed to be no program so designed.

The co-ops certainly were elitist enterprise in certain ways. Their food policies were clearly too restrictive, even silly at times. Ordinary folks may have had some interest in participating in the operations, but they were put off simply trying to shop. At the same time, these amateur grocers did create some needed alternatives for a specific market and attempted to create a viable economic network, which at some point might have provided for the much-neglected working class. Nevertheless, Comeau and Haugen's analysis made several good points about the community's elitism. "Changing diet," Rebecca Comeau said later, "is an escape route that few can afford. Concentrating on diet and nutrition satisfies a few and diverts fire from attacks on the economic system. Pure food co-ops turn off the working class, keep the few satisfied, give them a sense of purpose and keep the heat off the system."[6]

There can be no peaceful transition to a more equitable society, she argued. At the Beanery, organizers want to concentrate on "political direction," not food policies. It's important to sell nutritious foods, she admitted, but it must come about through working-class revolution. "Concentrating on food merely deals with the symptoms of an ailing society." The question, she said, is one of priorities. "Where do we put our time and energy— into figuring out diet or maintaining the stores, or do we see the revolution coming from the masses and get beyond the co-ops?"

The paper ignited a war of words in the co-op community. Chuck Phenix and Nancy Evechild from Mill City, writing under the pseudonyms Jeb Cabbage and Emma Evechild, fired the first salvo.[7] In their tract, they argued that the Beanery Paper indicated a typical rerun of political hostilities between Marxism and anarchism, between conservative party dogma and radical libertarianism. The Beanery version of co-op history, Jeb and Emma wrote, was a "pseudo-Marxist revision full of generalizations and accusations." If, for example, being "grounded" in the colleges makes one bourgeois, they argued, then Professor Marx wouldn't qualify as a revolutionist. The Mill City leaders also challenged the claim that "anti-imperialism" was the only factor in the creation of the co-ops. "A political context" didn't descend on the co-ops out of the blue, they said. It must then have been a conscious decision made by someone. According to the Beanery Paper, it must have come out of some "bourgeois influences." The breadth of the allegations is bewildering, they continued. "The nameless leaders all began with the same motivations and haven't changed? The hippie-baiting tone of the paper," they wrote, "reads like *Time* magazine."

Jeb and Emma went on to admit that the co-ops had exhibited many "mistaken tendencies." However, some came from good motives, they argued. Because of the co-ops' desire to break through the stifling employee-customer relationship of most regular stores, many customers were confused by this new way of doing business. An "intense dislike of conventional business practice" led to informal attitudes about money and accounts. The decision-making process was often inadequately explained to new member/shoppers. "Caught in the hassles of just maintaining the day-to-day operations," they asserted, "people let down in explaining what the store is about and how it works. People didn't take seriously that they were establishing new ways of distributing foods."

Co-ops never pretended to be all things to all people, they continued. No one had been physically prevented from shopping or from opening their own co-op. "How revolutionary can any group be when they compromise strongly held principles just to reach the masses?" The alternative food system represented an attempt to move away from the university scene, away from protest in general, they explained, toward a "rooting in community—a commitment to a neighborhood, to settling down.... The co-ops were born of the spirit of all liberation movements—to hell with the rich and bosses—people working together can do it and do it better."

Jeb and Emma went on to refute, point by point, criticism aimed at them and other leaders, on the issues of working-class service, organic food policy, class biases, and economic determinism. There had been no attempt at Mill City, they claimed, to "serve the people"—only to provide an alternative to established ways of eating and food distribution. "The neighborhood... was the focal point." There had never been a "co-op policy" to "eat organic," either, they added. The policy had always been to buy the best food at the cheapest price. Besides, "Who are the food purists?" they asked rhetorically. "Is that the same elitist escapism that said no to participation in the imperial destruction of Vietnam?"

Who was the enemy? they asked. The reformers shouldn't condemn people because of their class background. Engels operated his father's factory in England, they pointed out, and was Marx's financial benefactor.

They also rejected any analysis of social change based on pure economic determinism. The socialist state, they noted, can still be a bulwark of sexism and racism.

"The co-ops are a living example of Mao's dictate to 'let a hundred flowers blossom, a thousand thoughts contend,'" they concluded. "The sight of people struggling to master their own lives free of dogma and bosses is disturbing to some—they need to be told what to do and who to follow, to be guided by the 'correct line'. But are these authoritarian tendencies compatible with the liberation struggle against patriarchal corporate-state imperialism? We think not."

Jeb and Emma's response, both in its tone and its substance, put them and Mill City immediately at odds with Comeau, Haugen, and the Beanery sympathizers. The response to the Mill City analysis, authored by warehouse workers Kris Garwick, Michael Biesanze, and Judy Long, took on a more strident tone, then, counterpunching with heavy-duty rhetoric. Jeb and Emma, they wrote, "threw a nasty bourgeois-intellectual stone from the unsanitary cesspool of anti-communism." This "Nixon-type tactic," they said, was meant to discredit their political opposition. They're doing it for two reasons: to protect their control of Mill City and to protect the "class clique" that owns and controls most of the co-ops.

Reiterating their version of co-op history, the Beanery crew accused "hippies and other forms of cultural cliques" of escapism, self-righteousness, and an absence of class solidarity. "Working-class customers at North County Co-op and other co-ops have been driven away by many documented attitudes and practices of class snobbishness and contempt." All these tendencies, they explained, emerged from the "puritan morality" stand taken on the war by white upper-class war resisters whose chief aim was to escape the draft and the war, not to change the system. "The struggle against imperialism is a class struggle. Not to take a class stand—for the revolutionary workers and against the imperialists—is to not really be anti-imperialist at all. Just a new kind of Puritan Morality."

The co-ops, they argued, claim to be antiimperialist. They profess to abhor capitalism, practice no-profit beliefs and selective boycotting of products, but they don't practice what they preach and must be changed. "The co-ops were a progressive development in the Twin Cities. But now it is a new day and if the co-ops are going to keep abreast of the times, they are going to have to advance from their present position of escape from evil for a few people to really taking on evil, i.e. monopoly capitalism for and with the masses of oppressed people. This means the leadership must be constantly transformed or be replaced."

Right now, the authors continued, co-ops don't represent any sort of liberation and alternative for most working people. What they are is simply a liberation for a few people, allowing them to escape from the working-class struggle. Indeed, the co-ops smack of petty capitalism. "At least a million people are involved in the Peoples' Bakery. . . . And yet some of the people at the Peoples' Bakery feel like it is their bakery . . . their property, to do whatever they want with. This is petty capitalism disguised as worker control."

The co-ops, finally, must move beyond these class-biased tendencies if they are to be a tool for building a revolutionary base, the paper continued. In a direct reference to Jeb and Emma, the authors concluded that this might be beyond the current leadership. "Any time an organization or a person feels that strongly held principles must be compromised to reach the masses of workers, then there is no doubt that the organization or person is counter-revolutionary and the strongly held principles are anti–working class."

The Marxist-anarchist conflict that underlay this controversy was addressed explicitly in a tract published among this opening flurry of the paper war by a member of the Red Star Herbs collective, Cliff Sloane. Attacking the narrow-mindedness of the Beanery position, Sloane pointed out the sometimes ambiguous, though always important, motivations and goals of the co-ops. "This black-and-white vision that you maintain is so hard on people and it's very simplistic, but worst of all, it makes NO ROOM FOR DISSENT OF ANY KIND. Isn't personal freedom what we're after? Then why attack it so cruelly? As people gain more freedom in life, they become even more different, not less," he wrote.

"It seems weird to me to go out and save the world but remain an emotional cripple inside," he continued. "And then you say that racism and sexism come from capitalism? Or class background? Oh really! You're wasting energy trying to clean up the world when your own backyard is a mess. . . . We have to strive to reflect in our personal dealings the society we wish to create, or we'll repeat the same mistakes all over again."[8]

Other position papers vied for the interest of a suddenly awakened community: more anarchist viewpoints ("we're just beginning to learn how to feed ourselves"); a statement by the Revolutionary Marxist Study Group of the Fourth International ("Co-ops cannot change the basic conditions that the vast majority of people live under.")[9]; and a statement "On the Radish Threat to the Process of Dialectical Self-Interpretation in the Co-op Movement: A Coughing Spasm."[10]

Although the dialogue sparked by the Beanery Paper seemed at times brutish, at times comical, the issues raised were serious and enlivened what had become a stagnant movement in the Twin Cities. At a debate on the Beanery Paper, March 23, 1975, eighty people braved a fierce snowstorm to discuss the direction of the co-op network. Although the outcome was inconclusive, the battle lines clearly had been drawn. The challenge, voiced succinctly at one point in the debate when a Beanery worker rose in defense of reform, rang clear: "You gotta stop being hippies," she said. "These people need leadership and that is where you are lacking."

Later, a sign appeared in each of the co-ops, placed there by members of the Beanery staff. It read simply: CRITICISM—DISCUSSION—TRANSFORMATION.

# CHAPTER SIX

## The Facts of Life

Comeau, Haugen, and their faction of co-op reformers moved quickly to "transform" the warehouse and Mill City—the warehouse because they wanted to control its political and economic clout, Mill City because its leaders had committed egregious political errors by opposing the new analysis. A week prior to the co-op's monthly community meeting in April of 1975, the reformers, now known publicly by their affiliation with the Co-op Organization (CO), began berating, questioning, and prodding workers about their politics. At one point one of the critics announced his intention to end the workers' control of the store.

At the April 2 meeting, where participants agreed to debate food policy, members of the CO, accompanied by seven or eight allies from outside the neighborhood, made public its demands. The CO was also building a majority among warehouse workers, and pestering those who veered from the party line. Behind the scenes, the group was preparing to challenge the legitimacy of the warehouse Policy Review Board at its May meeting. Rachlin, Haugen, and warehouse financial coordinator Michael Biesanze assembled a mountain of analysis for the fledgling directors of the organization: a seventeen-page history of the co-ops, a six-page economic analysis, and an eight-page restructuring proposal. So confident were they of their chances of overriding the PRB that the group included among this literature an invitation to discuss co-op transformation at nearby Walker Church on Sunday morning, when the second day of the PRB meeting was scheduled to begin.

The warehouse governing body was not quite a year old when co-op representatives gathered May 3 in Minneapolis, and its grasp of issues and decision-making capabilities had not evolved much during that time. The

CO, on the other hand, had been busily gathering allies within the movement, courting disaffected cooperators with its new sense of direction, purpose, and discipline. In formal and informal meetings with key co-op leaders around the network, movement critics had effectively expanded their ranks prior to the meeting. They were prepared that Saturday to demonstrate their strength.

The gathering was called to order at 10 A.M., and after roll was taken and announcements made, the chair, Aggie Fletcher of North Country, turned the floor over to Biesanze for the financial report. Biesanze distributed two sheets of paper to co-op reps, a balance sheet for first-quarter business and a warehouse break-even chart. Questions poured forth from slightly bewildered directors, but Bob Haugen asked that they be held until the floor presentation. Biesanze then launched into his financial report, a rapid-fire litany of warehouse troubles featuring current ratios, assets, liabilities, quick ratios, net working capital, operating ratios, earnings ratios—all designed to demonstrate how complex warehouse business had become. As might be expected, the befuddled PRB members responded with blank stares to the indecipherable figures on the pages before them.

The warehouse, Biesanze continued, is currently running on $38,000 in short-term loans, $14,000 of which are in personal accounts of warehouse workers. Labor costs are also increasing, he noted, and the warehouse space is too small; they can only store 65 percent of the items on their price list. The bottom line? The warehouse, so vital to the co-op network, is in trouble.

The co-ops have from the beginning operated on two false premises, he argued: that you can operate a nonprofit business in a capitalist economic system, and that co-op people would always reach into their bank accounts to bail out their co-ops. These loans and donations, he said, have created a class clique of co-op supporters who actually control the co-ops. "From historical evidences, we see that there wasn't a concrete strategy for the existence of the co-ops except for the innate class behavior of the leadership to exercise continuous ideological control of the co-ops," he explained.[1]

Further, an antagonistic contradiction emerged from the first-day of the first co-op store, he claimed. On one side of the contradiction was "the subjective desire of the co-op leaders to create an economic socialist structure in isolation from the working-class movement." On the other side there was no strategy based on "the economic laws of production," he noted. "Hence, we have characterized this contradiction as co-op leadership forcing its idealistic plan upon objective laws of reality."

Something has got to give, he argued. "The present co-op leadership has forfeited its right to lead for it has no sense of economic reality. The average worker on the street knew that the inflation rate was soaring, unemployment was steadily on the rise and the prices on all commodities hadn't been checked by any government controls which means the cost of living is still going up. In spite of all of those signals indicating economic danger, the co-op leadership hasn't done anything to circumvent an economic collapse of the co-ops."

Essentially, what Biesanze was saying was that the antiprofit, antibusiness philosophy of the co-ops had set them up for failure. Either the old leadership would have to move over, or the utopian dream was going to die a painful death. "Idealism and business don't mix," he concluded, and it was time to usher in a new era with new leaders "trained and fitted for the task of bringing the co-op system to a new level of economic development with emphasis on employing more productive forces."

The CO strategy caught the PRB totally by surprise, creating an atmosphere of confusion and crisis. Random questions filled the air, and panic set in. The body, incapable of confirming or repudiating the figures Biesanze supplied, was paralyzed.

Following a lunch break, the PRB reconvened to discuss the financial report. The chair set up a random list of speakers and discussion continued until Mark Larson, a CO supporter from Powderhorn Co-op, yielded the floor to Michael Rachlin. For the next half hour, she read from the CO's history of the co-ops, railing on "in a singularly obnoxious tone of voice," according to one listener. Before she could move on to another tract, the startled PRB moved on to the next agenda item. The CO and its sympathizers, about twenty to thirty people, walked out of the meeting.

The remaining group got down to business then and moved slowly through the cumbersome agenda until about five P.M., when CO members returned and a made a motion to reconsider its presentation. Shouting matches and general pandemonium ensued, and while a roll call vote was in progress, the reformers stormed out of the room again, shouting, "If anyone wants to get down to the real work, we'll be meeting in the back room." With the quorum disintegrating, the PRB adjourned.

Later that evening, while cooperators were winding down at a dance at the Oddfellows Hall, the CO was laying claim to the warehouse. Sometime that Saturday night, a group of CO members walked into the offices of Peoples' Warehouse and grabbed the checkbook and financial records. "The Peoples' Warehouse now belongs to the people!" CO member Jerry Path announced to startled co-op leaders the next morning at Seward Cafe. A similar announcement was made at another co-op hangout in St. Paul, Commonplace Restaurant. The news came with an invitation to join the CO at 10:30 that morning for a restructuring meeting.

Mark Larson officially announced the coup when the PRB reconvened at 10 A.M. By late afternoon, the group had released a public statement condemning the move. Four PRB members, Tracy Landis of Red Star Apothecary, Randy McLaughlin of the warehouse, Terry Hokenson of North Country, and Seward Co-op's Kris Olsen, were selected to serve as executive officers for the suddenly threatened corporation. These four would negotiate for the PRB and act in the body's absence.

That night, the faithful gathered at the warehouse for a tactics meeting. Some felt they should stay the night in order that the business could reopen Monday morning without complications. Ten elected to spend the night, among them Phill Baker, who later filed a report and analysis of the events that transpired there.

"I was there Sunday night when the iron pipes were swung and the phones were ripped out and the doors were blocked," he wrote. "I was one of the ten who had been asked to stay at the Peoples' Warehouse overnight. 'Just in case,' it was said, 'they'd come in the middle of the night.' They did come, and they came with a military plan of action and with weapons.

"There were about 35, with a few more hiding in the front office. They came looking for violence, trying to pick fights; they acted like the worst barroom hoodlums you may have seen. Who are these people? Many of them are former co-workers of mine, some were former friends or people I was just becoming friendly with this past year. At least two had lived with me. Not a few had been on the streets with me, with me, against the Tactical Squads of Minneapolis, Madison and D.C. Now they were the goons. Standing grim and paramilitary, ready to hit and restrain. Ready to intimidate and control. And they did these things.

"Some have asked, 'Who had the clubs? Who did the hitting?' As if a Storm Troop has individuals with choices. Apparently, not all the invaders carried weapons. But that is not the point. This action was premeditated. It was supported by them all. There is no difference between a club-wielding Storm Trooper and one who barricades you in the room so you can't leave the brutality. There is no difference between a club-wielding Storm Trooper and one who restrains a brother from helping a beaten sister. They did these things. They all agreed upon them. They supported these actions.

"When the Co-op Organization came into the warehouse at 3 A.M. we offered them food and smiles and talk. 'Let's rap,' we said. They said, 'No. We came here seriously.' Then they drew the lines. 'You've got 30 minutes to get out, join us or get the shit kicked out of you. We'll burn you, we'll shove your balls up to your ears. We came here to offer you a choice; either join us or get your asses kicked. Do we make ourselves perfectly clear?' In no way did we choose sides or draw lines. They were drawn for us.

"What about the issues they've raised? These people talk about some important things. They use language I tend to use and study social problems and situations I'm interested in. They've raised criticism. I also have. But they have no monopoly on revolution. Simply because they scream the loudest and back up their analysis with weapons does not mean other analyses are wrong, or that other revolutionaries aren't working hard for the same stated goals. Some people are impressed with the violent, macho dramatics of these people. Some people have longed for a party to join, to militarize their life—this I've heard from some of them, my former co-workers.

"This week's act is only the beginning of a very bad drama. I believe that what the Co-op Organization has done so far is part of a sophisticated and orchestrated program. I believe that as the followers are led from questionable act to another, heavier tactic, they will be committed to ever-increasing levels of outrage to justify the previous ones. It is a spiral of self-induced frenzy that feeds on itself and is manipulated by its leaders.

"There are many fronts in the struggle for increasing human consciousness and happiness," Baker concluded. "If Stalinist materialists have a path, an analysis, I encourage them to follow it—to set up their community projects, their political education projects. But don't try to take over what has been created by other committed people. Don't try to fight the people closest to you. Don't try to get in our way because we'll sidestep your immature ravings and violence as history always has shown progressives to do."[2]

Word of the occupation spread quickly through the community. By eight o'clock Monday morning a crowd had gathered in the warehouse yard. Some talked with members of the CO occupation force, urging negotiations; others engaged in shouting matches. Mike Dunn, a longtime co-op supporter, tried to take matters into his own hands. Grabbing a shovel, he hoisted himself onto the roof of the two-story building and began smashing windows until he was subdued by the CO. Collective members unsympathetic to the new direction at the warehouse were turned away from work. Edward Winter was met at the door and barred entry. Bob Haugen confronted another worker, Koti, telling her things had changed. "Your political views are not correct," he told her. "You may not take part in decision-making. You will have to leave."

A few blocks away at Whole Foods, warehouse customers began lining up alternative food sources and talking about a boycott and mass march on the warehouse. At 9 A.M., PRB leaders gathered at the bank to claim legal control of warehouse funds. They found that the CO had already withdrawn $6,000, but the bank nevertheless agreed to recognize them as legal representatives of the occupied business.

That evening, co-ops around the Twin Cities held emergency meetings and reported to the PRB that there was strong support for a boycott and march on the warehouse. There was, however, unanimous opposition to calling in the police. The question of police involvement brought a sharp renunciation from CO members Dean Zimmerman and Paul McClusky. Zimmerman, like Keith Ruona a well-known co-op personality both in the Twin Cities and out of state, had been recruited for his standing in the community. His response to talk of police action was indicative of his own transformation. "Once again the struggle in the co-ops has advanced and heightened the contradictions," he wrote in a paper distributed widely in the network. "Before, all the forces involved at least paid lip service to being progressive and anti-capitalist. Now, those whose primary allegiance is to the capitalist system have begun to show their hand clearly.

"By calling on the cops, the courts and the big corporations to carry out the interests of one side in the warehouse struggle, these people showed whose power they respect."[3]

From a community that had learned of police and FBI/CIA infiltrators during the antiwar days, any move toward police protection would have seemed reactionary indeed. The CO, at least for the moment, could count on there being no police response to their actions. They were thus free to negotiate with the inept PRB from a position of power. The two parties met formally Monday evening at 10:30 to begin serious talks. The PRB said it wouldn't bring in the police; the CO said that it hadn't changed its position, and it meant to transform the warehouse structure to give more control to the collective, a group, it said, that would soon be composed of members of the working class.

The discussions were hampered more by confused process, however, than by either party's intransigence. The PRB leaders, though elected to represent the co-ops, were afraid to take a stand before consulting with the stores. The CO occupation forces seemed to lack leadership as well. No one seemed to know who was calling the shots at the warehouse. In fact, one negotiator revealed that the CO was being phased out in favor of a new "democratic centralist organization."

The next morning, about seventy-five people gathered a few blocks from the warehouse at Fair Oaks Park to receive alternative prices and product-ordering lists. There, they decided against a march on the warehouse, fearing provocateurs. The support for a boycott remained strong, however, with ex–warehouse workers organizing a temporary distribution system.

One day after the warehouse bank account was reclaimed by the PRB, the bank reported that it had found in the Beanery Co-op account the $6,000 taken from the warehouse account. The funds were returned to the PRB–held account, leaving the occupied warehouse without any money with which to do business. Meanwhile, the Southside Community Garage, which had been repairing the warehouse truck, turned it over to the new Ad Hoc Distributing Committee after hiding it from the CO occupation forces.

After negotiations adjourned Tuesday night, the CO made its first serious bid for legal recognition. Larry Zepp and Mark Johnson, two of the three original signers of the warehouse articles of incorporation, went to the bank Wednesday morning to assert their control of the business and the much-needed checkbook. Bank officials, confused by conflicting claims made by the two parties, froze the business accounts altogether, preventing either group from writing checks. Later that afternoon, the real crunch of the controversy hit home. The PRB was informed that its May contract-for-deed payment check had bounced. The warehouse was in default; its former owner could begin legal proceedings to claim the building himself.

This development, devoid of rhetoric and political meaning but laced with real-world urgency, was enough to bring the parties together for the first time. The bills had to be paid, regardless of who had the upper hand, regardless of who had the most convincing line. While the political circus continued, the two combatants agreed to designate check signers from both camps to keep the business afloat.

Out in the community, the two forces vied for the support of the co-ops and the masses. Most of the co-ops threw their support behind the boycott forces; only the Beanery, Powderhorn, the Riverside Cafe, and the new St. Paul bakery, Our Daily Bread, continued to buy from the occupied warehouse.

Distributing food to the disaffected was a delicate operation. Dean Zimmerman had confronted the driver on his first run and threatened to report the truck stolen. As a result, security measures were tightened; only a few insiders knew the exact delivery route. Receiving goods was a similarly secretive undertaking for this suddenly mobile warehouse. Suppliers would meet the delivery truck at a prearranged location, where, parked back to back, they would load the co-op-bound goods.

The CO was more public in its efforts to get goods out to the people. Fliers printed and distributed throughout the neighborhood on Friday announced a cheap food sale at the warehouse on Saturday and Sunday. The sale attracted a few curious shoppers and a picket line of co-op leaders. More successful was the free potato-distribution project. In two days over the weekend the CO gave away some fifteen thousand pounds of spuds (and a similar amount of weighty rhetoric) to appreciative neighbors.

Sunday evening at a meeting of CO supporters, the vanguard organization was replaced by a new group called the Mass Organization. This juggling of labels by essentially the same personalities with the same mission was both a response to the boycott and an indication that the struggle, at least in the eyes of the occupation force, had risen to a new level. The occupation had shaken the co-op community, causing it to question its priorities and examine its leaders. Now was the time to take the struggle out to the individual stores and to the working class it had been neglecting.

Dean Zimmerman called the warehouse takeover political theater, an effort to wake up the co-ops by attacking their central activity. Whether or not the resulting boycott, and the subsequent weakening of the warehouse as a central business activity, were part of their script is anybody's guess. Their contempt for the PRB members as decision-makers probably didn't prepare them for the actions carried out against them: the boycott, the picketing, and the alternative distribution system. Nevertheless, it can be plausibly argued that with negotiations underway, the new Mass Organization remained in the driver's seat. The PRB was not going to let go of the warehouse and it was not going to go to the cops. The takeover had accomplished its mission.

Ready now to negotiate seriously, the occupation forces sat down on Monday, May 12, with mediators from the West Bank Tenant's Union and with PRB representatives Tracy Landis and Terry Hokenson to draw up a joint statement. Tempers flared over a clause condemning the use of violence in the takeover, and Hokenson stormed out of the meeting. Landis remained, and the parties finally produced an agreement. The draft statement traveled back and forth from the negotiators to the various interested groups, and the next two days were spent revising clauses repulsive to one group or the other. The clause condemning violence was disposed of altogether, and the negotiators agreed to leave any restructuring issues up to the June PRB meeting. On Thursday, May 15, in a vacant warehouse, the occupation ended with both parties' signing a statement.

Reviewing the strained negotiations in a letter to the co-ops, PRB executives noted that there were really two series of negotiations.[4] The first set involved direct talks between PRB officers and CO representatives. Different representatives of the occupation forces kept showing up, they explained, and much ground had to be re-covered at each meeting. They encountered a good deal of resistance and evasion; often the CO representative could not answer important questions, nor did they have the authority to take a position on key issues.

The second set of talks began, they said, after the boycott began to tighten the economic noose around the warehouse. These were mediated effectively in the writing of the joint statement. "We feel that the establishment of clear lines of accountability summarizes the formal side of the agreement. The major content is made up of the provisions for how decisions will be made concerning new products and other warehouse policies. A majority of ten out of the 15 warehouse collective members will be required for a decision, and there will be a moratorium on adding any new foods for ten days after the warehouse re-opens. The criteria for adding new foods will be reasonable demand from the co-ops and the comparative efficiency of either handling the new items in the warehouse or using some other means of distribution."

The agreement opened the warehouse for business on the following Monday and brought an end to overt hostility between the two factions, but it set the stage for a showdown in June. CO leaders, confident of their appeal outside the Twin Cities, visited numerous co-ops outside the metro area prior to the June 21 meeting, urging co-op representatives to come to the next meeting "with a thorough grasp of the central issues, [representing] the broadest possible interest in their local co-ops." PRB loyalists countered with a June 1 meeting to draft a restructuring proposal that would strip the warehouse of its influence in the network.

In the meantime, the papers analyzing the warehouse takeover and related events continued to fly back and forth, heating the controversy still further, and heightening the prospect of an explosive June PRB meeting. Terry Hokenson noted the similarities between the current situation and the struggle in the Finnish co-ops on the Iron Range in the 1920s, advocating a balance between the subjection of the co-ops to narrow sectarian politics and the movement away from politics altogether.[5]

"What course may be steered between subjection and neutrality?" he asked. "I believe the answer lies in education and a constructive program which are consistent with the character of cooperatives as popular or mass organizations. Within the formal structures of the co-ops there is room for funded programs which can build and educate in areas of great indirect political significance, while leaving potentially divisive political programs to formally independent organizations.

"The directly political organizations would be informally related to the cooperatives through dual membership of persons, social relations between persons, and through various educational projects and communications media. The indirectly political programs within cooperatives would focus on multiplication, expansion and diversification of cooperative enterprises and on education in areas of consumer products and production."

Hokenson's analysis implicitly demonstrated the error of the CO's warehouse takeover and of its strategy of transformation. The co-ops, he argued, must maintain their independence and autonomy from formal political organization in order to serve any sort of revolutionary function. Blurring the two, as the CO had done, hampered the work of each. A communist analysis, distributed in a paper by Pam Costain and Laura Davis, highlighted the differences between "mass organizations" and "cadre-type organizations," and took the CO to task for mixing the two.[6] Mass organizations, they wrote, serve to introduce socialist politics to the working class. They can help form cadre organizations, and serve as "arenas" for sharpening the cadre's political understanding in specific areas of concern. The co-ops, however, were mass organizations of a fairly low level, they explained. People were attracted only on the basis of price and nutritional value. Communists must patiently explain the role of the capitalist system in these food issues and make it clear that the co-ops alone can never really solve even their food problems. The CO, they concluded, erred in taking the warehouse and demanding the transformation of the co-ops because such a transformation "is entirely incompatible with the co-op's character as a mass organization."

The warehouse, they said, should be controlled by a democratic system under which the various co-ops and the warehouse workers share power. Communists shouldn't give up on the co-ops, either. They should simply be more patient. "Communists must learn to work in mass organizations properly, even if the mass organization does not yet have a good political perspective."

Other papers were less diplomatic. Leo Cashman, a worker at Seward Co-op, blasted the CO for creating a "sham issue" of PRB performance: "It was simply a pretext used to grab the warehouse. Of course, the PRB is slow and unwieldy, because so many co-ops want to be represented on it, and so many of them want to be heard," he explained. "The Co-op Organization detests the PRB because the PRB is democratically run, and the CO has never had any hope for democratic change. They came with every intent to disrupt the PRB, to render it ineffective. If their objections were truly to combat apathy and informality at the PRB, they could have replaced informal selection by formal votes. Instead, their whole contempt for the democratic process was clear to most who were at the PRB meeting."[7]

The CO, for its part, sought to explain in the weeks prior to the pivotal meeting the reasons behind its actions at the warehouse. In a paper entitled "What Has Really Been Happening at the Peoples' Warehouse," CO analysts once against presented their argument that the co-ops were elitist, class-biased businesses dominated by people who viewed them as their own private property.[8] They warned that the warehouse was threatened by individuals who had financed the business in its early days.

Opposed to the call for transformation, these moneylenders and their allies among the co-op leadership have torn down CO posters, thrown out their leaflets, and threatened them with "personal attacks." Just prior to the May PRB meeting, they explained, CO leaders at the warehouse were told that the business was dependent on loans of $38,000, "and that if we continued to push for transformation, many of the money lenders would take back their money. On Saturday at the PRB meeting, we attempted to present these facts," they continued. "We were declared out of order, although the subject on the agenda was the financial situation. When we finally got the floor, we were shouted down and then debate was cut off.

"We brought in 30 people, not the official 'PRB representatives' for sure, but mostly working-class people who were asking for transformation. Again the PRB refused to allow discussion, although this time a majority voted for it. The time had come to take some action! We had been patient too long. We had hundreds of signatures on petitions demanding an end to private ownership of co-ops. We had tried community meetings, as well as the PRB, and found the official controlling organs of the co-ops unwilling to even listen to this mass criticism from below. It was clear that the issue had to be forced or the ruling powers of co-ops would continue to be able to ignore it. So we yanked the money out of the bank before the owners could. We want to make it clear that we did not take this money to spend on ourselves, we intend to use it to buy the kinds of food that has been demanded by masses of people and denied by the co-op leadership."

More than a hundred people gathered at the Powderhorn Park building in south Minneapolis June 21 to decide the structure and ownership of the warehouse. Four restructuring proposals were submitted for consideration by the PRB: a charter for the co-op movement, a decentralist structure, a working committee structure, and a proposal for legal incorporation as a cooperative.[9]

The charter proposal, written and presented by Noush Kauskis, a professor of political science at Moorhead State College and a member of Plain Foods Co-op in Fargo, North Dakota, called for a thrice-annual General Assembly of Co-ops and the creation of new committees meeting to discuss issues between the assemblies. The warehouse, under this proposal, would be financed, staffed, and controlled by the co-ops.

The presentation of the proposal was muddled. It was criticized as impractical, and lacking in familiarity with the current realities of the co-op system. Regardless of their relative merits, it became quite clear from the first comments that the anarchist "decentralist" proposal and CO–sponsored "working committees" approach were really the ones to be considered here.

Chuck Phenix of Mill City presented the decentralist proposal next. It was based on the simple presumption that the warehouse should no longer be treated any differently than the rest of the co-ops and collectives in the system. The workers, regardless of alliances, should be allowed to control their own business. Projects currently undertaken by the warehouse should be the responsibility of the community as a whole. Outreach, education, and communications functions would then be fulfilled by committees operating under a new organization, the All Cooperating Assembly (ACA).

The proposal regarded the concentration of many network activities in the warehouse as the main weakness of the co-op network. Though in its early stages the warehouse service encouraged and depended upon co-op volunteer support, the growing sophistication of the operation had demanded a solid core of workers and a new sense of specialization, driving co-op activists increasingly into a narrower, store-centered vision of the movement. The decentralists did not favor this narrow view necessarily, but the ACA could perhaps pull the community together once again. They simply wanted to take some power and control from the warehouse, and by implication, from the CO.

The proposal also "acceded explicitly to the unworkability of the PRB and implicitly to the control of the warehouse by persons identified with the Co-op Organization." It stated that "workers should have direct control over their workplace" and that the warehouse, controlled by its workers, should be an autonomous entity, just like the co-ops that bought from it.

The decentralists were clearly anti–CO, owing to their investment in the community status quo and their anarchist tendencies. The proposal, when seen in the light of the successful boycott of the warehouse after its occupation, was clearly designed to alienate the CO–controlled business even further, in effect allowing the CO to go down with the ship.

The CO–sponsored "working committees" proposal, presented by warehouse worker Kris Garwick, stressed the importance of committee work in the structure and operation of the network. Most of the committees mentioned in the proposal had been or were currently operating (purchasing and expansion, distribution, farm, and others). These would be coordinated by a Workers Administration Committee composed of representatives of the other committees. The PRB would remain in place for information and communication functions and to provide a legal umbrella.

All committee work at the time was dominated by CO sympathizers, so it was clear that the proposal was designed to consolidate CO control of the warehouse, while maintaining the illusion of democratic processes through the much-maligned PRB. In fact, the Workers Administration Committee, the body that would have final authority over warehouse decisions, was not even mentioned in Garwick's presentation. In a paper distributed at the meeting, the CO stated: "The Workers Administration Committee would consist of members from each of the other committees and function as the place where all the ends and pieces come together. This committee has not yet been established and will not be until the other committees are functioning and accepted."

In other words, any democratic structure that might emerge from this proposal would not come until after the PRB had approved a CO–controlled warehouse and distribution system. Considering events of the past few months, it wasn't likely that the gathering was going to place that kind of trust in the hands of the opposition. When asked whether present committee members would allow CO opponents to assume leadership positions on these committees, Garwick replied that "leadership would be accepted from people doing the necessary work, but . . . that [I] would have difficulty working with someone who didn't share [my] political ideology."

The final proposal, a bylaw change incorporating the warehouse as a legal cooperative, had generated some enthusiasm prior to the meeting. A legal co-op would settle the ownership problem once and for all, giving the PRB official governing authority and removing any legal challenge to its legitimacy. The tax and rebate questions would be answered as well, with the co-op's owners receiving a percentage of profits based on their patronage. This was, however, a showdown between the communists and the anarchists, and although the proposal had some merit, the body pronounced it overly bureaucratic. Few had traveled to the Twin Cities looking for a compromise; the community's polarization was virtually complete. Sunday's vote was going to be for the CO or against the CO. The middle ground had been removed.

In the discussions that took place that evening at the Peoples' Center, it became clear early on that the decentralists were going to carry the day, despite questions of control and ownership of the warehouse. When the meeting reconvened on Sunday morning it was with a sense of smugness that a voice in the crowd moved immediately to fire the warehouse collective. The motion, however, was quickly withdrawn when the chair informed the body that no such action could be pursued with the Joint Agreement still in force, which it was until the end of the day. Although the CO had dodged that particular bullet, it was clear that the reformers were not going to prevail on this occasion.

The decentralist proposal was approved 33 to 0 with three abstentions, following a long and confused discussion centered on the issue of hiring and firing. This bit of uncharacteristic decisiveness immediately crumbled, however, as the group fought valiantly to ignore the just-completed resolution. After an amendment creating a purchasing and pricing committee failed to pass, the PRB launched into another discussion of warehouse ownership and control, resulting in the "remarkably unclear" position that whatever proposal was finally approved should have the "same sense of ownership" as the present bylaws. By a 22 to 9 to 4 vote, this resolution was passed. As usual, the PRB was waffling: By their earlier vote, thirty-three co-op representatives had given up the warehouse to the workers there. Before the end of the day, twenty-two had taken it back.

This bit of confusion did not prevent the group from going ahead with the business of setting up another organization. They may not have known what to do with the distribution function at the warehouse, but they certainly wanted to pull the rest of the power out of the hands of the CO. Despite the confusion, these actions did represent a solid repudiation of the CO. Not one of the seven members of the new organization's Coordinating Committee had ties to the reformist faction.

With the meeting winding down and people getting restless, Randy McLaughlin, one of the three original incorporators of the warehouse, read a statement announcing his resignation as the business's official president. Other executive officers moved to dissolve the executive officer positions. "You can't do that," McLaughlin yelled. "You have to have someone in those offices." Kris Garwick's suggestion that the collective serve as executive officers was met with a resounding "NO!" Somebody nominated Ed Winter to fill the vacancy, but he declined, and for a moment, the body was stumped. Finally someone suggested leaving the position vacant: "That's what the vice president is for." Reprieved by common sense, the PRB gratefully passed a motion to that effect.

Through all this sat Susan Shroyer, patiently awaiting a chance to speak. Peoples' Pantry seemed a long way off; the good vibrations of West Bank cooperation had somehow been lost. Divorced now from Keith Ruona and estranged from the political vision they had nurtured at Winding Road Farm and Georgeville, she herself had become a target of CO threats and harassment.

It had all been planned in advance, she said later, all the tactics approved, the targets selected, the weaknesses probed. They knew exactly what they were doing. As she read to this crowd of spent idealists her statement calling for an end to political and personal harassment, she knew that somehow the dream had finally gone sour.

As she sat down, someone suggested the meeting reconvene in five minutes to discuss the issues she had raised. But there were no takers, and the PRB adjourned.

# CHAPTER SEVEN

---

# Invasion of the "Stalinoids"

I t is a tribute to the discipline of the apparatus from which the CO had sprung that, despite all the debate, all the papers, all the ruckus that came down upon the co-op community during the wild spring of 1975, the organization still managed somehow to shroud itself in mystery. The fighters on the front lines, the Comeaus, the Haugens, the Rachlins, and the rest, were familiar faces in the movement, for the most part, but the leader of the organization, Theo Smith, was known to only the innermost circle of followers.

Indeed, Smith maintained his anonymity for nearly twenty years, until organization defectors filtered back to the Twin Cities from Chicago (where Smith's organization is headquartered) and began slowly to tell the story of his cultlike operation.

According to internal organization documents, Smith grew up in Alabama, where he joined SNCC in the early 1960s. A devoted follower of James Forman, Smith worked as director of economic programs through the summer of 1968 in Mississippi, where he helped organize rural cooperatives for SNCC. With the organization disintegrating (a proposed merger with the Black Panther Party collapsed in 1969), Smith moved to Chicago to organize the Revolutionary Action Movement. There he met Dan Stern, a white academic married to a Sears-Roebuck heiress. Meanwhile, Forman was busy organizing black auto workers in Detroit and forming the Black Workers Congress, the group from which the Co-op Organization, and many other Marxist-Leninist groups connecting the Black Liberation Movement and the white youth movement, sprouted.

In late 1973, Stern's wife, who owned a farm commune in western Wisconsin, introduced Smith to Bob Haugen and Keith Ruona at Winding Road Farm, and they began formulating the CO strategy. "It was all planned from the very beginning," said Susan Shroyer, who'd witnessed the early meetings at the farm. "They knew exactly what they were doing." While Haugen and Ruona made regular forays into the Twin Cities co-op scene, Smith set up a construction business in Minneapolis, and recruited co-op workers for drywall and painting jobs in order to check out their political sensibilities. In Marxist-Leninist study groups, those sensibilities became more apparent, and Smith carefully selected the most disciplined of these new reformists to be part of his organization.

Given specific tasks and assigned to units with a contact person inside the organization (usually several levels below Smith), these early CO recruits were never told who ran the organization. Their job simply was to carry out orders and maintain a strict silence about the inner workings of the group. CO member Fred Ojile, who professed to have been an insider, said he'd know the rest of the leadership if he "saw them on the street," but he never knew their real names. Smith's control of his followers was so complete, according to CO sources, that he was able to arrange marriages, divorces, and births, as well as to relocate members according to his whim.

CO members assumed there was a connection between Smith and Forman and other Black Workers Congress refugees, and indeed a number of other like-minded groups were operating around the country. Less than a month after the Peoples' Warehouse takeover, members of the Revolutionary Union in Ithaca, New York, invaded three alternative organizations in a manner that seemed remarkably similar to the Twin Cities uprising. According to one firsthand observer, "All three thefts occurred on the same weekend and all followed a similar internal struggle: at least one or more members of the group strongly pushed the RU line, later influencing one or more members of the group. RU cadre and supporters conducted what they called a 'political line struggle' in which other members are bombarded with reasons why the RU line is absolutely correct. After endless meetings, papers and counter papers, attempted purges, resignations and heated arguments, RU had to 'destroy the organization to save it.' In each case the claim is made that the masses will continue to be served by RU, only better, and that the people whom RU forced out did not see the importance of the work—especially in light of 'the present crisis of the imperialist state.'"[1] In the mid-1970s, RU members also invaded the Chicano Workers Center in El Paso, Texas, and took over the Vietnam Veterans Against the War national office.

Although such incidents spawned much speculation about the origins of the CO leadership in the Twin Cities, the organization never stood still long enough to allow much scrutiny. By the time co-op representatives met in mid-August to create the organization mandated by the June PRB meeting, the CO had shifted gears again, choosing to ignore the gathering altogether. The All Cooperating Assembly (ACA) was, after all, a direct challenge to warehouse power and influence in the co-op network and was created against the wishes of the reformist faction.

The new organization was also less important to the CO than the individual co-ops comprising it. Although the June meeting did little to clarify ultimate control of the Peoples' Warehouse, it did effectively isolate CO power within that business, which emerged from the pivotal weekend gathering with a different identity. No longer the official centerpiece of the local co-op movement, the warehouse and the CO would now be forced to vie for influence in the network by working through the individual stores.

There was another challenge. On August 3, a small group of co-op activists met at North Country to discuss plans to develop an alternative warehouse to serve those co-ops still disenchanted with the CO line and skeptical of its promises of moderation in the future. This was the group that most concerned the reformers, for their already shaky business depended upon the return of the co-op flock to the warehouse. Another warehouse would destroy the economic leverage they had once enjoyed, and force a radical change in tactics.

Three CO members arrived uninvited at the North Country meeting. When they were asked to leave, two of them complied, leaving Larry Zepp alone to force a confrontation. He did, refusing to budge unless he was thrown out of the store. The meeting adjourned, and, rather than provoke a struggle, the seven organizers left the downcast Zepp behind as they reconvened in the home of a sympathizer.

The group arranged a weekly truck run to the Martin Company in the Minneapolis warehouse district for nuts and dried fruits, and talked of coordinating honey distribution from Charlie Hurd in Marshall or David Brett in Northfield. There also was talk of buying grain directly from an organic farmer in North Dakota and placing orders for miso, sea salt, and tamari from Erewhon, Paul Hawken's for-profit natural foods warehouse in California.[2] All this was designed, of course, to bypass the existing warehouse. To some extent, it was purely a practical move. The CO–controlled collective at the warehouse had discontinued stocking a number of products basic to the co-op inventory, replacing these with a larger canned goods inventory. The alternative distribution network was mostly responding to political pressures, however. The warehouse was out of its hands now; changes there would continue without input from the co-ops. As long as it was forced to rely upon warehouse services, it would be forced to contend with the accompanying political static. These activists sought to create something better, an institution that would work alongside the new ACA and in harmony with the co-op community.

In some respects, the dream was regressive; the new warehouse would once again be an inter-co-op activity, owned and run by the community. Whether this was practical or not, considering the size of the network and volume of business, was of less importance at the time than the desire to pull the movement back together, united behind a single enterprise.

Because the earlier warehouse boycott had been so successful, CO leaders knew this alternative warehousing plan would gather wide support unless they were able to gain control of the individual stores through their surrogates in the movement. Earlier transformation attempts had been met with mixed responses. CO members had in many cases been able to gain a foothold in the stores and push the working-class line. At the warehouse, the Beanery, the Riverside Cafe, and other businesses, the CO enjoyed strong support. The warehouse takeover dampened that enthusiasm somewhat, but by the fall of 1975, the organization was prepared once again to make a move.

Despite the warnings sounded by the community, many of the stores remained ripe for the taking. Few co-ops had initiated the kinds of structural and procedural changes necessary to stave off the whims of a packed community meeting or the designs of a newly transformed worker. Tom Copeland, an editor of the *Scoop* and a member of Selby Co-op, toured nine Twin Cities food co-ops that summer and concluded that most were extremely vulnerable. Of the nine, only one co-op kept adequate financial records. Four of the stores had only rudimentary bookkeeping systems, and the rest kept only a bank balance and record of gross daily sales. Jon Havens, interviewed at Whole Foods, argued against a "tight financial trip. When things get tight we tighten up; when things get loose we loosen up."

Politically, most of the co-ops, like the warehouse, felt little pressure from their communities and constituencies to pursue policies that seemed inimical to those who ran the stores on a daily basis. A community meeting might, as it did at Mill City in April, demand a survey of neighborhood grocery needs, but the workers still were required to follow through on the initiative, and often it simply wouldn't get done. The "transformation" threat, then, seemed less than urgent—especially in view of the movement's reaction to the warehouse occupation. Indeed, the CO's rhetoric had cooled somewhat in the wake of the June PRB decisions. Although the community remained polarized, it seemed that the CO was too busy trying to keep the warehouse afloat to bother with more takeovers.

The warehouse survival strategy depended upon CO control of key co-ops. How Theo Smith chose the targets is unclear, but in the late summer of 1975, with an alternative warehouse looming on the horizon, the CO had to move fast to consolidate its strength in the network. Two co-ops presented particularly appealing targets: Selby and Powderhorn—Selby for its black, working-class constituency and Powderhorn for its lack of structure.

Powderhorn Food Community, nestled in an older residential neighborhood near Powderhorn Park in south Minneapolis, had operated for some time with no paid staff. A decentralized operation, the store was run by small groups of volunteers fulfilling specific tasks—a storekeeping group, buying groups, bookkeeping group, maintenance group, and a communications group. The structure was so loose, in fact, that when the CO moved in to take control in July, there was really nobody to attack.

A community meeting, responding to the "order out of chaos" theme used on these occasions by the reformers, resulted in the hiring of two paid coordinators, an expanded inventory and membership base, and a mandate to educate the membership about food and politics. It was all so quick and painless, according to one observer, that the CO seemed "downright humble."[3]

The reformers had no clear power base to attract at Powderhorn, co-op member Lowell Nelson wrote later, because things were so loose there were few people exercising even subtle control. The very mushiness of the operation also prevented any significant inroads. "The same naive tolerance that allowed them to get a firm foothold has prevented them from getting any more than that so far," he noted. Nelson, like many other Powderhorn members, was not particularly alarmed by the takeover. The changes, after all, would be reevaluated in six months, and they might, in fact, turn out to be good for the kind of store Powderhorn seemed to be. He argued that there were actually two food co-op movements in the area: a natural food movement and a community store movement. They should both be allowed to develop independently, he insisted.

Powderhorn organizers, he contended, always placed whole foods a rung below community control, so the transformation was really only a logical step. "If your aim is community control of the storefront, then in most cases you'd be hypocritical not to sell shit food," he wrote. "Unless it's all changed since yesterday, that's what most of America eats."

The Selby transformation was accomplished with none of the graciousness of the Powderhorn takeover. Armed with revolutionary rhetoric, CO supporters campaigned vigorously in the predominantly black neighborhood and emerged with a majority on the store's Co-op Council. The campaign featured regular attacks on CO opponents and on the mostly white leadership of the co-op. Charges of "racism" and "elitism" filled posters distributed prior to the election. When the dust settled, the CO had won control. The new Co-op Council distributed a flier three weeks after the elections explaining the goals of Selby Co-op and its new leadership:

1 Transform the store to serve the material needs of poor and working-class people in the neighborhood.

2 Unify and integrate the struggles of Selby Co-op with the struggles of poor and working-class people in the neighborhood, e.g., around food education and monopoly capitalism.

3 Develop and follow leadership of poor and working-class people in the neighborhood.

"For the first time in its history," the flier concluded, "Black working-class people are making decisions about what happens in the store."

Also making decisions was Tom Copeland. A longtime volunteer at the co-op, Copeland challenged the transformation and came up a loser. Held up for special criticism by Michael Rachlin and her supporters, Copeland, when it became clear who would control the business, closed the attached bookstore and T-shirt business and kept the inventory. The T-shirts, which read Strength through Cooperation, were manufactured and sold to raise money to buy the building in which the co-op was housed. That issue, more than anything else, polarized the membership and consolidated CO power at Selby. The new Co-op Council wanted the money to be used to buy more inventory, specifically meats and canned goods. Leaflets arguing their case with the slogan People Can't Eat a Building appeared in the neighborhood signed by "The Movement for a Working Peoples' Co-op."

CO supporters called on Copeland the night before the June PRB meeting in order to persuade him to give up the shirts. At midnight, two CO members confronted him at his house, and they argued in the kitchen for a couple of hours about who really owned them. In the end, Copeland offered to give the shirts to those who worked on them based on how much time individuals had contributed. By this formula, about 10 percent of the inventory would have been given to CO supporters. The two emissaries, Rick Owens and Sara Stedman, called the offer ridiculous and threatened to take some of Copeland's property and hold it until the shirts were returned. "Rick said that he represented the co-op and that I was a thief and would suffer the gravest personal consequences for my action," Copeland reported in the *Scoop*.[4]

Elsewhere in St. Paul, CO member Bob Malles, purged from the Peoples' Bakery collective after his bid to transform that business, turned up at the new co-op bakery, Our Daily Bread, to present a restructuring proposal there. The workers bought it, and Malles was made general manager. Created to serve St. Paul co-ops, Our Daily Bread was soon selling and delivering bread to Seward, Northside, and the Beanery in Minneapolis.

Although skeptical of the transformation process and the CO in general, the local co-op community could not be said to have completely dismissed the reformers and their message. For one thing, most of those involved in the network were aware of the fact that there were indeed problems of class bias and elitism. For another, the CO was full of people who were known and respected in the movement. "They got the benefit of the doubt for a long time, even after they took over the warehouse," said Susan Shroyer.

Those unfamiliar with the political rhetoric and the history and ideology behind it were particularly susceptible to the CO line. New 1970s radicals, like the naive "fellow travelers" among the 1930s bourgeoisie, entered the political maelstrom with little sense of leftist history, beyond the widespread disgust with American foreign policy in Vietnam. The Soviet Union and communism in general was seen by many new radicals as a greater good than capitalism in any form; the horrors of Stalinism and the brutality of repressive regimes practiced in the name of Marx were unnoticed by the most of the neophyte revolutionaries, ignorant of history, drawn to the co-ops by some vague vision of utopian communitarianism. The message, the direction, the new, pragmatic militancy, all filtered through a liberal conscience unburdened by historical perspective, brought new recruits into the CO fold. Even among those disgusted by the warehouse takeover, there was a sense that maybe the message wasn't all wrong; the tactics were heavy-handed, but maybe some changes were in order. As a result, the CO was given the leeway necessary to regroup its forces and devise a new strategy.

The CO made all of its decisions in private, but reports from the warehouse in the summer of 1975 indicated something of a leadership vacuum at the site. Bob Haugen was still in town, though not working at the warehouse. The direction at the time was toward presenting a working-class front to the public and the co-op movement, and prior to the September PRB meeting, the CO had begun to hire and train "ordinary" people for warehouse work. Theo Smith still made the major decisions behind the scenes, but on the surface the warehouse was moving toward its proper relationship with the working class. The strategy that emerged was one of preventing the creation of a competing warehouse by transforming key co-ops and thus assuring their future patronage of the original warehouse. Beyond that, it's difficult to determine with any accuracy the intended long-term direction of the organization.

On the eve of its September meeting at the Peoples' Center, the PRB seemed similarly directionless. This, of course, often seemed to be its natural state, but after the decisions in June, it seemed not unreasonable to expect some new sense of purpose. That meeting left a number of issues unresolved. If, for instance, the warehouse was a separate entity, stripped of communications, education, and sundry movement functions, why should it answer to a movement-based governing body? If the warehouse was no longer the hub of the local co-op universe, did its workers have any responsibility to the movement beyond getting the food out to the customers? The business was not, after all, a consumer co-op.

The PRB wanted some input into the operation of its warehouse (only a privileged few knew the plans underfoot to create a new one) and gathered on the West Bank on September 27 and 28 to try to iron out some sort of compromise. Three proposals were to be discussed at the meeting: the creation of an executive committee, the negotiation of a contract between the PRB and warehouse collective, and the reincorporation of the warehouse as a legal cooperative. All three had the common aim of involving the PRB in warehouse decision-making.

The various arguments were presented on Saturday morning at three separate workshops. At a warehouse-store relations workshop, CO critics characterized the warehouse collective as being dominated by a political faction that was nonresponsive to the PRB. The collective, in turn, presented itself as being open to criticism, but independent from the PRB. They would not obey PRB decisions with which they didn't agree.

At a workshop on the PRB, the CO charged that the PRB was illegitimate because it did not represent all the co-ops. The group also came out against an executive committee, arguing that it would be too bureaucratic. A legally incorporated co-op was also out of the question. It would always be dominated by its more economically powerful members. Political direction, they said, should be the only criterion for control. PRB representatives countered with a historical argument: The warehouse, they said, was created to be operated by and for the co-ops, and the PRB was created to make that arrangement more workable. It was the appropriate arena for warehouse policy decisions.

At the third workshop, warehouse financial coordinator Michael Biesanze presented current financial statements. The information, sketched on two scraps of paper taped to a wall, were, as a result, difficult to decipher, and Biesanze encountered some pointed questions. The warehouse, it seemed, had been granting credit and making loans based upon the political affiliation of the applicants—thumbs-up to CO–controlled co-ops; thumbs-down on the rest. Noticeably uncomfortable, Biesanze argued against a suggestion that an audit be done, saying that it would be relatively meaningless because of the lack of efficient bookkeeping prior to the past year. He also made a not-too-subtle point about any moves away from the warehouse by in-town co-ops. The warehouse was burdened by a large amount of fixed assets (the building and truck), he explained. Because of this, the warehouse was dependent on credit from suppliers in order to bring food onto the warehouse floor. If the big metro co-ops were to pull out, this would affect the sales volume at the warehouse, which in turn would hurt its line of credit. This would eventually hurt the small co-ops outside of the Twin Cities that depended on the warehouse's buying power.

Before the meeting, CO members had traveled around the state, drumming up support among the small rural co-ops unfamiliar with the struggle underway in the Twin Cities. Biesanze's attempt to play their interests against those of the city metro co-ops represented the culmination of that campaign on the eve of what all expected would be another pivotal gathering of the co-op tribes.

Tom Copeland and "Emma Evechild" called the business meeting to order that afternoon at 3 P.M.[5] Almost immediately, the Selby representative challenged Copeland's position as chair. "What principles does this man represent when he has rejected the leadership of blacks, has stolen t-shirts from Selby Co-op and is not actively working in any co-op at present?" A shouting match ensued, and a vote was taken to remove him from the chair. Five voted yes, eighteen no, and six abstained. The five votes represented the CO faction of the meeting: Selby, Beanery, Powderhorn, Our Daily Bread, and the warehouse. The battle lines were drawn.

The Executive Committee proposal was offered by its author, Cy O'Neil, who tried to sketch the issue in its basic terms. The PRB owned and was responsible for the warehouse, but it was having a hard time meeting its responsibilities, he explained. A committee would identify problems and present to the PRB choices that would make the warehouse more efficient and productive.

As expected, the CO criticized the proposal on the grounds that out-of-town co-ops would have a hard time participating in such a committee because of the distances required for meetings. They urged that the body decide what "material work" it could do instead of setting up yet another committee. Supporters of the proposal countered with the claim that the structure would provide an effective way of maintaining control of the warehouse operation. Their argument, however, ran into trouble with the rural co-ops and those who saw themselves as neutral. The meeting moved slowly toward the boiling point.

A representative from one of the outstate co-ops spoke up. She said she thought the warehouse collective had been doing a good job, that she trusted them, and that she opposed any new committee unless she knew specifically what role it was going to assume in warehouse operations. The rep from SAP (St. Anthony Park Co-op) said he was confused about the proposal's intent, but if it was to exert real control over the warehouse, he would vote against it. "Trust ha[s] been broken," the Commonplace rep cried. "We're changing direction," said the rep from the Beanery, "and we need to be struggling in response to that change of direction. The PRB is useless in bringing that struggle to resolution."

Another voice chimed in, saying that the real issue was whether or not "we're going to fire the collective," a point with which everyone seemed to agree. The Executive Committee proposal was tabled (even the CO supported the motion), and the body addressed a motion to fire the warehouse collective. Fifteen minutes later, the body backed down, tabled the motion, and returned to the earlier proposal, which it eventually approved on a 12 to 11 to 6 vote. The proposal clearly lacked consensus, however (the Riverside Cafe rep changed his vote from a yes to an abstention; Famine Foods of Winona changed its from a no to an abstention to a yes). Only twenty-nine of the forty-three PRB members bothered to show up for the meeting, an indication of ambivalence that would surely prevent any direct implementation of the vote anyway. As in the past, the PRB had acted, but to what end no one could be sure.

After a fifteen-minute recess, the body reconvened for another vote. Some representatives, particularly from the outstate co-ops, were unsure of the issue before them and caucused with the intention of giving the proposal another chance to fail officially. After some debate, the rep from the Marshall co-op presented a CO–sponsored proposal that criticized the Executive Committee idea as "a step backwards towards bossism." In its place, he proposed the creation of an advisory communications board. The chair ignored the proposal and called for a vote on the Executive Committee proposal.

Shouting matches erupted all over the room, while someone called for a quorum. When roll was taken, all five CO–aligned co-ops and a number of sympathetic outstate reps had left the room. There was no quorum— therefore no vote. "This proves the illegitimacy of this body," a rep from the Beanery shouted. "Shut up, you're not here." Calls for a boycott arose from the crowd, while others roundly criticized the "CO lackeys." Five months after the first salvo had been fired in the Co-op War, people started to say what they felt. "People talk about broken trust," a warehouse worker yelled. "A co-op was started in the West Bank community several years ago. That trust has now been broken." "You helped break that trust!" someone countered. "What we're talking about is serving the working class in the community!" a CO member proclaimed.

Edward Winter got the floor. "Last May, when there was the occupation of the warehouse, one of the direct results was that all the credit we've built up and the building were in jeopardy. It was close," he said. "So we got together and signed an agreement to work together to get the bills paid. I was part of that agreement. I went back to work fully expecting that we could work together. Since that time I've become completely discouraged. I've been excluded from the decision-making. The decisions are no longer collectively made. And I guess I see this as a reflection of the warehouse collective's attitude toward the co-ops in general. I feel there is not cooperation motivating the warehouse collective."

Another warehouse worker stood to say that she didn't feel she needed to be involved in all the decisions there. She trusted Edward to make decisions affecting his job.

"Are you new at the warehouse?" someone shouted. "How long have you been there?"

Another woman rose, sobbing. "There is shit in this room. It is shit. And we won't get back together until it's dead and gone. All that's going on in this room is warfare."

A man nearby stood up to agree. "Something has happened here," he said quietly. "Bob and Dean. They were my friends. I worked with those people. I was surprised when they disrupted the PRB. I didn't understand. Okay, so we left seven people in the warehouse that night because they'd said they weren't gonna let us in the next day. And then a woman I live with came home at four in the morning hysterical because someone had hit her and dragged her out of there. It was my friends that did that. My friends. And that's the fucking truth."

A woman from Selby took the floor. "I'd like to put to rest some of the emotionalism that's coming down over what we've gotta do to move things forward," she said. "Some people live at a level where they gotta struggle every day. I can see that violence is frightening. Nobody likes violence. But it is a reality. So we gotta get real. I'm not saying this isn't real, what we're doing right now, but there are other things that are real and we've got to deal with it and not throw everything out the window because we see something that we don't like."

"It's in our hands this weekend," somebody else stood to say. "Either we hold it together or we blow it. If we can't work together, then let's walk out of here. If people are unwilling to let go, then we can't work together. The Advisory Board proposal speaks of isolation, but I think the real issue is the lack of trust. If we can't work out some kind of mechanism between us, then we'll have to walk out, we'll have to throw away five years of growing and go our separate ways. I'm just sorry we can't get together, I'm sorry if we can't compromise."

By the time the meeting fizzled out, around nine that evening, the fate of the warehouse was clear. There could be no compromising on either side, no sacrificing of ideals to save what had once been a symbol of movement growth and vitality. No longer could the PRB be used as a forum for discussing warehouse issues. The trust had been broken, and smashed with it were whatever fragments of legitimacy the body once enjoyed. The CO's challenge for control of the warehouse had succeeded, but it was left with damaged goods.

Those who knew a split was in the making—CO supporters and their critics—came to the Sunday meeting prepared to solidify their positions and to justify decisions made in the heat of the Saturday battle. They'd cleared the air the day before. Now was the time to take action.

Sunday's meeting moved quickly to dismiss any proposals that distracted the group from its primary task of severing ties with the warehouse and the CO. Plans to contract with the warehouse collective for services and a proposal for incorporating the warehouse as a legal cooperative were voted down. It was time to finish off the CO, not to contemplate a new struggle to find compromises. After four hours of hopeless wrangling, someone from Selby Co-op invited all who wanted to "move the co-ops forward" to meet at one end of the gym. Another voice boomed above the commotion: "All those who wanna boycott the warehouse meet at this end of the room."

Once again the movement chose up sides, but this time it was for keeps. This was what they'd come together to do. All the discussion, all the debate, all the rhetoric and oratory of the meeting—of every meeting since the takeover in May—was nothing more than a postponement of this action. It was time to kill the warehouse.

Annie Young, one of the seven organizers of the new warehouse, stood up and read a statement: "As members of the cooperative community at large we are concerned that the issues have been obstructed and confused to everybody here. We have tried to work with you. Even if we had fired you, you would not have left without a confrontation. In order to move forward and restore the true spirit of our movement we must make a firm stand. It is time for a split. Those of you who wish to work in cooperation may join us."

In the end it was almost anticlimactic. After five months of struggle and pain, the co-ops had finally made a choice. On the wall, unfurled high above the tables and the cacophony of clashing political dreams, a banner proclaimed the final battle cry. It was Emma Goldman's anarchist oath: "IF I CAN'T DANCE, I DON'T WANT TO BE PART OF YOUR REVOLUTION."

# CHAPTER EIGHT

## War!

Appropriately enough, the new warehouse was called DANCe, or the Distributing Alliance of the Northcountry Cooperatives. Not surprisingly, it immediately cut sharply into the business of its competitor. In its first month of operation, the new warehouse did $25,000 in business and Peoples' slipped to about $30,000. The old warehouse had averaged about $90,000 a month during the previous winter.

This was open warfare in the capitalist arena, not the political ring, and in the weeks following the split both warehouses sent representatives out to sell their particular line. (The struggle extended all the way out to the West Coast, where suppliers in the Bay Area were courted by each warehouse and were forced to choose sides.) The CO, now decimated and increasingly desperate for business and political support, made a case against DANCe. The new warehouse, it said, was trying to kill the Peoples' Warehouse and by extension, the small co-ops that depended on it for business. DANCe, on the other hand, argued that the old warehouse used a secretive, nondemocratic decision-making process. The new warehouse, a true cooperative in which stores reigned over policy decisions, sold an economic and political alternative.

For the first time, the Co-op War entered the world of finance. The DANCe–affiliated co-ops, in an effort to deal the Peoples' Warehouse and CO a fatal blow, decided to demonstrate their allegiances by refusing to pay their bills at the old warehouse. DANCe never officially endorsed the action, though the new warehouse clearly was to benefit from it. According to Aggie Fletcher in the *Scoop*, the action represented a final slap in the face of the reformist faction. "There remains a strong feeling among many non-CO workers that they took everything we built together, and we should have gotten something out of it."[1]

The DANCe truck went out the first week in hopes of finding support among the non–CO food co-ops. The new warehouse was rewarded with large orders from Seward, North Country, Whole Foods, Mill City, Good Grits, Wedge, and Southeast co-ops in Minneapolis, and Merri Grove in St. Paul. On the first Saturday, October 3, sales were $1,577. Still ordering from the Peoples' Warehouse were the Beanery, Selby, Powderhorn, Our Daily Bread, and SAP in the Twin Cities, as well as co-ops outstate in Marshall and Mankato. Clearly, the CO had to take some action before its most influential force in the co-op community went under. It decided once again to get tough.

"DANCe must close its doors permanently," read the new booklet authored and distributed within the community. "The Indictment of DANCe" accused the new warehouse of responding with a "subjective and selfish emotional reaction" in an attempt to destroy the Peoples' Warehouse and "thereby cause the permanent loss of hundreds of thousands of hours of work to build the co-op movement and take it forward." (The epistle neglected to mention, of course, that many of the people who created DANCe had also built the Peoples' Warehouse.) Because they ignored "the laws of development of society," DANCe, the booklet claimed, was illegitimate.

"The economic contradiction in the Twin Cities co-op system has been raised to the point that the objective condition can't any longer give reality to the existence of two warehouses," the booklet continued. "The two warehouses being mutually competitive because of political differences which stem from class allegiances." The CO pointed to evidence that, it claimed, exposed a plot to destroy the Peoples' Warehouse financially, trying to take the co-op movement backward. Indeed, in early meetings planning the alternative warehouse, specific plans had been made to take business and other political support from the CO–controlled warehouse. From notes about those meetings that the CO had obtained, it was clear that DANCe was created to bleed the other warehouse dry. The booklet concluded with a demand that DANCe close its doors within twenty-four hours and negotiate the liquidation of its inventory with the Peoples' Warehouse. "Failure to respect this verdict will have far-reaching consequences for the co-op system and the co-op movement."

There was indeed a conspiracy among DANCe organizers, but the charge of bleeding assets from the warehouse didn't hold much water.

More than $20,000 of Peoples' Warehouse working capital had come in the form of loans from DANCe supporters, and after the CO takeover at least half of that was pulled out of the warehouse and eventually invested in the alternative warehouse. DANCe also received about $770 that was owed to the old warehouse but never paid. Although the indictment asserted the new warehouse was using Peoples' Warehouse assets, records indicated that it was the buying power of co-ops that broke with the old warehouse that most helped to fund the new one.

Amid rumors that December would be a make-or-break month for the old warehouse (their annual $10,000 balloon payment was due November 1) the CO began in November to work on Minneapolis's newest food co-op—Bryant Central. The store had been organized by a small group of neighborhood activists led by a longtime gadfly/revolutionary named Moe Burton. Burton was a fairly respected figure in this predominantly black neighborhood on the south side of Minneapolis. An ex-con, he had organized a Revolutionary Peoples' Community Information Center in 1970 before being arrested in violation of his parole. Four years earlier he had been convicted of "non-cooperation" with a police officer and sentenced to two more years at Stillwater state prison. In an interview in the *Scoop*, Burton explained the evolution of the new co-op and the strange coercion he experienced at the hands of the CO.

"In May of this year . . . this little guy—white—come up here and said, 'What do you think of starting a co-op up here?' And we said, 'We like that idea, yeah.' This guy, Bob Haugen, talking as a representative of the Peoples' Warehouse, said, 'Well, we've changed and we've gone into canned goods and more mainline foods.' When he explained the changes about canned goods I said, 'Yeah, that would work, and I would devote some time to that.' So we went and sat down in the garden and talked about it some more. Later I invited him to my house. Other people in the community were talking about a co-op too. It wasn't just one or two of us. This thing was building, but it was still just a lot of talk. So we wrote a leaflet and called a meeting at St. Peter's Church here.

"This first meeting was a madhouse. People with past co-op experience dominated the meeting. Some of this was coming from the CO people, but mainly it was other people who claimed they had experience, and wanted to be organizers. Later, when needed, they didn't show up. It wasn't a lot of people there from outside the neighborhood, just over-anxious energy in the neighborhood, itself. First meetings are always the most chaotic.

"A couple of weeks later we had a meeting at Sabathani Community Center, and at the third meeting we decided on the store site we now occupy.

"One thing that hasn't been clear on a public level, but was very clear to Bob Haugen, myself and others in contact with either of us," Burton continued, "was that there is and always was a deep political grievance between Bob and I. We did agree on most of the pragmatic things about organizing the store. But he always came off like he thought he was the leader . . . even in this neighborhood he would come on like a white Jesus or something, he was here to save the Afro-Americans, bring us to co-op heaven or CO heaven.

"My ego was involved too. But it was really on two different levels. I don't have to compete with Bob Haugen . . . it rubbed me wrong to watch this guy come up here and think that he was organizing us.

"Bryant Central was not under their wing as CO propaganda said and this misunderstanding is partly my fault here. We never did take the time to investigate what the other side was saying, until real late in the game. You know? The first time I took any time to see what was happening with the other side—the DANCe Warehouse and the All Co-op Assembly people—I was, all of us were, kind of shocked.

"That was the end of October. We heard there was a party for Bryant Central over at one of the DANCe stores to talk about getting support from all the co-ops and not just the CO party-line stores and warehouse. They were worried that we at Bryant Central were being told that certain non–CO stores were racist.

"I told Haugen before the meeting, 'Let's go and confront DANCe.' I thought the CO political analysis was right about the co-op system up until that time.

"At the meeting we walked into there were people from DANCe Warehouse, Mill City, Whole Foods, Co-op Outreach, Seward Co-op and some others. They weren't expecting us; four of us from Bryant Central and Bob Haugen. We were welcome to stay and start talking face to face in the same room for a change. Before this, our only contact with non–CO workers was occasionally one to one. No group process . . . seeing a lot of leaflets go back and forth, etc.

"That night was the first time we got a glimpse at the total picture. Up

until that time we had been too accepting of other people's points of view—
the CO—because coming from just one side it sounded right.

"That night we saw where there were inconsistencies. One was that
these CO people, who were talking like they were working class, were
really just the same old hippie intellectuals that have been laying a rigid
hippie line on everyone before. Now they had 'transformed' their line, cut
their hair, but they were the same old hippies."

Bryant Central opened for business on November 3, 1975, and almost immediately became a battleground for the rapidly escalating Co-op
War. The fact that Bob Haugen was on the front lines indicated how important it was to the CO that Burton and Bryant Center be annexed.

Like Selby Co-op in St. Paul, Bryant Central's predominantly black
constituency was a prize the CO would go to almost any lengths to win. The
successful wooing of economically disenfranchised minorities was the primary goal of the campaign, as it demonstrated that their political rhetoric
could really reach its intended audience and could thus further discredit the
hippie elite the reformists hoped to shove aside elsewhere in the co-op community. The movement and its leaders were overwhelmingly white,
college-educated political activists whose message had failed to attract
members of other ethnic groups to the stores. Indeed, the struggle against
racial injustice was never addressed as a major issue in the movement.

Part of the reason for this was the fact that there were so few African
Americans, Native Americans, and other members of minority communities in the stores. The issue simply never came up at most of the co-ops.
Sexism, by contrast, was an ever-present topic of discussion, because
women had risen to leadership positions at all levels of the movement.

At Bryant Central, Burton and other African-American activists
found themselves being courted aggressively by the CO. Linda Janssen, a
CO leader, took Burton around with her when she tried to collect money
owed to the warehouse, he recalled, and offered four Bryant Central
workers jobs at the warehouse. Although DANCe supporters did little to
bring Burton and his store into their column (the co-op started out ordering
from the Peoples' Warehouse), the co-op was more than a little suspicious
of the CO, especially after a weird confrontation between Burton and
Haugen.

"Haugen had been calling me in the middle of the night for two
nights to tell me, 'Hey, meet me out in front of Bryant Central at one

o'clock tonight because I'm gonna get you,'" Burton remembered. "The first time he said this I said, 'What you mean, meet me at one o'clock at night in front of Bryant Central? I ain't gonna do that shit.' Then I said, 'Hey Bob' and he hung up. It got me kind of worried. I didn't know where he was coming from," he said. "Then he called through the night, you know? Ten times in one night and wouldn't say nothing. He'd ring it and ring it, and then when I would answer the phone he'd just be sitting there, quiet," he said. "And I don't know who this was . . . it didn't have to be Haugen, it could have been a whole group of them."

Burton recalled that this went on for two nights, before he got a call at noon on Friday, November 21. It was Haugen, challenging him again. Burton went to see what was up. "When I got to Bryant Central and started walking up to the door, Haugen came out from inside and started immediately at me," he said. "So when we got to each other we grabbed and started struggling-like. At that point these three other men from the CO started coming in on me, getting behind me and moving in. Now there was one person from Bryant Central who was supposed to be refereeing but a kid on the street got mad and popped Haugen in the head twice while I was just holding Bob. At this point it all gets hectic. Some people from around the store grabbed these other CO people so they don't get at me and Haugen. In the meantime I held Haugen from behind, and sat him down on the ground. We were both on the ground, me on top, and I said to him, 'I don't want to fight you, man. It's not gonna do me any good to fight you.' I held him down so he couldn't hit me. Then I let him up and kept him from hitting me.

"So we talked then, down the street, about that stuff. Haugen said, 'Well, OK, I just want to try you again. Let's fight one more time for friends' sake.' That's what he said. I said, 'No man, I don't want to fight you.' And he said, 'You gonna fight anyway.' Then he run and tried to tackle me. I just grabbed him, threw him down, and wrapped my legs around him and held him. He finally quit and said 'OK,' and I let go of him and he got up and left."

As a result of the fracas, the warehouse cut off deliveries to Bryant Central and Haugen reemerged with a leaflet criticizing the whole turn of events. "DISCREDIT MOE BURTON AND BOB HAUGEN," the paper shouted—an obvious nod to the CO's credo of self-criticism. In his leaflet, Haugen accused Burton of trying to take control of the co-op and reprimanded himself for being "wishy-washy and liberal" for opportunistically supporting Burton. Shortly thereafter, the CO announced that Bob Haugen had been expelled from the organization. In fact, Haugen, Theo Smith, and a small band of true believers had fled to Chicago, where they set up organization headquarters, eventually to be fronted by a computer software company.

Their action was not surprising. According to a former CO member, who had risen in the ranks to a leadership position during this time, the organization demanded a lot from its leaders, and Haugen's emotional outburst was simply not tolerated. "There was an incredible amount of discipline," she said. "They were told who they lived with, who they had social contact with, who they could talk on the telephone to." Those who were unable or unwilling to follow CO leader Theo Smith's instructions were simply discarded. "The CO wanted to groom people to the point that they could be little islands," she explained. "They wanted true revolutionaries who weren't dependent on anyone and could be set down anywhere to do their work."

Whether Haugen's silly confrontation with Burton and subsequent "purge" from the CO was staged to provide a plausible reason for him to disappear from sight is not altogether clear, but the organization was certainly going through some changes in leadership and its strategies were being subtly altered. Phill Baker wrote just prior to a December 3 "United Front Against Opportunism" meeting that the CO was in trouble, citing increasingly "vituperative" attacks, the Bryant Central incident, the apparent Haugen purge, the departure of a number of followers, the opening up of the CO bookstore to the movement, and what he characterized as the "poorer quality" of writings coming from inside the organization.

The meeting was attended by CO members and a handful of anarchist co-op workers, as well as people from the Native-American and Southside black communities, people from the West Bank Tenants' Union, an alderman from the Minneapolis City Council, a couple of people from the radical New American Movement, some Marxist-oriented neighbors from outside the co-ops and the CO, and a half dozen "old boys"—longtime local politicos. The co-op war had leaked out into the community at large.

Somebody from Bryant Central heckled CO members for their racist attitudes, a criticism that was also voiced by some of the local Native Americans in attendance. The local Marxists talked about how the CO wouldn't let them in because they didn't agree with the group's tactics and style. Others pointed to examples of personal slander, disruption, and the shattering of community.[2] CO members admitted to instances of bad judgment, but explained that Bob Haugen had been leading them and had now been purged. The analysis of the co-op system they had circulated so persistently during the past year, they said, had been wrong.

Almost three weeks later, on December 22, the CO held the first in a series of meetings designed to "reunify" the co-ops. They presented there a paper entitled "Update on Co-op History," which set out to smooth over some of the differences that had been hampering their relationship with the movement up to that point. The CO's "historical task" in the co-ops was to create "ideological unity," the paper asserted. Once they accomplished that, the CO would disband.

The group was not going to ignore its biggest problem while trying to mend fences in the community, however. The DANCe Warehouse was still a "class enemy," they asserted in this latest analysis, and had to be abandoned—or destroyed.

What better place to begin than at the Mother Co-op? The CO had made some inroads at North Country over the past few months and, despite a storewide referendum that directed the co-op's staff to buy "as much as possible" from DANCe, six of North Country's eight coordinators refused to abide by the decision and on December 30 began to resume their buying at Peoples' Warehouse. They argued that they could override the co-op's membership because Peoples' Warehouse served the working class, which made their decision legitimate.

A week later, at a hastily convened community meeting called to discuss the issue, about thirty irate shoppers voiced their distrust of the co-op staff for overriding the referendum. By this time, the six-member pro–CO contingent had shrunk to four workers, who asked politely for a three-month trial period to buy only from Peoples' Warehouse and try to bring more working-class shoppers into the store. The shoppers (who, you must remember, legally owned the store now) were faced with a dilemma—they no longer controlled the store, had no way to force the workers to abide by a decision short of firing them, so what was there to decide?

Not much, it turned out. The collective was split, four for DANCe, four for Peoples' Warehouse. After getting an earful of complaints from the store's owners, North Country decided to split its orders right down the middle.

The North Country debate—or nondebate—demonstrated that, although the movement was beginning to learn how to deal with the vagaries of politics and business, the stores themselves remained extremely vulnerable to bullying by reformist troops. It was not surprising, therefore, to see the CO exhibit a certain contrition in public meeting billed as "reunification" efforts while maintaining the pressure at the storefront level. In fact, the reformers had actually decided to turn up the heat a little in the new year.

The morning after the North Country meeting, Moe Burton's neighbor called the police after she observed two men cutting the telephone lines to Burton's house at 3 A.M. Moments later, she said, Burton's truck was engulfed in flames. By the time police and fire engines arrived, the vehicle was destroyed. "Whoever did this is crazy," Burton said. Almost as if on cue, Peoples' Warehouse issued a statement disavowing any knowledge or responsibility for the act.

Two days later, it became increasingly clear that the CO had redefined its strategy. In two separate assaults—at Seward and Mill City—storm troopers sought to do by force what the CO had not been able to do with rhetoric. "I was standing up front by the checkout," said Kris Olsen, who was managing Seward Co-op with Leo Cashman that morning. "I heard Leo shouting for help, so I started to turn around, and this wall of faces jumped toward me. Right away they started kicking, punching, and dragging me out of the store." A shopper who was just leaving the store when the troopers stormed in escaped and called the police, while inside, the invaders were busy barricading themselves in the store.

The onslaught at Mill City, less than a mile away, was a bit more gracious, but just as serious. Coordinator Pete Simmons said that ten or fifteen people stormed the premises, announcing they were taking over and that he would have to leave. They were equipped with sleeping bags, pieces of plywood, and a change of locks. Simmons complied, but immediately notified the police.

As in the case of the warehouse occupation seven months earlier, police arrived on the scene without a clue as to how to determine which group had what rights to the stores. In the absence of any legal owners or proprietors, they temporarily shut the stores down, while coordinators scrambled to provide legal documents to the city attorney's office. By late evening, both stores had been cleared to reopen under their former ownership.

The next day, at an emergency community meeting, Mill City shoppers and workers voted to prosecute those involved with the break-in. The question of collaborating with police that had arisen to stymie CO opponents after the warehouse takeover was hardly a factor this time around. They had made a distinction between collaborating with the police to fight the CO and using the legal system to prosecute particular individuals. All but a handful of the fifty to sixty people attending supported the idea of police prosecution.

Phill Baker wrote later that the co-ops were too quick to run to the authorities.[3] "Someday, as we become more of a challenging alternative, the police will come to close us down and who will we turn to then?" he asked. "Better we learn now how to deal with our social deviants. Turning to the police to save us from an infiltrated, provocateur-ridden organization would be pathetically blind. This is what the co-op struggle is all about—gaining control of our own lives. Do we run to the State when the 'big boys' give us trouble? If so, then we are playing store in mommy and daddy's house."

Of course, that's what the CO had been saying from the beginning, and although Baker's critique may have been unfairly harsh considering the circumstances, it held some weight. If, after all, the movement sought some sort of independent, alternative standing—a "good world within a bad world" bubble of sanity—then perhaps the utopia should be expected to police itself. On the other hand, the war had moved quickly and violently into the stores themselves now, the level of activity most uncomfortably close to home. Take the warehouse and we'll build another one, the community seemed to be saying. Take my co-op and you're messing with the neighborhood.

It shouldn't have surprised even Phill Baker, then, when on January 10, members of Seward Co-op unanimously passed a motion to seek a restraining order against those involved in the attempted takeover the day before. The meeting also directed the co-op's board of directors to file suit for "actual damages and to file for punitive damages not in excess of one dollar." Olsen and Cashman had decided to file assault charges, a move the membership heartily supported.

All this activity, not coincidentally, occurred the Friday and Saturday (January 9 and 10) that DANCe members were gathering to incorporate the warehouse as a legal cooperative. Were the takeover attempts designed to intimidate DANCe members? "What happened Friday was necessary to get some co-op coordinators to listen to us," CO leader Linda Janssen told the *Minneapolis Tribune*. "If violence occurred it was necessary and it will be used again if needed."[4] The CO had distributed a flier prior to the DANCe meeting telling representatives that the meeting had been canceled. The group had widely redistributed its Indictment of DANCe, promising harsh consequences if the new warehouse refused to close its doors and give up its effort to take customers from the Peoples' Warehouse, so, once the incorporation was completed January 10, it wasn't surprising to see a last bit of rage issue forth from the increasingly desperate CO and a bit of reprisal from the victors in the other camp.

About 4:30 on the morning after the incorporation, two beer bottles filled with gasoline were tossed through the windows of Bryant Central Co-op. The owner of the building discovered the small blaze and extinguished it before any extensive damage was done. Later that day, a former accountant of the Peoples' Warehouse was beaten in his home. The man identified his assailants as members of Bryant Central. The co-op denied the charges.

The next day, January 12, coordinators at Selby Community Foods found the storefront sprayed with the words "shit foods" and "commies." The word "Community" was obliterated by paint.

That evening, members of SAP Foods reversed an earlier decision to buy primarily from Peoples' Warehouse, voting 13 to 3 to buy wholesale items from the cheapest source available, but giving preference to DANCe when the prices were the same. The switch in policy was attributed to the attacks at Seward and Mill City.

On January 15, coordinators from Mill City and Seward Co-ops filed charges against their attackers. Pete Simmons signed a burglary complaint against the four CO members who had broken into the store. Meanwhile, the four suspects met with Minneapolis Mayor Charles Stenvig and asked him to investigate the basis of the charges against them. Later, they justified their action by saying, "When present co-op workers use the police or legal system, it is to suppress progressive forces. When the CO had reasons to use the police, it will be against the reactionary forces in the co-ops." If the sight of the radical CO trying to ally itself with the ultra-right-wing Stenvig wasn't enough to send some flags up in the co-op community, the leaflets circulating two days later in the Phillips neighborhood certainly would. "Kick out Chuck Phenix, the dope dealer, and his clique—and turn Mill City into a Peoples' co-op store," the fliers read.

That afternoon, about fifty CO supporters marched on the tiny co-op. Inside, an estimated two hundred Mill City shoppers blocked the entrance. While police looked on from the sidewalk, the CO marchers chanted, "WORKERS UNITE, SET THE CO-OPS RIGHT!" and pushed against the door. Mill City supporters sang "Row, row, row your boat" and stood their ground. Some observers reported that the Mill Citizens hurled sticks of butter at the intruders, but no one was injured in the fracas.

One CO insider said later that after the failed takeover attempts "all the struggles were internal." A lot of people were purged from the organization as a result. "After a while it just got so crazy. The night the CO was going to take over Mill City Co-op that was kind of frightening to me because people had clubs," she said. "It scared me what they were doing that night."

Less than two weeks later, Mill City coordinator Paul Janssen (Linda Janssen's former husband) got a call informing him that there was a bomb in the co-op's basement. He notified the police, who searched but found nothing. "The more I think about it, the more I think it was just neighborhood kids," he said. "It's just the climate, ya know?"

Actually, it was hard to figure the climate at the time. Was the CO getting ready to pull out the heavy artillery—rumors were circulating that the police had discovered a cache of arms at a CO member's home—or were they just fooling around? Seward received an eviction notice from CO member Mark Johnson the day of the Mill City march.

Tom Copeland and Cy O'Neil, writing in the *Scoop*, argued that it was all just business as usual. "All the January 1976 fuss can be traced to the economic pressures brought to bear on the PW by the emergence of DANCe. Sales there totaled $96,000 by the end of its first quarter of business. . . . it was getting about one-third to one-half of PW's business," they wrote.[5] "Reunification attempts (via co-op community meetings) were dismal failures because people were angered by the CO role at Bryant Central.

The storming of Mill City and Seward were desperate moves doomed to failure, but they had to try to stem the economic erosion somehow."

It was fitting, then, for economic as well as political reasons, that the final battle of the Co-op War would be fought back where it all started, on the West Bank. North Country was not only the most successful of the co-ops, it was the most influential. So the CO took aim at the Mother Co-op, where it would either win or retreat.

# CHAPTER NINE

---

# The End of Innocence

Though the Co-op War touched nearly everyone connected with the blossoming movement in the region, each co-op dealt with it in different ways. In some of the stores, all the commotion simply made for interesting chatter and fuel for the rumor mill that sometimes was busier than the movement's retail trade. In others, the rhetoric and tactics were serious matters.

The Mother Co-op, North Country, transcended the war to a certain extent. Its representatives were lobbied stridently from all sides, of course, owing to its economic clout and historical influence, but the worker collective that ran the store and the co-op's membership that determined policy both were held above the fray initially. As it has from the beginning of the co-op network in the Twin Cities, North Country occupied (and still occupies) a sacred place in the movement. Its philosophies and practices, the way it does business, the way it relates to the community and the world, informed so much of the movement's development that there were seldom any attempts made to publicly question its leadership or challenge its tactics. Further, the co-op's foothold in the Cedar-Riverside neighborhood, a community of activists that had proven time and again its ability to destroy enemies from the outside, prevented the sorts of heavy-handed strategies that were attempted elsewhere.

Still, the war did have an impact at North Country. The CO had not attempted to take the store by force, but had infiltrated the collective with its rhetoric successfully enough to cause a split within the co-op by February of 1976. At a February 14 workshop held to negotiate the differences between the two factions, the four CO–affiliated workers agreed with the rest of the participants to pursue six concrete goals to help the co-op serve the neighborhood better. The goals, as they did in other stores under CO influence, essentially sought to spread the word about the co-op outward, beyond the counterculture circle that dominated the store, and to broaden the decision-making base. The collective specifically agreed to implement a grocery delivery service to local shut-ins, involve neighborhood kids in the store, clean up the place, garner the support of "progressive neighborhood organizations," and get the word out about the store's "new direction."[1]

The CO could agree to such a program because it didn't obstruct its mission to reach the working class. The non–CO members of the co-ops could get on board because they knew that if the rapid transformation did not occur, they would not lose the support of the already ingrained membership and a community that had little time for autocratic Stalinists impatient for a revolution.

The CO botched it again. Less than twenty-four hours after the so-called truce agreement was approved, one of the CO–aligned coordinators produced and distributed a leaflet criticizing North Country as a "transformed filthy hippie whole foods store." This put the neighborhood in an uproar again, and set the stage for yet another community meeting to reprimand the loose cannon on the co-op ship. The culprit, Bob Carter, apologized at the February 24 meeting, claiming his political inexperience led him astray, and the assembled residents agreed to give him another chance. Two weeks later, though, on March 9, the CO faction unilaterally announced that the co-op would discontinue the 10 percent discount awarded to volunteers who worked four or more hours each month (a common practice the CO had campaigned against from its inception). None of the other coordinators, the truce committee, or the co-op board was consulted. The four workers also attempted to fire one of the members of the rival faction on the grounds that she was slowing the co-op's transformation. She had apparently refused to step aside, arguing that only the board or the community at large had the power to terminate an employee.

That "community," essentially an imposing army of local neighborhood activists, fired a salvo of its own in response. In a paper announcing the decisions arising from a March 11 meeting, the "progressive community" on the West Bank announced that the four "reactionary" workers were fired.[2] They had "botched" the implementation of the delivery service, they wrote, failed to run the store efficiently, and alienated everyone in the community. "In incident after incident [they] have actively provoked divisiveness rather than unity around a progressive program," they argued.

"When Cedar Riverside Associates [local development lords] go bankrupt in the near future this neighborhood faces serious attacks by HUD and the City; low income residents of Cedar Square West, especially, face massive rent increases. Unity is necessary to win these fights; factionalism cannot be tolerated. These upper-middle class, pseudo-intellectual college punks and their sectarian antics can no longer be tolerated."

The seventy residents who met March 11 talked at length about boycotting the store to show their displeasure with the bungling reformist faction that seemed to be running the co-op, but decided it was time to get tough. A boycott, they agreed, would be "too liberal"; tougher measures were needed. They would fire the four coordinators, a rare action in the typically "worker-friendly" movement.

The community had taken the precaution of legally incorporating an "interim board" to take control of the co-op's books, and earlier in the day members of that board had transferred all the store's assets to the board's bank account, to be managed by a group of workers accountable to the board. Peoples' Warehouse had taught people some lessons. They had also prepared for a typical CO response to their action and had organized an extensive phone tree designed to alert sympathetic neighbors in the event of an invasion.

The following evening, when about forty CO members showed up at North Country to have "a discussion with the community," the phones started ringing. Moments later, sixty North Country supporters gathered at the Peoples' Center down the street. They marched the two blocks to the store and announced that they had no interest in having a discussion at the moment. (Some residents, in fact, wanted to duke it out with the CO once and for all, but cooler heads prevailed.) The store was closed, they told the surly crowd, and if they weren't gone in five minutes, the police would arrive and escort them out of the neighborhood.

Twenty minutes passed, and nobody was moving. Finally, a member of the interim board phoned the police. The CO cleared out, informing the defenders of the co-op they were "going to the Peoples' Center to struggle with you people." Some of the North Country loyalists followed and engaged in a brief shouting match on neutral territory, but besides a couple of shoving incidents, the crowd had lost its taste for confrontation, and the meeting fizzled.

The CO regrouped and distributed another leaflet in the high-rises nearby (where the local middle-class and mainstream student population resided) announcing a meeting for later that evening at the co-op. About twenty-five CO cadre showed up with five curious neighbors, only to find that the store had been wrapped up tight since three that afternoon "to avoid a potentially dangerous confrontation." The meeting was hastily reconvened in a meeting room at Cedar Square West, where the group orchestrated an election of a new board of directors for North Country. The new board was immediately challenged by the deposed board, which called it "utterly without legal foundation." One of the new board members, a resident of the high-rises recruited by the CO, later proclaimed that she was "in over her head" and was afraid she was being used.

The new Committee to Support the Aims of the Co-op Movement, another in a series of CO front groups, sent thirty of its members back to the store the following day to force another confrontation. They were met by coordinators who asked them not to stand in front of the checkout counters and said that if they wanted to have a meeting during business hours they'd have to hold it in the basement. When they again refused to budge (the CO line, borrowed so effortlessly from Lenin, was always to force the confrontation), coordinators behind the counter called the cops. The four who still refused to make the graceful exit were arrested, although no charges were filed and they were quickly released.

That evening, at a meeting of the West Bank Tenants' Union, a group of CO members demanded that the co-op's use of police force as a weapon to thwart political discussion be put on the agenda. The Union was a widely respected organization in Cedar Riverside, much applauded for its struggles against a local developer named Keith Heller and his grand plan to level the housing in the neighborhood and replace it with high-rises. The Union, in fact, was in the middle of a bitter rent strike against Heller and had collected a quarter of a million dollars in withheld rent. The Union board listened to the CO request and agreed to place it at the end of that evening's agenda. Most of those board members, of course, were not only aware of the threat the CO posed to North Country (and, by extension, the close-knit counterculture community on the West Bank) but also knew that the cadre had been leafleting the high-rises with papers accusing the Tenants' Union of working on the side of the corporate landlords. The board adjourned just before the CO's agenda item came up for discussion.

Former members of the CO, who were working in leadership positions inside the local organization at the time, explained that the óbstacles thrown in their path by so-called liberal community forces proved frustrating, but hardly dampened their taste for the fight. Co-ops, after all, represented only one of the fronts where they were actively seeking to transform the hippie elite. Fred Ojile, a member at the time, said that the fury with which the co-op protectors responded to the confrontations that did occur indicated just how out of touch they were with the revolution they pretended to be making. At various times during the wars within the Twin Cities co-op movement, in fact, it seemed as if the CO simply wanted to make the movement see itself for what it was: a group of well-intentioned radicals who had no idea what to do with the tool they had in their hands.

That's not to say that the CO could wield the piece of economic and political machinery that the co-ops had become any more effectively, but at least they had some goals beyond making a principled living and hanging out with other radicals.

As they strove to do at every opportunity, the CO, at a giant community meeting March 16, asked the leaders of North Country and their followers to consider the hard questions and leave their defensiveness at the door.[3] "If we are to sit down and struggle this question together it will prove both our unity and disunity," explained CO supporter Mary Altendorf. "We will come to understand our differences, and it is important in doing that to admit our errors on both sides. We must engage in principled struggle. I want to say that there is going to be a lot of people who are going to come up here tonight, and the way we are going to serve this struggle best is to be principled, not get into shouting matches, to not say, 'You said and she said but she said' etc., but to talk about issues and in that will come up incidents when both sides have made errors."

The errors to which Altendorf and other reformers would refer during that meeting (and during any discussion in which questions of tactics were raised) were mistakes of judgment or miscalculations. They had nothing to do with the overall campaign to transform the co-ops, from which the CO never wavered. Nevertheless, if the reformers came to the meeting prepared to confess their sins, North Country loyalists were less than willing to provide absolution. To some, it all sounded like the same old schtick.

"I think [this] is indicative that some of the same old nonsense is coming down," said Jack Cann. A well-respected neighborhood activist whose work against Keith Heller and the city had garnered him almost a legendary reputation on the West Bank, Cann went on to point out that Carter's arrogance was more than a character defect; it was a pattern of response he and the CO used to further their goals. "It was a product of a line that was coming down from the CO," he said.

"I want to see, in fact, the base of North Country broadly expanded, and I want to see it be a working-class grocery store," he concluded. "I want to see it be a working-class cooperative, where people from that class decide what they are going to eat and what the pricing policy will be. I don't want Bob telling us what the pricing policy is going to be."

From there, the meeting quickly disintegrated. The two forces exchanged Marxist analyses and charges of elitism and political impurity, until finally a young woman, an outsider who simply shopped at the co-op because the food was cheap, stood up and asked a question that cut right to the heart of the matter.

"OK, I live in the Cedar Square West high-rises and I am on ADC [Aid to Dependent Children] so you know I don't have much money," she began. "In my opinion North Country has been stumbling along fairly nicely. I do a lot of my shopping there. I would like to know if you four coordinators believe so much in what you're doing why can't you leave North Country alone and start your own store?"

"Is your question why don't we have a store for the way it was and another store for progressive changes?" Lisa Dickman, a CO supporter, replied.

"Why can't you leave North Country alone and start your own store for whatever you want, whatever political beliefs you want it to have?" the young woman replied.

Dickman bristled. "Because I don't think we want to have different stores for different classes," she said.

"I have a response for her and I'll be glad to respond," Mary Altendorf yelled above the stirring crowd.

"WE DON'T WANT TO HEAR YOUR RESPONSE!" the loyalists chanted.

"HOLD IT! HOLD IT!" the chair screamed.

"You weren't the leadership in our store," somebody hollered. "We were talking about the leadership of our community store."

"Leadership in your store," Altendorf bellowed angrily, "Got up and walked out of here about an hour and a half ago because they were so fucking bored with this meeting that they turned to me—some of them—and said, 'This is typical of a co-op meeting, this is exactly why we don't go!' "

Her CO colleagues chanted in unison, "MARY, MARY, MARY!" and a gray-haired man stood to make a final point. "It was the leadership who called the cops," he cried. "That for the working class?"

"YOU are not the working class."

"Who are?" he asked.

"HOLD IT!" the chair yelled, trying to maintain order as shouting matches broke out all over the hall.

"We're getting back into 'you said' and 'they said' and 'I said....'"

"My question still is, Why can't you leave North Country alone and work on your own store, start your own operation—anything you want?"

"CO-OP, LOVE IT OR LEAVE IT!" Linda Janssen chanted. "CO-OP, LOVE IT OR LEAVE IT. CO-OP, LOVE IT OR LEAVE IT!"

"HEY, QUIET!"

"The reason I'm concerned with what North Country's gonna do is because I've been working at North Country, and I've wanted North Country to do the best thing that it could," Dickman said above the tumult. "And I wanted to work at a working-class store, and I was working there."

"Why can't you start your own store?" cried somebody else.

"I can't start my own store."

Altendorf took the floor again. "What I was talking about was the people from the high-rises who were here tonight who have been drifting out all evening," she said. "And people here who give a damn about people from the high-rises have been very careful to go and find out 'Why are you leaving?' and down the line what they said is that, 'This is typical of why we don't go to that store, it is not democracy."

"THAT'S RIGHT!" her CO supporters chanted.

"This is not what it's all about."

"THAT'S RIGHT! THAT'S RIGHT!"

"That's right," Jack Cann said. "And I think, Mary, that you have to see that you're half the problem."

"That's not true," she argued.

"Yes, it's true," he said. "This meeting is exactly that same old horseshit, your actions—"

"What actions? Your actions, Jack!"

Hold it! Hold it! Hold it! Hold it!" the chair pleaded, until the commotion subsided slightly. "I am the chair of this meeting. I now see why people don't like to be chairs of meetings. I was handed a fairly vague thing to discuss tonight, it got vaguer all along. I can't tell who wants it to go on."

"I'll chair the meeting," somebody from the CO cheering section offered.

"FUCK YOU!" came the refrain from the loyalist group.

"I call for the resignation of the temporary board!" the CO group cried loudly. "All in favor say aye!"

"AYE!"

"All opposed say no!"

"NOOOOOO!"

"The ayes have it!"

"NO, we yelled louder than you did!" someone screamed.

Altendorf and her CO colleagues began to march out the door. "We will now institute the board from across the street, who was too fucking scared to come here tonight," she said.

"HOLD IT! HOLD IT!"

"LET'S MAKE NOISE, LET'S MAKE NOISE!"

"This is a free-for-all," the beleaguered moderator finally admitted. "I see absolutely no purpose to this meeting continuing."

The Peoples' Center meeting proved to be the last grand confrontation in the year-old Co-op War. There were minor skirmishes at Powderhorn (where police once again were called in to determine who really controlled the store) and Northeast and Northside co-ops, but the reformers had clearly been routed. Loyalists recaptured Selby Co-op in St. Paul in March, and at the Peoples' Warehouse a move was afoot to seal the CO's fate for good.

Its resources depleted as, one by one, local and outstate co-ops transferred their business to DANCe, the old warehouse by March 1976 was operating with a skeleton staff led by CO regulars Jeffrey Frank, Linda Janssen, and Michael Rachlin. The PRB still officially owned the business, but exercised essentially no control over its operation.

In fact, nobody was really sure who was pulling the strings there (Theo Smith and his most loyal compatriots were busily organizing in Chicago and Milwaukee by that time) until a mysterious bookkeeper, recently paroled from a Wisconsin prison, showed up in town. Steven Brandereit arrived in the Twin Cities in December of 1975 to visit his sister, Linda Harris, who worked at the warehouse. Harris told him then about all the financial difficulties the business had encountered since the boycott, and Brandereit agreed to meet with Jeffrey Frank and give him some financial tips. "I asked him if his inventory was encumbered; he didn't know what I meant," Brandereit said in an interview later in the *Scoop*.[4] "I asked him if his receivables were pledged; he didn't know what I meant."

The cadre was impressed, and Brandereit began to hang around the warehouse, providing some free financial consulting. "The idea of needing some help here, needing some organizing, was no big demand as far as I was concerned," he said. "And a lot of emphasis was placed on the strength of volunteer labor. My private appraisal or assessment was that you had a lot of people here who were willing, who had high ideals, but the place was sorely lacking for anybody with any business experience."

For a couple of months Brandereit puttered around with the books, trying to give the warehouse a little financial direction. He was getting antsy, though, thinking of moving to Alaska—getting his own financial house in order—and toward the end of February told Frank they would have to find somebody else to help them out of the hole they were in.

"Three or four days later, Jeff Frank called, and we were supposed to have a meeting to tell him what approach he should take in securing money from the bank. They had a store they were hoping to open at Seventh and Arcade in St. Paul," he told the *Scoop*. "They wanted to establish a relationship with a bank over there close to that store. I told him he didn't need to borrow money here. By then I knew you could run Peoples' Warehouse without it."

Still, Frank said he wanted the money. Brandereit said he would get it, but that he would have to be paid to direct the warehouse's finances from here on out. He wanted $250 a week and a clear line of authority. They agreed, but Brandereit soon wondered what he had gotten himself into. "All I got out of them from the minute we had the agreement was 'Get the money from the bank, get the money from the bank,'" he said. "This was contrary to everything we'd discussed in the past. I said you don't need the money from the bank. If you're willing to work at just maintaining a food distribution center, you can do it."

Of course, that wasn't the idea at all. The warehouse had become the chief political financing tool to which the CO had access. Brandereit would learn that every decision was made on the basis of political, not business, factors. "Whether credit was extended was ultimately a CO decision—by Jeff Frank, Linda Janssen, Michael Rachlin," he said. "Each time I objected to something—hey, how come this account is way the hell out here?— 'Well, they're in our corner.' Now, that's a nice reply. How in hell can I find out what our corner is unless I want to get into their politics, which I did not want to do and do not want to do."

All Brandereit knew was that the CO was desperate for money. "Once I had told them point-blank that this place can survive financially and they could see what was going on, they continued to harp about liquid capital," he said.

There wasn't much of that kind of cash flowing through the warehouse, though, that hadn't already washed up on political shores elsewhere in the Twin Cities. When Brandereit discovered "a whole fistful of checks that had been made out to cash," all hell broke loose.

"I confronted Jeff Frank and Michael Rachlin with them. I said, now explain this bullshit to me, will you please? People are volunteering a portion of their wages, trying to do anything they can to keep the place from falling apart, because they're convinced that there's a financial crisis on hand. And all along, they're taking out hundreds of dollars," he said. "These checks are dated like December, January, February, March. And I said then, take your politics and nonsense and get it the hell out of the warehouse. They said OK."

Monday morning following the Friday confrontation, Brandereit arrived for work and found the warehouse doors locked and himself and two other "opportunists" fired. Linda Harris had not been purged; she had apparently given in to some Sunday evening threats about herself and her brother going to jail for some kind of conspiracy. Brandereit conferred with some lawyer friends, anticipating some trouble. (He had received a probationary sentence in 1970 in Milwaukee after a similar incident: The company he was working for was keeping an illegal set of books, a practice with which Brandereit didn't agree. He removed them, and was charged with theft. Four years later his probation was revoked when he did not report properly, and he served fifteen months of a five-year sentence.)

"That following day, I called [PRB attorney] Dick Rahders and said there's something you should probably know about," he said. "My position being that if there's still some kind of question about who owns the place, what's going to be left?"

On April 1 Rahders obtained a restraining order that removed the last CO leaders from the warehouse, and he asked Hennepin County District Court Judge Allen Oleisky to slap a temporary injunction on the business, giving control of the warehouse to the PRB until a hearing could be held to decide officially who was to be left with what remained of the warehouse.

For a few months, the episode fueled a resurgence in political hostilities. Three days after the CO forces were booted out of the warehouse, the organization issued a statement at Sabathani Community Center in south Minneapolis accusing Brandereit and acting president of the PRB Kris Olsen of being police agents and quoting James Forman on how to deal with them: "The greatest danger facing revolutionaries in the U.S. is not police infiltration, but a refusal to organize in such a manner that police infiltration will be minimized and eliminated," the statement read. "The revolutionary movement in the U.S. has not reached the point where police infiltrators are killed after they publicly reveal their role in helping to destroy an organization or frame one of its members on trumped-up charges or a conspiracy, but this day is fast approaching."[5]

Brandereit, the statement argued, went to the law because he was losing his cover. "As time progressed, Steve's lies began to catch up with him. His practice was inconsistent with his rhetoric. He was losing his cover story; and then orders came for him and Chris [sic] Olsen to consolidate their forces in order to pull off a legal coup d'état. It is important to note that at the time Steve was losing his cover, he would disappear for days and weeks at a time. Let us take note, their action will be proven to be fatal in days ahead."

Nothing came of it, of course, because the organization was split at the seams. Smith had introduced a fiercely critical individual "assessment" process inside the organization, and for the first time his followers began to openly question his leadership. Devoted cadre had long since departed, frustrated by the rhetoric, the social control, the violent threats. None of them was in it for the fun of it, but few were willing to stay through the craziness. Smith responded by creating a secret structure within the CO, and dispatching "military units" (loyalists in dark glasses) to confront internal opponents, seize their organizational documents, and purge them from the group as "pseudo-Marxists." True believers were moved into secret households and prohibited from giving out their addresses or phone numbers to anyone.

Meanwhile, at the floundering warehouse, Jeffrey Frank wrote a letter to Brandereit's parole officers, outlining his "crimes" against the warehouse and urging them not to grant him parole, but the incident soon faded into the background. After a brief trial in July (in which Mark Johnson and Linda Janssen, so much a part of the reform movement, both denied knowing anything about the CO), the court found the PRB to be rightful owners of the warehouse, and the PRB moved slowly to sell the warehouse and disband the business.

What had gone wrong? Plenty, if you looked at all the critiques and analyses that emerged in the wake of the warehouse's death. The CO was unsuccessful, according to one paper ("The CO, Love 'em or Leave 'em"),[6] because it was only fooling around with the co-ops, "sharpening their analytical and organizational skill in preparation for the real task, the building of a revolutionary party."

In the end, the authors concluded, the only organizing weapon the CO used effectively was one that wouldn't keep people in the fold for very long. "It doesn't seem really, to be class consciousness at all which is motivating the CO. Rather, it looks like guilt, plain old guilt: guilt for not being, or not having been, conscious of class distinctions, conscious of the social injustice they foster. Rather than encouraging practical changes in work style which might make left activity more accessible and meaningful to working people, the CO nurtures guilt, treating class background as original sin. After creating an impossible psychological burden, they offer salvation—absolution by transformation."

That absolution never came for Dean Zimmerman. One of the fathers of the local movement, Zimmerman had been forced into exile in the fall of 1975, labeled a "dangerous deviationist" by CO leaders and a traitor by his former comrades on the other side. "I didn't make any bigger mistakes than anyone else there," he said later. "It was just that it had a far-ranging effect because of my particular position at that historic point. You see, I had visited all these co-ops in these rural areas and had developed some good friendships with the people involved there and had met them three or four or five times and they often stayed at the Yellow House when they came to town so that when all this argument came down, these people tended to side with the way I saw things, just because I was their main contact with the whole city movement." Following the warehouse's demise, he returned with an apologetic treatise on his and the organization's weaknesses that quietly punctuated the armistice the courts were about to declare.[7]

The organization was flawed in several ways, Zimmerman argued, not the least of which was the way it treated its present and prospective members. "When I sent an analysis (that Moe Burton has a history of opportunism) up the tube, the analysis was ignored and the person who made it was trashed," he wrote. "I was guilt-tripped because the person making the analysis (not a CO member) was an old friend of mine—OK, we all make mistakes. I spent a great deal of time during this period defending the CO in co-ops where my past work and personal associations acted to lend credibility to my propaganda effort. Yet even with a correct analysis, my own personal reputation among many co-op people, and our apparent success at capturing the warehouse, the abusiveness and abrasiveness of our style appeared to be making us enemies rather than allies."

Zimmerman went on to note that he had called for some public "self-criticism" by the organization, but that the proposal had been ignored. That analysis, he wrote, would have to include the CO's confusion about the difference between a "cadre" organization and a "mass" organization. "A cadre organization finds unity first around a desire to build proletarian revolution and through practice, study and struggle comes to more clearly define what it means to build a proletarian revolution—how one establishes the democratic-dictatorship of the proletariat," he explained. "A mass organization on the other hand is unified around a much less grandiose goal such as 'to provide ourselves with good quality low cost food'—as in the case of a food co-op. . . . A revolutionary individual or group when considering whether or not to work within any particular mass organization must first determine whether or not the basis of unity of that organization objectively benefits the working class in the long run."

What the CO failed to do in its struggle within the co-op movement was to recognize the "basis of unity," he said. "If the basis of unity of an organization is objectively progressive, but its social practice is not progressive, then there is room for struggle within the organization. The role of revolutionaries within these organizations is not to 'take them over,' but to struggle to get the organization and its members to live up to their own goals and standards."

There was nothing wrong with CO members' aspiring to leadership roles within the movement in an attempt to move the co-ops into a more progressive direction, he argued, but those leaders should be elected to those roles based upon the good work they've done within the co-op—not because they are more politically pure than their fellow workers. Similarly, any attempt to forcibly transform a mass organization into a cadre organization is doomed to failure. "Mass organizations must be allowed to have a life of their own, for it is through them that the masses take their first steps toward a proletarian consciousness."

Ultimately, the CO lost its opportunity to influence the direction of the co-ops by disregarding democracy in its campaign, Zimmerman noted. "The history of the struggles on the West Bank is replete with lessons for all serious revolutionaries. Within this microcosm can be clearly seen the struggle between the tendencies toward secrecy and propaganda (the need to win) and the tendencies toward openness and telling the complex truth, however confusing (the need for democracy)."

Both the co-op loyalists and the reformers were guilty of selling political lines and half-truths about their opponents, he said, but the CO clearly failed to understand that balance between those two tendencies and made several specific mistakes: attacking those who should have been allies; showing contempt for the ability of the masses to grasp fundamental issues; reneging on agreements; substituting agit-prop for grassroots organizing and "wishful thinking" for considered tactics; developing a "cult of secrecy" that stifled the flow of information within the organization; and isolating itself from the masses.

"In summary," he wrote, "it appears to me that the primary result of the CO's work has been to create anti-communism. The practice has been so far off-base and has isolated us so completely from the masses that the damage is irreparable. I consider most of the people in the organization to be good people, most will make an important contribution to the struggle in the years ahead. There is a victory to be won, there is work to be done, I don't think we have time to be saddled to an organization so counterproductive. I quit."

# CHAPTER TEN

## The Golden Age

T he end of the Co-op War by no means ended the debate begun years earlier by reformers intent on changing the co-op system. The dialogue simply took on a significantly less strident tone and was now couched in the sort of anarchist rhetoric with which co-op loyalists had long been most comfortable. People still talked about the movement's direction, community power, and even canned goods, but the language was noticeably softer. "Group process" had begun to replace "principled struggling" as the preferred community dynamic. People were tired of arguing.

There wasn't much to argue about anymore, anyway. In many ways the old countercultural revolution was over. The Bicentennial summer boiled over into an orgy of patriotic flag-furling, the war in Vietnam was history, and revelations about atrocities in the newly liberated land had long since dampened celebrations by those who once deified Ho Chi Minh. Disco and soft rock had begun to dominate the mainstream radio, and barber shops were experiencing a revival.

The co-ops continued to act as a harbor for many of the wayward radicals who held out against the persistent wave of conformity and conservatism that would become the Reagan Revolution, but even inside the movement there was a slow, almost inexorable flow away from the political and countercultural waters in which it had been spawned. The CO battle, certainly, had created some refugees who quickly fled the movement for more placid lives. Others who stayed were profoundly shaken by the political and personal eruptions that characterized those twelve months. As a result, the co-op movement that arose from the ashes was quite different from the one the CO had destroyed.

People were getting older, for one thing. Although there had always been an entrepreneurial streak in local co-op organizers, many of them were beginning to wonder when the payback was coming. Good friends and a politically correct life-style might feel good, but they weren't necessarily going to pay the rent and put new shoes on the kids' feet. Life was another kind of war altogether.

The radical community had been ripped asunder. Marriages had fallen apart over ideology, relationships had collapsed, and the fabric of trust that had always been so much a part of the countercultural experience was left dangling in shreds. Faced with the prospect of rebuilding that cultural and spiritual network at a time when there seemed so little support for doing so, movement leaders found it much easier to continue their personal revolutions in subtler, less obviously political ways.

There were, of course, notable exceptions to this trend. War resisters Dave Gutknecht and Don Olson (who both served prison time for their activities) continued to labor for their particular sense of community empowerment. Gutknecht became board secretary for DANCe, helped cultivate a national warehouse and trucking network, and served as a sort of editor emeritus of the *Scoop*. Olson published the anarchist review *Soil of Liberty*, taught pottery classes, and could be seen at every demonstration. Others kept the faith, as well; Susan Shroyer reemerged to help organize a supermarket co-op on the West Bank. Increasingly, though, people inside the movement began to get more serious about building a business than constructing a utopia. The co-ops didn't look much different—a bit cleaner perhaps, a can of corn here and there—but the movement was slowly becoming less of a community and more of an economic network.

At the center of that network were the two organizations that had sprouted from the Peoples' Warehouse: the ACA and DANCe. Created to ensure that the movement's distribution and propaganda arms would forever dangle harmlessly apart, the two organizations revived and refined the "personal is political" mission that had been under such a fearsome attack for the past year.

In its bylaws, the ACA and its founders explained that the organization was created "so that people coming together can meet their needs without competition, authoritarianism, violence or exploitation of people or nature. In order to achieve control over our lives we seek to integrate the health, ethical, economic and other basic concerns of people through supportive human interaction and a cooperative network."

DANCe had a similar view of its purpose, a response to the just-completed war. In a statement released in February 1976, the warehouse collective admitted that the movement did have some "bourgeois tendencies" but argued that in order to reach those people "caught in a bourgeois nightmare" it was important to be unified in an "egalitarian and decentralized manner.... We are united in our struggle to meet these needs in non-sexist, non-racist, non-ageist, and aggressively non-violent fashion.... The process takes time, and while cataclysmic events will speed the process, they will also destroy us if we lack trust in each other, if we are not prepared to offer direction and hope to large numbers of people caught in a frenzy of capitalistic contradiction."[1]

The key, they wrote, was the same as it had always been—trust. "Trust is the foundation of cooperation and cooperation is the essence of unity. We must be able to trust that our cooperation enhances the cooperating community, enhances the unity of people struggling to be free. Just as we must not lose our vision of a new and better society, as we expand our economic cooperations, we must not allow the unmet needs of people to become tools in the hands of dogmatic sectarians."

Not much had changed. It was just that sort of namby-pamby style that so infuriated the CO. Where was the revolutionary mission? Where was the drive, the discipline, the chutzpa needed to bring the masses along for the ride? Where was the path to a new society? There wasn't any, of course. The ACA was in the business of helping people start co-ops and helping those who had started them to keep them going. We were back to the old anarchist, do-your-own-thing atmosphere—only this time, there were a few more resources available to help us do it.

There were also a few more people interested in the model. With nutrition becoming less of a fad and more of a concern among the mainstream, people in the suburbs were increasingly demanding assistance in setting up their own stores. The self-help alternative also attracted a fair amount of attention among government and quasi-government agencies, which were anxious to explore models of community development that would require little government involvement and would reach those most in need of a service.

Unfortunately, the rhetorical support voiced for the young federation during the CO struggle had pretty much evaporated by this time, and the task of answering the call for help fell to a few diehards who, volunteering their time and energy, slowly extended the network outside the Twin Cities. Among the most determined were Seward Co-op workers Kris Olsen and Ellen Wersan and Mill City maverick Chuck Phenix.

"We really had no direction," Olsen recalled. "Ellen, Chuck and I spent some time trying to think of what to do and then we simply tried to do outreach. We'd get a card from somebody wanting to start a co-op and we'd go out and give it a try. They both did some good work in making presentations in public schools to high school students and did some speaking, but basically, when it came down to getting co-ops off the ground, I pretty much shouldered the burden. If somebody wanted to start a co-op, I tried to make a commitment to go out there and help them get it off the ground."[2]

Another Seward alumnus, Leo Cashman, did legal and financial consulting, and Evelyn Roehl of Winona's Famine Foods provided some food research information, but that was about all there was of the ACA a year into its operation. There certainly wasn't any money. Dues collection was erratic at best. In the quarter ending June 1976, the federation took in $630 from its loyal members.

Nevertheless, the work went on because the calls kept coming in. "Generally, a lot of it was just PR work—trying to get ourselves in the paper, trying to make ourselves visible, myself making a real strong commitment to respond to any correspondence or calls," Olsen said. "And anybody who wanted to start a co-op, we would just do it, even if it came out of our pocket. We had to start someplace—getting a reputation that we could do things. Let the buck stop there, so to speak."

The group did manage to compile the first co-op directory in the Upper Midwest, printing and distributing twenty-five thousand copies through area co-ops and alternative organizations. The federation's work otherwise focused almost exclusively on creating new stores. That had more to do with Olsen's priorities and skills than any federation direction. An Army veteran-turned-community-organizer whose political sophistication was well hidden behind an "aw shucks" exterior, Olsen had little time for the vagaries of organizational management. Although he had played a major role in the PRB–CO negotiations, his real love—and his real priority—was to see the network grow. So whenever anybody called for help, it was most often Olsen who climbed into his pickup truck with his dog and headed out to deliver the sort of practical advice even people in the suburbs could appreciate.

The message was simple: Working together, you can do almost anything. No political line was needed, Olsen argued, because self-empowerment and community empowerment were in themselves intrinsically political notions that required no dogma to sell. Co-ops, after all, provided economic benefits only as an offshoot of the larger product: individual and community self-esteem. To Olsen and most of the ACA faithful, creating co-ops created social change by convincing ordinary people that they weren't powerless to change their circumstances.

Of course, to the folks at DANCe, creating co-ops meant more than that: Every time Olsen answered the call, the warehouse got another customer. By November of 1976, nearly seventy stores and buying clubs had become members, and the warehouse trucks were traveling as far south as Albert Lea, west to Sioux Falls, South Dakota, north to Duluth, and east as far as Hayward, Wisconsin. Although the warehouse reaped a bonanza from the ACA's work, the federation gained very little.

DANCe had agreed to pay as ACA dues .1 percent of its monthly sales, but by the time Olsen came to them with a proposal for "special temporary funding" for a staff position at the February 5, 1977, membership meeting, the warehouse was three months in arrears on its dues and seemed hardly to acknowledge the importance of the federation's outreach work. The DANCe membership did agree to fund the ACA position with a $530 monthly contribution for the period March through June 1977, but the board voted the next day not to pay its back dues. It wasn't as if the ACA was squandering its dues on power lunches. Only in the summer of 1976 had Olsen found the federation an office, which it shared with the *Scoop* staff in the basement of Walker Methodist Church in south Minneapolis. He was still volunteering his time; total staff salaries amounted to about $200 a month, he recalled.

Things weren't all that rosy for DANCe either. The fall of 1976 saw sales of nearly $200,000, but where it all went was anybody's guess. One of the early collective members, in a letter announcing his resignation, noted that there had been errors in billing, lost member equity, and sloppy accounting.[3] "Out of $13,000 capitalization, close to $10,000 seems to have been lost," he wrote. "It doesn't seem responsible to talk about further capitalization, expansion, or anything new until operations improve to a point where it is not throwing money away without explanation."

Worse, the member-elected board seemed either blind to it all or simply unwilling to take any action. "The Board of Directors of DANCe must meet its obligation to represent the membership's interest in DANCe and its equity and not fall prey to cliquish in-group politics and shrug their shoulders because it's easier to drift along," he said. "Otherwise, all will be revealed as a sham masquerading as a direction towards a new society."

The CO was gone, it seemed (actually it had burrowed deeply underground), but it looked like the PRB had returned. Just as had been the case in the operation of the Peoples' Warehouse, the representatives of the co-op movement were ill equipped to deal effectively with real-world business issues that cropped up at DANCe. Though the board-collective dynamic in this case was a great deal more cooperative, the task of leading the business out of the woods fell, as usual, to the workers.

Operations were refined sufficiently by the February 1977 membership meeting that most in attendance were satisfied with the progress. Indeed, by midyear both organizations were beginning to look as if they knew where they were going. DANCe was operating out of a new space on the West Bank; the ACA was firmly entrenched at Walker Church.

By the end of the year, both Kris Olsen and Barb Jensen had paid positions at the federation ($200 a month each). Olsen was concentrating on outreach and Jensen on education and communication functions. They put out another directory (this time in the *Scoop*), organized a couple of conferences, and struggled to collect dues and increase membership. By the spring of 1978, the federation was strong enough to take on a third staffer, Judy Stevenson.

DANCe, too, was getting stronger. Every month a new group of buying clubs and co-ops approached the board with applications for membership. Every day more food moved between the warehouse and the stores. In spite of the well-publicized Co-op War, shoppers everywhere were flocking toward the co-op model in greater numbers than at any time since the Depression. More than five thousand food co-ops had sprouted nationwide by mid-decade, accounting for more than a half billion dollars' worth of sales.[4] It wasn't just local counterculture veterans who were noticing this. In Washington, D.C., legislation to create a National Consumer Cooperative Bank had been introduced early in the Carter Administration and was considered by no less than Ralph Nader to be "one of the three most important consumer bills in the past generation."

In testimony before the House Banking Committee dated June 29, 1976, Nader called the proposal "a novel approach because it aids consumers directly, avoiding the faults of the producer-oriented remedies while assuring the one requirement which most food operations, especially those in the inner city, have found to be essential for success: community support."

The problem, Nader said, was that banks typically refuse to deal with co-ops, even the largest, most successful ones, when they come to them with expansion proposals and ask for capital to fund them. In his testimony, Nader cited the difficulty Commonwealth Terrace Co-op, a student housing organization in St. Paul, had had trying to capitalize services such as day care, baby clinics, play areas, a bookstore, and an auto repair center. Similar problems had stymied optical co-ops, auto repair co-ops, co-op supermarkets, and inner-city housing co-ops, he said. "None of these cooperatives has the government among its interests, as so many producers do, so they must wait until their own members can provide the capital," he concluded. "Given the expense of large capital outlays, that day may never come."

What the Co-op Bank supporters proposed to do for the movement was simply this: make market-rate interest loans available for the larger, more successful consumer co-ops and help struggling new wave co-ops—especially those serving low-income members—with technical assistance, below-market-rate loans, and grants. Judging by the hosannas that erupted around the country when the proposal was announced, one might have thought the U.S. Treasury was ready to ship boxfuls of cash to anyone who made a request.

At the traveling congressional hearings held across the country in 1978 (one landed in Minneapolis), co-op activists trooped gleefully forward to offer yet one more example of the wonders of cooperation, and as the bill limped doggedly through one after another committee on Capitol Hill, the movement prepared to reap the largesse that was sure to come its way in the next decade.

In the Twin Cities, co-op leaders viewed the proposal with some skepticism. In meetings of a local bank task force, members spent the bulk of their time trying to fashion a proposal for a regional office in Minneapolis. Government money was fine as far as it went, they argued, but it could go a lot further if the delivery system were connected to organizations that were already delivering the kinds of services the Bank proposed to provide. "We don't want to continue technical assistance as a piecemeal activity," said the Bank's Regional Operations Director David Dunbar.

"We forsee a network of technical assistance capacity set up by regional bank staff and Washington staff. . . . There will be a lot of new co-ops starting with the money that is now available."[5]

In other words, movement leaders argued, since the local network already was providing technical assistance through various resources, including the ACA, why not fund the assistance from the Bank's regional office rather than set up a federally sponsored entity? Also in operation at the time was a small lending organization called the North Country Development Fund (NCDF) that helped to bail out the weaker stores from time to time. Why not create a relationship between that organization and the Bank?

The bottom line was that few people involved in the local network trusted the government to design something that would work. "David's notion of a regional structure is to plunk four people into a region and have them report back to Washington," said task force member Ann Waterhouse. "If the Bank is to have credibility with co-ops, we must design it to be organizationally accountable to co-ops."[6] True to form, the local movement was demanding accountability and taking steps to assure the network would maintain control of its destiny. The co-ops were ready to move into a new era, but only on their terms.

Despite the bravado from task forces and at the endless seminars and meetings designed to prepare the network for the coming of the Bank, nobody was really ready to deal with the true consequences of this development. Before the first dollar of government money came down the Co-op Bank pipeline, before the proposal was even ratified by Congress and signed by the president in 1979, the Bank delivered something that few in the movement were prepared to accept: credibility.

Nearly a decade into its growth, the movement's prime product remained its process, the notion that people working together could empower one another. If the stores succeeded economically, all the better, but the real measure of success had been and continued to be seen in the eyes of those ordinary people whose self-esteem had somehow been dragged out of the mud and who were ready to help do the same for their community. What the Bank was all about was something entirely different and, indeed, was often at odds with the prevailing goals of the movement. The Bank was all about performance.

Even though many local co-op leaders opposed the proposal and vowed to ignore it should it become reality, the debate itself had begun to change the essence of the movement. You can't talk about the difficulties co-ops have in dealing with lending institutions, for instance, without discussing the reasons that loan officers blanch at every co-op business plan that floats across their desks. That discussion is bound to lead to talk about performance, priorities, appearances, and dreams—as in pipe dreams. Bank or no Bank, co-ops in the 1980s were going to be quite different than they ever were before.

It's not entirely fair to blame the Bank for the great expectations that seemed to crop up so suddenly in 1978 and 1979. The people attracted to co-ops at that time, the members of this second generation of activists, were in many ways different from their predecessors. They were on the whole more mainstream, less committed to the political and countercultural revolution that had fueled the movement.

Many of those who became involved in the local network were surprised to discover that there was little or no sophistication in the way things got done. That had never bothered earlier cooperators, who saw the funkiness of the co-op scene as part of its charm, but this second generation of activists clearly wanted to see something happen beyond the creation of good vibes. They wanted to see the warehouse and the federation streamline their operations, they wanted to set up regional offices within the network, they wanted to see the ACA provide seminars, and they wanted the warehouse to deliver marketing advice with the brown rice.

That was all well and good, Kris Olsen said, but all this new credibility was keeping him plenty busy as it was. In the winter of 1978, he convinced the ACA board to allow him to move the office from beneath the leaky pipes and peeling plaster of the Walker Church to relatively posh digs east of the U of M Minneapolis campus. Olsen was putting in sixty to sixty-five hours a week as the federation's only full-time staffer. A part-time assistant helped to handle the books and organize the next conference.

"As we became more efficient, we had a tremendous amount of requests," Olsen recalled. "I think there was a general growth and development of awareness about the co-ops' work. We had much more demand for outreach at that time. We had more demand for everything. There was a lot of growth going on. It was very difficult to cope with that many times. We were frantically short of funds, though we did have a dues collections system. We simply lacked a lot of things."

From the outside, though, it looked a lot like the ACA was doing a bang-up job. Around the country, it had built a reputation as the largest and most diverse co-op federation in the United States. In its 1979 co-op directory, the ACA boasted of an expanding network of more than 280 co-ops, buying clubs, and worker collectives, scores of which had gotten their start with Olsen's help.

It all sounded good on the phone, or at a co-op organizing meeting, when Olsen would reel off the services the federation could provide in return for the nominal membership fee and monthly dues. In reality, the ACA was Kris Olsen, great at providing what it takes to get a co-op started, but not too polished otherwise.[7]

By mid-1979, starting co-ops was the last thing the ACA board wanted Olsen to do, anyway. At its summer conference that year, the federation membership decided the organization would shift its focus drastically: from outreach to education and from a centralized to a decentralized staff. Olsen had no quarrel with the decentralization issue; he had been working for some time to develop contact people out of state to ease his traveling burden and to extend the reach of the federation. The education question, though, was a different matter. Outreach—starting co-ops—*was* education, for one thing, and shifting focus in that way certainly wouldn't stop the requests from pouring in.

"To me, education and outreach are one and the same thing," he explained. "Outreach creates an educational format for people—a structure for people to establish different forms of education such as nutrition programs and adult education classes, internships in their co-ops, places where people can volunteer, develop local resources, use local resources. That was never made clear at the summer conference—except that we were going to switch our focus from outreach to education and we were supposed to wind outreach down."

To make matters worse, his assistant quit after the conference, and for nearly two months, Olsen ran the office by himself. Meanwhile, a hiring committee frantically searched for somebody who could come in and transform the office into the sort of professional educational clearinghouse the board hoped it would be.

The woman they chose, a relative newcomer to the network named Cynthia Olson, brought with her an affinity for management, a penchant for goal-setting, and a vision of the ACA that very quickly clashed with reality. "I didn't expect to be any kind of savior or to single-handedly do anything, but rather be a facilitator," she said later.[8] "It looked to me like what needed to be done was some facilitating. That there are many people out here with some ideas and a lot of people out there with some ideas and that somehow communications needed to be facilitated. As I moved along in my job it dawned on me—it actually hit me like a ton of bricks—that even that was a step down the road, a pipe dream."

Administrative efficiency was not found very often in movement work of this kind. Most of the co-ops were still incredibly lackadaisical about bookkeeping and management; the warehouse often didn't know where all the money was going. The problem, wrote psychologist Kenneth Keniston in his groundbreaking study of the New Left, was that radical leaders had difficulty dealing with power and authority.[9] "In their personal manner and values," he wrote, "these young men and women favor open, equal and direct relationships with other people; they are psychologically and ideologically hostile to formally defined, inflexible roles and traditional bureaucratic patterns of power."

Cynthia came on the scene with a totally different view. Although she belonged to the same generation as Kris and other co-op pioneers, she refused to be intimidated by traditional forms of organizational management. "I'm a firm believer in discipline, in some kind of structure," she said. "I think you can move faster, you can be more creative, you can grow more if you limit yourself in certain ways. Many people in the alternative culture are into yoga, or meditation, or other disciplines, yet we're expected to be this loose, happy-go-lucky group of people who can just work everything out and work beautifully together. That's crazy!"

That the Olson and Olsen team should clash was not surprising. One saw his job as extending the movement, empowering people, and organizing communities, while the other saw her job as cleaning up the files and drawing an organizational chart. Cynthia came on to make the organization slick enough to fulfill the communications and education task it had undertaken; Kris argued that it was already being done.

"I came into the office and couldn't find anything in the files because they [were] not indexed for access by the public. Those small day-to-day things needed to be shaped up," Cynthia said. "The reality came to be that we needed a clear sense of who we were. I guess I see the problem as being one of always pretending to be a little bit more than what we were and in the long run that catches up with you."

The myth to which she referred became something of a rallying point for federation critics, who, buoyed by the movement's new credibility both in Washington and closer to home, often noted that the ACA was somehow less than what they had thought it was, that they'd been fooled by its reputation. Soon after Cynthia came on staff, DANCe got into the act. A paper authored by two members of the warehouse's Communications Committee and critical of Olsen's outreach priorities was distributed among ACA board members in the fall. Implicit in the criticism was a threat: Clean things up, or no more dues from your biggest contributor.

The paper stung Kris, who admitted that his administrative skills may have been lacking, but argued that, myth or no, the ACA had accomplished a good deal. "I think realistically the ACA has done much more than anyone would have dreamed possible with the limited amount of finances and people involved," he said. "It's incredible that we've been able to knit together a federation that's geographically the largest in the country and probably one of the most diverse. And for a long time it was the only federation which involved all types of co-ops, collectives and buying clubs. There was no blueprint for that, nobody had ever done it before.

"I think we've done an excellent job of developing regions, initiated 60 or 70-odd co-ops and buying clubs over a three- or four-year period on a shoestring budget. When you consider the dollar volume in sales of those co-ops and the number of people involved and the effect they have on their community and, as a whole, as a federation, I don't see how it could be compared."

The ACA board's hand had been forced, first by Cynthia Olson and, more forcefully, by DANCe, and on February 17, 1980, it voted to "restructure" the federation staff by letting both Olsen and Olson go. The decision shocked Cynthia, who said she felt the board was "blaming the victims," but later chalked it all up to the fact that the co-ops may have wanted to grow up, but still weren't sure what would happen if they did.

"We're not quite sure we're a viable movement," she explained. "Well, my view is that everybody is not quite sure they're a viable movement or if they've got their shit together, or whatever. And you have to trust yourself, you have to have faith in yourself. Sometimes you have to have blind faith in what you're doing and just put your foot out there and do it. It's better to me to do it and accept the consequences of your behavior than to not ever do anything."

By refusing to listen to all the evidence and come up with a way to make the federation better than it was, the board tore it all apart. What was left of the movement would never recover.

# EPILOGUE

## Dreams Die Hard

The ACA office got a good cleaning in the weeks following the tumultuous firing of Kris and Cynthia (and my own resignation as *Scoop* editor). The board hired an interim staffer who mainly answered the phone, sent out brochures, and created a decent filing system. Cynthia Olson went to work as a communications coordinator for West Bank Co-op Supermarket, and Kris did odd jobs until he was injured on a roofing job. Paralyzed, he gets around now in a wheelchair, and operates an information clearinghouse on co-ops from his south Minneapolis home.

Elsewhere, the co-op network barely skipped a beat. The ACA sputtered, but DANCe took on a marketing and outreach worker, and sales continued upward. The co-ops that struggled before continued to struggle, fail, and reemerge. The successful co-ops began to discover Management By Objective.

The movement died.

In 1984 the ACA, several thousand dollars in debt and riddled with personality conflicts, closed up shop. There was some talk among the more successful stores about setting up another networking organization—this time to deal specifically with business issues—but nobody showed much interest, and the initiative soon faded among the day-to-day commercial exchange that had come to dominate the stores.

In 1988, DANCe was sold to another co-op warehouse based in Iowa. The warehouse reportedly had undergone radical management surgery in an attempt to push the business into its next phase of growth, but had failed. Though representatives from North Country Co-op opposed the sale and embarked on an eleventh-hour campaign to keep the warehouse locally

137

owned, the lobbying effort failed to generate serious opposition, and the transaction sailed easily through a membership meeting.

Seen against the backdrop of the Co-op War, these two developments are tragic reminders of the fragility of the victory won by those who defended their original co-op vision—with all its warts—in the 1970s. For all their effort, these pioneers were never really able to fashion institutions that could help to build the movement instead of eroding it.

In their heartfelt attempt to spread the co-op doctrine through an independent organization like the ACA, they unwittingly institutionalized an outreach program that had once operated from a community base. As a result, the movement became represented by a single, vulnerable organization, rather than by a stronger and more diverse collection of resources. Kris Olsen started a lot of co-ops and extended the network into five states, but there's no evidence to suggest that the movement, the vision of a larger co-op community, ever extended much beyond south Minneapolis.

The history of New Left activism is full of people who were looking for a niche in the world, a reason for being, and found themselves radicalized in the process. For movements to extend beyond their leaders, however, those who follow need to be given an opportunity to grab hold of the vision and pursue it. For all its good work, the ACA tended to obstruct rather than to clear that path for all but a few.

DANCe, like Peoples' Warehouse before it, remained the center of the movement despite the widespread concern of people who hoped that the creation of the ACA would curb its power and influence. What actually resulted from the move were two organizations attached by their overlapping memberships (food co-ops that were members of the ACA also were members of DANCe, which used their sales to pay its own membership dues to ACA, a sort of double tax that many food co-ops loudly decried) and waltzing semi-independently, trying not to step on any toes.

The warehouse had a serious interest in seeing the co-op network expand; more co-ops meant more sales. Whether its leaders were particularly interested in extending the *idea* of cooperation—the essence of the movement—to a wider, more diverse audience is not nearly as clear. Spawned in the midst of a battle over what that idea meant, DANCe could probably have been forgiven for not wanting to return to the debate for a while. Besides, even if its leaders did want to spread the movement, to do so would mean stepping on the ACA's toes—and calling into question the whole decentralized arrangement in the bargain.

Other decisions—paying lip service to the needs voiced by outstate or rural co-ops, allowing the Winona warehouse to die, ignoring the communications and educational potential of the *Scoop*—also contributed to the death of the co-op movement. In fairness, and within the context of sixties activism and the vagaries of the free enterprise system, a funeral was inevitable. By the beginning of their second decade, co-ops no longer had a larger countercultural movement to draw upon for energy and credibility; the political imperative had become an economic one as mainstream supermarkets began to lure co-op shoppers with alfalfa sprouts and tamari; leaders and role models split for "real" jobs; and, even though others emerged attempting to lead the co-op community, there was no community left to lead.

In his examination of the radicalizing process among youth involved in the 1967 Vietnam Summer project (which sought to channel antiwar sentiment into the electoral process), Kenneth Keniston notes six fairly distinct steps each of his subjects took on the road to membership in the larger Movement.[1] These were: a change in one's perception of the social reality, some personal confrontation with social inequity or injustice, the beginnings of disillusionment with existing social reform institutions and systems, a radical reinterpretation of sociopolitical reality, some sort of personal activation, and, finally, a personal engagement in a project that led to an identification with the Movement.

The pioneers of the Twin Cities co-op frontier had all been through the radicalizing process. They'd watched the civil rights and the antiwar movements unfold, had changed their way of thinking about the world, and had confronted injustice on voter registration drives in the South or at their local draft boards. Most had tried to change things through the existing reform system before becoming disillusioned (Don Olson especially comes to mind), before going the way of demonstrations and other direct action. Eventually, they came around to co-ops—a project that could be sustained as part of a larger commitment to social change.

The second generation of co-op activists did not take the same path. Few had been directly involved in civil rights or antiwar activity, and thus they did not experience the sort of confrontation with injustice (excepting the sexism every woman must deal with) their predecessors had brought to the movement. Their disillusionment with government agencies wasn't any less genuine, perhaps, but it came about less from having tried to work within the system than by simply hearing that it didn't do any good. No matter what their radical reinterpretation of the world, then, they came upon it more intellectually and less from any direct experience. The revolution was perhaps as real for this second wave of radicals in the co-ops as it was for the pioneers who preceded them, but the principles, values, and attitudes that characterized it had already been laid down by the time they arrived. For the movement to survive and grow, they'd have to conform to its ways.

To participate in its future, they needed mentors, role models who still believed in it all. "To be of general assistance in the process of activation," Keniston wrote of radical role models, "such individuals had to be physically available to the incipient radical: For no matter how important his identification with distant or historical figures, the latter rarely can substitute for real people whom he actually knows. In the early stages of radicalization, such real people serve to concretize the meaning of radicalism, to relieve the sense of aloneness, to focus vague discontent into a new interpretation of American society, to provide specific ideas, tactics and models of effective action, and to enable the fledgling to begin to identify himself as a part of a Movement."[2]

But there were no role models in the co-op movement by the early 1980s—at least none who were particularly accessible. The movement here had a way of chewing its leaders up and spitting them out. Those who hung on often became cynical or selfish or both. Many graduated to national co-op organizations (the Consumer Cooperative Alliance, a fifty-year-old organization, not coincidentally, experienced a dramatic rebirth in the early 1980s) looking for new challenges, a wider cooperative movement to influence, or just a good-paying job.

For many of the co-op pioneers the early 1980s were a time of searching—not for a way to strengthen and revive the co-op movement, but for a way to grow up without sacrificing the ideals they'd accepted during their own radicalization. Dave Gutknecht left DANCe and became the director of a fledgling federation of co-op warehouses; Dean Zimmerman helped found a direct mail computer service for progressive organizations. Don Olson started his own magazine distribution business. Others—perhaps frightened by their "increasing estrangement from the system," as Keniston explained, tired of tilting at increasingly immovable windmills, or realized finally that "movement work, far from relieving their psychological problems, merely exacerbated them"—simply packed it in. They went back to the real world hoping that the lessons and attitudes they brought from the Movement would help build a better system from the inside or, failing that, at least would allow them to cope with the failure.

Part of what the sixties left its refugees in the decades following was an unfortunate inability to commit either to the stupefying insanity of mainstream life or to the wild-eyed fantasy of the Left's counterculture. "The distinguishing characteristic of that generation, as it grows older and as many of its members choose reluctantly to enter more conventional careers than they once hoped or imagined," write John Case and Rosemary C. R. Taylor, "may be a persistent malaise, an inability either to embrace wholeheartedly the putative rewards of success in America or to throw themselves without ambivalence into challenging them."[3]

It's questionable whether even the most persevering of the original co-op activists would have been able to revive the local movement anyway. Like all New Left movements, it wasn't really designed to transform the food industry in the Twin Cities. Its "personal is political" foundation was simply designed to transform the individual. Once transformed, the individual moved on. Eventually, the movement transformed more leaders than it could replace.

Participatory organizations are like that. They mature, they become bureaucratized, they lose track of the larger world. Paul Starr has noted that the energy, informality, and wonderful spontaneity of alternative organizations such as the co-ops may have been due more to the age of its members than the spirit of its ideology.[4] As members age, the organization becomes gradually less interesting, less fulfilling, less revolutionary.

In order to survive and flourish, in fact, co-ops and other alternative groups need to stay small, on the fringe, always on the brink of collapse. Their workers must be underpaid and transient, or the organization loses track of its real purpose: changing society.

People assume alternative organizations won't last, Joyce Rothschild-Whitt has argued, because members tend toward "an accelerated pace of social, psychological and physical change in their lives."[5] In her studies of alternative groups, she found that anyone who had been involved in a specific group for more than two years had probably stayed too long.

"Careerism" was never welcomed in the co-ops until after the movement had slipped into a coma in the early 1980s. According to Rothschild-Whitt, any move toward professionalization in an alternative group guaranteed that the movement upon which the group was built had been forgotten. "If work is to retain its value-purposive quality, the alternative must try to avoid the economic incentives that generally encourage the development of careerism," she wrote. "If its pay scales are too high, it will attract and retain staff who are not fully committed to its purposes, and staff will develop a self-interest in preserving the organization as an end in itself. Relatively low pay ensures that staff are devoted to the collective's purposes and people. But, clearly, if pay is too low, staff cannot subsist and they will leave in spite of their commitments."

Without access to local role models who believed in the movement or to a larger national movement from which to draw support, energy, and creativity, the 1980s co-op activists began increasingly to look to people with business expertise to lead them. Attracting these experts meant higher pay scales and less attention paid to higher purposes.

The arrival of the Co-op Bank certainly did nothing to discourage that new leadership, as co-op business consultants and "technical assistance" teams sprouted all over the Upper Midwest. Local activists may have been suspicious of the Bank, but few of them turned down the help when offered or the cash when they were doing the consulting.

There was a new competitive market to consider in the 1980s, they argued, supermarkets were trafficking in bean sprouts and granola and the co-ops needed to keep pace somehow. They were right—the big boys finally had begun to tap the market demanding nutritious food, but even with the new Bank, these small enterprises never really had a chance in the big-time world of food wholesaling and retailing.

"While co-ops attempt to create an alternative food system beyond the control of the food industry octopus, they need precisely the same nourishment that Safeway does. That's money—and lots of it," Daniel Zwerdling has noted. "And the key to accumulating money is adequate size. Yet from the first day a food co-op forms, its fundamental nature guarantees that money and size will be painfully beyond its reach."[6]

Besides, loyalty to the neighborhood co-op never had much to do with price, selection, or convenience. People had always shopped at the co-op because it carried what they wanted at reasonable prices and because they owned a piece of it.

Several co-ops in the early 1980s did attempt to capitalize on the ownership factor by pushing member-equity programs, trying to get people to put their money where their hearts were, but few succeeded. By that time the local co-op didn't really represent anything new and revolutionary anymore. It was a place to buy groceries, a slightly curious specialty store; there was nothing larger attached to it.

Those who stay in these sorts of movements, Keniston wrote in *Young Radicals*, do so out of "a growing sense of rightness," a moral righteousness that once may have formed the foundation of the co-op movement, but that by the 1980s had become as anachronistic as bell bottoms and the peace sign. In the end, maybe that's the way it should be. As Morris Dickstein noted in his study of sixties counterculture, the revolution didn't change institutions very much. People changed in extraordinary ways, and the co-ops in some cases helped consolidate those changes, but all that personal growth really had little effect, in the long run, on the way the local food industry operated.

A grocery store is still a grocery store, even if behind its checkout counter lie the remnants of revolutionary ideals. After more than a decade of zealous struggling for the hearts and minds of the innocent shopper, that's the real bottom line. The food co-op movement, after all, lasted longer than most spawned by the New Left and, if you accept Keniston's version of sixties revolution, accomplished everything it had set out to do. Unlike those on the Old Left (the CO would be included here), sixties activists from the New Left school never promised revolution—only personal transformation and personal effectiveness. The New Left, he wrote, tends to "alternate between hopes of effectiveness in the very long range, and the sometimes stated view that the essential rightness of the task makes the issue of ultimate success irrelevant."[7]

More than anything else, the co-op movement, because of its roots in the New Left, its countercultural connections, and its bitter conflict over values that nearly destroyed it in the 1970s, succeeded in furthering the subtle revolution on the battlefield within each human who passed through its school of hard knocks, what Theodore Roszak called the "war of the instincts."

"Liberation must therefore become, at one and the same time, a more sweeping, yet more subtly discriminating project than most social rebels have realized. Those who believe that the liberation of man can be achieved by one sharp revolutionary jab, by the mere substitution of a well-intentioned elite for a corrupt one, are courting that element of self-defeat which

Marcuse sees in all the revolutions of the past," he wrote.[8] "From this viewpoint it becomes abundantly clear that the revolution which will free us from alienation must be primarily therapeutic in character and not merely institutional."

Roszak's point is well taken. Despite the scars left by the Co-op War, a lot of people took liberating attitudes and values from the co-ops when they moved on to the real world. The co-ops created in them an appreciation of consensus-building, a recognition of the power of community, and the discipline and self-esteem to carry the revolution with them. The world may still need transforming, but they've been changed unalterably for the better.

# NOTES

## 1 Dancing on Dogma

1 Dr. James Peter Warbasse, *Consumer Cooperation and the Society of the Future* (New York: Apollo Editions, 1972).

2 Milton Viorst, *Fire in the Streets* (New York: Simon and Schuster, 1979), 189.

3 Sara Evans, *Personal Politics* (New York: Vintage Books, 1980), 104.

4 Theodore Roszak, *The Making of a Counter Culture* (Garden City, New York: Anchor Books, 1968), 203.

5 Daniel Zwerdling, "The Uncertain Revival of Food Cooperatives," in *Co-ops, Communes and Collectives*, edited by John Case and Rosemary C.R. Taylor (New York: Pantheon Books, 1979), 92.

6 Ronald Fraser, *1968: A Student Generation in Revolt* (New York: Pantheon Books, 1988), 108.

7 Ibid., 288.

8 Jack Whalen and Richard Flacks, *Beyond the Barricades: The Sixties Generation Grows Up* (Philadelphia: Temple University Press, 1989), 156.

9 Ibid., 136.

10 Fraser, *1968*, 309.

11 Ibid., 313.

12 Ibid., 313. Weatherman Jeff Jones, in recalling the action, lamented the lack of conviction among Movement youth, who slightly more than an a year earlier had been so indignant over Mayor Dailey's police riot. "Thank God the Vietnamese weren't depending on us—mounting a national effort with six hundred people!"

13 Cy O'Neil, *Origins and Legacies* (Minneapolis: Scoop Collective, 1978).

14 David Moberg, "Experimenting with the Future," in *Co-ops, Communes and Collectives*, 278.

## 2 Reconstructing the World

1 Morris Dickstein, *Gates of Eden* (New York: Basic Books, 1977), 21.

2 C. Wright Mills, letter to the *New Left Review*, 1960, cited in *The Sixties*, ed. Gerald Howard.

3 See Fred Halstead, *Out Now* (New York: Monad Press, 1978) and Thomas Powers, *The War at Home* (New York: Grossman Publishers, 1973).

4 Powers, *The War at Home*, 189.

5 Dave Gutknecht, interview, December 1981.

6 Paul Goodman, *Anarchy* 96, February 1969, cited in April Carter, *The Political Theory of Anarchism* (New York: Harper and Row, 1971), 9–10.

7  Ibid.

8  See Staughton Lynd, and Michael Ferber, *The Resistance* (Boston: Beacon Press, 1971).

9  For a classic piece of reporting on the Pentagon siege, see Norman Mailer, *Armies of the Night* (New York: New American Library, 1968).

10  Lynd and Ferber, *The Resistance*, 160.

11  George Bloom, "Ecology and the War," *Changes* 13, May 1971.

12  Dickstein, *Gates of Eden*, 27.

13  Whalen and Flacks, *Beyond the Barricades*, 156.

## 3  Revolutionary Food

1  "The Georgeville Commune," *Hundred Flowers*, 17 April 1970.

2  Loren Baritz, *The Good Life: The Meaning of Success for the American Middle Class* (New York: Alfred A. Knopf, 1989), 274.

3  For an in-depth look at the Diggers and life in San Francisco during the mid-1960s, see "A Social History of Hippies," by Warren Hinckle, in *The Sixties*, edited by Gerald Howard (New York: Washington Square Press, 1982).

4  Karim Ahmed and Janet Ahmed, "What Is Natural Foods," *Changes* 10, January 1971.

5  Richard J. Margolis, "Coming Together," *The New Leader*, 17 April 1972.

## 4  No Bosses Here

1  Whalen and Flacks, *Beyond the Barricades*, 128.

2  Hans Elf, "Mill City," *Changes* 21, Summer 1972.

3  Ken Meter, "Organizing a Community Garage," *Changes* 21, Summer 1972.

4  Howard, "The Politicization of Culture," in *The Sixties*, 33.

5  Jerry Winzig, "SAP Foods: From Corner Store to a Cooperative," *Changes* 21, Summer 1972.

6  In its March 1972 newsletter, *This Is About Us*, a report on a recent All Co-op Meeting announced the co-op money scheme. It was suggested by Ina Haugen, a worker at Whole Foods Co-op, who argued that it could be used at all the co-ops and given out to anyone who would accept it as change. In effect, she said, it would be a short-term loan to the co-op, helping them deal with "over-expansion." There could be some forgery problems, she admitted, but the benefits outweighed the liabilities. "There is always the small rebellious joy of having our own money—money that is based on co-op volunteers and immediately responsible to our people."

7  *This Is About Us*, March 1972.

8  Jonathan Havens, "Whole Foods II," *Changes* 21, Summer 1972.

9  *This Is About Us*, April 1972.

10  Dave Wood, "Looking Ahead: Freak or Free?" *Changes* 21, Summer 1972.

11 Both the Bakery and Warehouse controversies were reported in the May 1973 edition of *This Is About Us*.

12 *This Is About Us*, June 1973.

13 Michael Rachlin, "Expanding Networks," *This Is About Us*, September 1973.

14 Whalen and Flacks, *From Beyond the Barricades*, 135.

15 Fraser, *1968*, 308.

16 Ibid., 309.

17 Whalen and Flacks, *Beyond the Barricades*, 136.

18 O'Neil, *Origins and Legacies*.

## 5 "Criticism, Discussion, Transformation"

1 Cy O'Neil, Article on warehouse losses, *Scoop*, August 1974.

2 Cy O'Neil, "A Little Present From the Past," *Scoop*, September 1975.

3 *This Is About Us*, January 1974.

4 For a closer look at Forman's work organizing the Black Workers' Congress in Detroit in the early 1970s, see James Geschwender, *Class, Race and Worker Insurgency* (New York: Cambridge University Press, 1977).

5 James Forman, "Control, Conflict and Change." Undated paper.

6 Interview with Rebecca Comeau, *Scoop*, May 1975.

7 Chuck Phenix and Nancy Evechild, "A Response to the Beanery Paper." Undated paper.

8 Cliff Sloane, "Personal Reactions to Michael Biesanze's 'RECAP'." Undated paper.

9 "Whither the Co-ops?" by Gary, a worker at Good Grits and Peoples' Warehouse. Undated paper.

10 Terry Hokenson. Undated paper.

## 6 The Facts of Life

1 Report of the May PRB meeting, *Scoop*, June 1975.

2 Phill Baker, "I Will Not Collaborate With Storm Troopers." Undated paper.

3 Dean Zimmerman, and Paul McClusky, "The Legal Question Is a Class Question." Undated paper.

4 Untitled notes on the final joint statement regarding negotiations between the PRB and the Peoples' Warehouse, dated May 16, 1975, and signed by Kris Olsen, Terry Hokenson, Tracy Landis, and Randy McLaughlin.

5 Terry Hokenson, "Political Struggle in the Old Co-op Movement and in the New." Undated paper.

6 Pam Costain, and Laura Davis, "The Error of the Warehouse Takeover." Undated paper.

7 Leo Cashman, "What Is the Fundamental Issue?" Undated paper.

8  Anonymous. Undated paper.

9  Report on the June 21 PRB meeting, *Scoop*, August–September 1975.

## 7  Invasion of the "Stalinoids"

1  Ron Bunch, "The Dangers of RU," *WIN* Magazine, 7 August 1975.

2  From the so-called Conspiracy Notes taken at the meeting by Annie Young, 17 September 1975.

3  Lowell Nelson, "Powderhorn Notes," *Scoop*, August–September 1975.

4  Tom Copeland, "Why I Quit Selby," *Scoop*, August–September 1975.

5  Report on September meetings, *Scoop*, October–November 1975.

## 8  War!

1  *Scoop*, December–January 1976.

2  Both Baker's critique of the CO and a report of the "United Front Against Opportunism" meeting were reported in the December–January 1976 issue of *Scoop*.

3  Phill Baker, "Community Sense and Self-Protection," *Scoop*, February–March 1976.

4  *Minneapolis Tribune*, 11 January 1976.

5  Tom Copeland and Cy O'Neil, "Behind the Headlines," *Scoop*, February–March 1976.

## 9  The End of Innocence

1  North Country report from *Scoop*, April–May 1976.

2  "Reactionary North Country Coordinators Fired by Progressive Community." Undated paper.

3  Quotes from meeting notes taken by Warren Hanson.

4  *Scoop*, June 1976.

5  "Realignment of the Left Forces." Paper, 4 April 1976.

6  "The CO, Love 'em or Leave 'em." Paper signed by Jack Cann, Pat Christianson, Nancy Evechild, Fluffy Golod, Miriam Monasch, and Don Olson, 18 April 1976.

7  Dean Zimmerman, "And God Knows We Have Made Mistakes." Paper, May 1976.

## 10  The Golden Age

1  "DANCe Statement," paper by the DANCeCollective, February 1976.

2  Interview, *Scoop*, May 1980.

3  Resignation letter from "Tai," dated 24 September 1976.

4  Zwerdling, "The Uncertain Revival of Food Cooperatives," in *Co-ops, Communes and Collectives*, 91.

5  Cat Burns, "Co-op Training Institute: A Hopeful Proposal," *Scoop*, May 1980. CTI was proposed by the local task force as a channel for technical assistance funds from the new bank. Some critics of the proposal argued the new organization was a direct challenge to the ACA.

6  Ibid.

7  Olsen was once invited by some state agency to come out and talk about co-ops, but some ACA board members were hesitant to let him go unless he agreed to wear a suit jacket. Flannel shirts were his typical office apparel.

8  Interview, *Scoop*, May 1980.

9  Kenneth Keniston, *Young Radicals* (New York: Harcourt, Brace and World, 1968).

### Epilogue

1  Keniston, *Young Radicals*, 144.

2  Ibid., 135.

3  John Case and Rosemary C. R. Taylor, *Co-ops, Communes and Collectives*, 11.

4  Paul Starr, "The Phantom Community," in *Co-ops, Communes and Collectives*, 269.

5  Joyce Rothschild-Whitt, "Conditions for Democracy," in *Co-ops, Communes and Collectives*, 221.

6  Zwerdling, "Uncertain Revival," in *Co-ops, Communes and Collectives*, 92.

7  Keniston, *Young Radicals*, 141.

8  Roszak, *The Making of a Counter Culture*, 93.

# SELECTED BIBLIOGRAPHY

## Books

Baritz, Loren. *The Good Life: The Meaning of Success for American Middle Class.* New York: Alfred A. Knopf, 1989.

Belasco, Warren J. *Appetite for Change.* New York: Random House, 1989.

Boyte, Harry. *The Backyard Revolution.* Philadelphia: Temple University Press, 1980.

———. *Community Is Possible.* New York: Harper and Row, 1984.

Carter, April. *The Political Theory of Anarchism.* New York: Harper and Row, 1971.

Case, John and Rosemary C.R. Taylor. *Co-ops, Communes and Collectives.* New York: Pantheon Books, 1979.

Cluster, Dick, ed. *They Should Have Served That Cup of Coffee.* Boston: South End Press, 1979.

Dickstein, Morris. *Gates of Eden.* New York: Basic Books, 1977.

Evans, Sara. *Personal Politics.* New York: Vintage Books, 1980.

Fraser, Ronald, ed. *1968: A Student Generation in Revolt.* New York: Pantheon Books, 1988.

Geschwender, James. *Class, Race and Worker Insurgency.* New York: Cambridge University Press, 1977.

Halstead, Fred. *Out Now.* New York: Monad Press, 1978.

Horn, A. D., ed. *The Wounded Generation.* Englewood Cliffs, N.J.: Prentice-Hall, 1981.

Howard, Gerald, ed. *The Sixties.* New York: Washington Square Press, 1982.

Keniston, Kenneth. *Young Radicals.* New York: Harcourt, Brace and World, 1968.

———. *Youth and Dissent.* New York: Harcourt, Brace and World, 1971.

Lasch, Christopher. *The Culture of Narcissism.* New York: W. W. Norton, 1978.

———. *The New Radicalism in America, 1889–1963.* New York: Vintage Books, 1967.

Lynd, Staughton and Michael Ferber. *The Resistance.* Boston: Beacon Press, 1971.

Mailer, Norman. *Armies of the Night.* New York: New American Library, 1968.

Morton, A. L. *The Life and Ideas of Robert Owen.* New York: International Publishers, 1962.

O'Neil, Cy. *Origins and Legacies.* Mineapolis: Scoop Collective, 1979.

Powers, Thomas. *The War at Home.* New York: Grossman Publishers, 1973.

Reich, Charles. *The Greening of America.* New York: Bantam Books, 1971.

Roszak, Theodore. *The Making of a Counter Culture.* Garden City, New York: Anchor Books, 1968.

Ruble, Kenneth D. *Men to Remember.* Chicago: R. R. Donnelley and Sons, 1947.

Sekerak, Emil, and Art Danforth. *Consumer Cooperation: The Heritage and the Dream.* Palo Alto: Consumer Cooperative Publishing Association, 1974.

Stoehr, Taylor, ed. *Drawing the Line: The Political Essays of Paul Goodman.* New York: E. P. Dutton, 1979.

Viorst, Milton. *Fire in the Streets.* New York: Simon and Schuster, 1979.

Warbasse, James P. *Consumer Cooperation and the Society of the Future*. New York: Appollo Editions, 1972.
Whalen, Jack and Richard Flacks. *Beyond the Barricades: The Sixties Generation Grows Up*. Philadelphia: Temple University Press, 1989.

### Articles and Periodicals

Ahmed, Karim, and Janet Ahmed. "What Is Natural Foods." *Changes* 10, January 1971.
Baker, Phill. "Community Sense and Self Protection." *Scoop*, February–March 1976.
"Black Co-op." *Changes* 10, January 1971.
Bloom, George. "Ecology and the War." *Changes* 13, May 1971.
———. "George Bloom on the Environmental Movement." *Changes* 21, Summer 1972.
Brandereit, Steve. Interview. *Scoop*, June 1976.
Bunch, Ron. "The Dangers of RU." *WIN*, 7 August 1975.
Burns, Cat. "Co-op Training Institute: A Hopeful Proposal." *Scoop*, May 1980.
Burton, Moe. Interview. *Scoop*, December–January 1976.
*Changes*, January 1971 to June 1976.
Copeland, Tom. "Why I Quit Selby." *Scoop*, August–September 1975.
———, and Cy O'Neil. "Behind the Headlines." *Scoop*, February–March 1976.
Elf, Hans. "Mill City." *Changes* 21, Summer 1972.
"From the Beanery Paper." *Scoop*, May 1975.
"The Georgeville Commune." *Hundred Flowers*, April 17, 1970.
"Good Grits Co-op." *Scoop*, December 1974.
Gutknecht, Dave. "Co-op Warehouses Launch Brokerage." *Scoop*, April–May 1976.
Havens, Jonathan. "Whole Foods II." *Changes* 21, Summer 1972.
Leslie, Jean, and Steve Leslie. "Peoples' Company." *Changes* 21, Summer 1972.
Malloy, Tom. Essay on Anarcho-Syndicalism. *Scoop*, March 1975.
Marco. "Careless Marxism." *Scoop*, May 1975.
Margolis, Richard J. "Coming Together." *The New Leader*, 17 April 1972.
Meter, Ken. "Organizing a Community Garage." *Changes* 21, Summer 1972.
Nelson, Lowell. "Powderhorn Notes." *Scoop*, August–September 1975.
"North Country Transformation." *Scoop*, April–May 1976.
Olmscheid, Dave. Article on canned goods. *Scoop*, March 1975.
O'Neil, Cy. Article on warehouse losses. *Scoop*, August 1974.
———. "A Little Present From the Past." *Scoop*, September 1975.
Phenix, Chuck. "Federating." *Scoop*, February–March 1976.
Powderhorn Co-op article. *Scoop*, April–May 1976.
Rachlin, Michael. "Expanding Networks." *This Is About Us*, September 1973.
Report on December 3, 1975, meeting of the United Front Against Opportunism." *Scoop*, December–January 1976.
Report on June 21–22, 1975, PRB meeting. *Scoop*, August–September 1975.
Report on September 27–28, 1975, PRB meeting. *Scoop*, October–November 1975.
Rummelhoff, David. "Who Kneads Who." *Scoop*, August–September 1975.

*Scoop*, August 1974 to May 1980.

*This Is About Us*, March 1972 to January 1974.

"2002: A Peoples Department Store." *Changes* 21, Summer 1972.

Viebahn, Chuck. "How Us Malcontents Can Be Satisfied, Part II." *This Is About Us*, January 1974.

Vogel, Howard J. "Ecology and Social Justice." *Changes* 21, Summer 1972.

Winzig, Jerry. "SAP Foods: From Corner Store to a Cooperative." *Changes* 21, Summer 1972.

Wood, Dave. "Looking Ahead: Freak or Free?" *Changes* 21, Summer 1972.

Zimmerman, Dean. "Food Conspiracy in the North Country." *Changes* 21, Summer 1972.


## Papers

Anonymous. "The Indictment of DANCe." Undated.

Anonymous. "Reactionary North Country Coordinators Fired by Progressive Community." Undated.

Anonymous. "Realignment of the Left Forces." 4 April 1976.

Anonymous. "What Has Really Been Happening at the Peoples' Warehouse." Undated.

Anonymous. "Who Is the Beanery For?" Undated.

Baker, Phill. "I Will Not Collaborate With Storm Troopers." Undated.

Cann, Jack, et al. "The CO, Love 'em or Leave 'em." 18 April 1976.

Cashman, Leo. "What is the Fundamental Issue?" Undated.

Co-op Organization. "Discredit Moe Burton and Bob Haugen." Undated.

———. "Update on Co-op History." Undated.

Costain, Pam, and Laura Davis. "The Error of the Warehouse Takeover." Undated.

DANCe Collective. "DANCe Statement." February 1976.

Fletcher, Aggie. "Can the Co-op Movement Support 200 Warehouses?" Undated.

Foreman, James. "Control, Conflict and Change." Undated.

Garwick, Kris; Long, Judy; and Michael Biesanze. Untitled, undated.

Gary. "Whither the Co-ops? A Statement by the Revolutionary-Marxist Study Group of the Fourth International. Undated Paper.

Haugen, Bob. "Discredit Both Moe Burton and Bob Haugen." Undated.

Hokenson, Terry. Notes from *Scoop* meeting, 28 May 1975.

———. "On the Radish Threat to the Process of Dialectical Self-Interpretation in the Co-op Movement: A Coughing Spasm. Undated.

———. "Political Struggle in the Old Co-op Movement and in the New." Undated.

Marxist Study Group of the Fourth International. Undated.

Phenix, Chuck, and Nancy Evechild. Untitled, undated.

———. (Jed Cabbage and Emma Evechild, pseudonyms.) "A Response to the Beanery Paper." Undated.

Selby Co-op Council. "Transformation at Selby." Undated.

Sloane, Cliff. "Personal Reactions to Michael Biesanze's 'RECAP'." Undated.

Young, Annie. "Conspiracy Notes." 17 September 1975.

Zimmerman, "And God Knows We Have Made Mistakes." May 1976.
————, and Paul McCluskey. "The Legal Question Is a Class Question." Undated.

## Interviews

David Gutknecht, December 1981, September 1982.
Warren Hanson, January 1983.
Ellen Hawley, March 1979.
Scott Jackson, July 1992.
Mickey Kelly, July 1992.
Fred Ojile, May 1987.
Kris Olsen, May 1980.
Cynthia Olson, May 1980.
Don Olson, October 1981.
Martha Roth, February 1982.
Chuck Phenix, August 1978.
Debbie Shroyer, August 1979.
Jeannie Shroyer, August 1984.
Susan Shroyer, June 1978.
David Tilsen, December 1992.
Edward Winter, November 1981.
Annie Young, July 1979.
Dean Zimmerman, April 1979.

# INDEX

# The Art of Coarse Entertaining

# The Art of
# Coarse Entertaining

## SPIKE HUGHES

### ILLUSTRATED BY DEREK ALDER

## HUTCHINSON OF LONDON

HUTCHINSON & CO *(Publishers)* LTD
*3 Fitzroy Square, London W1*

London Melbourne Sydney Auckland
Wellington Johannesburg Cape Town
and agencies throughout the world

*First published 1972*

© Spike Hughes 1972
Illustrations © Hutchinson & Co *(Publishers)* Ltd. 1972

*This book has been set in Baskerville type, printed in Great Britain*
*on antique wove paper by Anchor Press, and*
*bound by Wm. Brendon, both of Tiptree, Essex*

ISBN 0 09 113300 9

*It snewes in her hous of mete and drinke*
*after* CHAUCER

# CONTENTS

# 1  First Principles

Ourself will mingle with Society
And play the humble host
SHAKESPEARE

Mankind, said Max Beerbohm, is divisible into two great classes: hosts and guests.

Or, we may add, men and women.

But where men can get along without women (as in some monkeries), and women can get along without men (as in some nunneries), neither hosts nor guests can get on, or even exist, without the other.

You can't be a host without at least one guest, and you can't be a guest without a host. Indeed, the French and Italians, so far from dividing mankind, unite it by using the same word to describe both a host and a guest. Which can be pretty confusing.

If a Frenchman tells you he's to be *hôte*, or an Italian that he is to be *ospite*, at Buckingham Palace, you can never be sure whether he's going to a royal garden party or has just bought the place and is giving a house-warming.

While in the sphere of Coarse Entertaining the nominal distinction between host and guest is recognised, in practice their functions are not only complementary, but overlap. One has only to think of the bottle party, one of the original and basic forms of the Art, where the guests provide their fellow guests with liquor as though they were hosts.

The Coarse Host may well find himself entertaining ordinary guests, just as the Coarse Guest may find himself being entertained by an ordinary host, but true Coarse Entertaining is not genuinely achieved unless host and guests are of the same happy breed. Only then can one be certain that there will be no social friction, no misunderstanding, no breach of a code of etiquette as strict in its way as anything ever laid down by Emily Post.

It must be stressed at once that, as in every other case, those who practise a Coarse Art are born to it. Talent shows itself at any early age, or not at all. Skill is improved, tact and ingenuity learned by experience and example, but the temperament, the imagination, the instinct is inbred.

You cannot suddenly decide, in middle age, that you,

The talent shows itself at an early age

too, would like to be a Coarse Host, or even shine as a Coarse Guest. You would be found out at once, betrayed by a careless gesture, an anxious look, or an involuntary and undisguisable air of disapproval.

Nevertheless, there is one point in their lives when hosts and guests of both worlds meet on neutral ground, and that is when they are christened and are entirely unaware of the fact that they are the hosts of the party that follows.

Or so they are deemed to be by tradition. The guests eat the cake, it is said, as a sign that they are 'partaking of the baby's hospitality and are therefore its friends'.

They are even more its friends, of course, if the baby lays on champagne. This is something that appeals to everybody present, but particularly to those of us who recognise the basis of the best sort of hospitality in the baby's skill in pushing the boat out in the grand manner, at somebody else's expense.

The serving of champagne at christenings is an ancient fertility rite, though this is not generally known. It is, however, still common practice in parts of Sussex. A local doctor, a friend of mine, celebrated the christening of each new baby with such effectively aphrodisiac doses of champagne that nine months to the day after every christening another baby was born. He collected a family of nine children by this method and has now moved to Canada—where, I suppose, there is more room.

Now, as we have seen, every baby with the right financial backing displays one of the most important features of good Coarse Entertaining at his christening, but there is no certainty that he will practise, perfect and adopt it as a Way of Life. He may turn his back on it altogether, and choose the way of Gracious Entertaining.

The crucial moment of decision is when the baby is a little older and for the first time asks if he can have a friend to tea. By choosing his own guest, instead of letting his mother do it for him, he expresses clearly his belief in the paramount principle of freedom to choose whom he shall entertain. From then on this principle is an indispensable element of the most important moments in a man's life. These moments are clearly defined.

The child's tea party is followed by coming-of-age parties, weddings, christenings (when *you* pay for what your father paid for when you were christened—this is known as the generation gap), re-weddings, housewarmings and wakes.

The custom of the wake, which I am glad to see is gradually coming into fashion again, completes the circle nicely. Like the protagonist of a christening, the protagonist of a wake is, without his knowing it, the host of a celebration in his honour paid for, and organised by, other people.

The generous host may, of course, leave instructions in his will that the remainder of his cellar should be shared among his friends, but if it's anything of a cellar, or anything of a wake, it won't be very suitable. As every Irishman knows, a wake is an occasion for the hard stuff, not for *premiers crus*.

The Stygian ferry at a wake should be pushed out by an intimate friend standing proxy for the host.

With any luck, the second and third important moments in the life of *homo hospitalis liberalis* are also to be enjoyed free of charge: the coming-of-age party and—if you are a man—the reception at your wedding.

How far the lowering of the age of majority from twenty-one to eighteen has affected the economics of the coming-of-age party I do not know, but I cannot imagine that it has been favourably received by parents. So long as it stayed at twenty-one there was an increasing

chance, in an age when youth's independence of everything is everything, that coming-of-age celebrations
would be paid for by the twenty-one-year-old himself, not
his parents. After all, nowadays twenty-one is almost over
the threshold of middle age for young executives, and
only a step from the age of retirement.

The decision that the English should come of age at
eighteen ensured not only that parents would have to
provide their children with the novelty of a slap-up
party while they were still at school but that the children
would not be denied the right to enjoy the second occasion
in their lives when they are hosts at a party paid for by
somebody else.

The tradition of the twenty-first is still active, I notice—
kept alive, I imagine, by those who see in it the chance of a
second celebration at someone else's expense. On the
other hand, they may find that, instead of fun and fire-
works, all they are likely to get is their name in one of
those announcements so long a feature of local country
weekly papers, but now eagerly solicited by *The Times*
in its anxiety to attract Bottom People. You know the
sort of thing:

DAVE. Congratulations, dear, on your 21st—Mum,
Dad, Gran, Aunt Lil, Uncle Reg, Ron, Rog, Norm,
Aud, Wend, Shirl and Samantha and all at No. 10
Downing Street.

One notable point was overlooked by the authorities
when they devalued the age of majority from twenty-one
to eighteen: how the hell can you scan 'eighteen' to fit the
tune of 'Twenty-one Today'?

## US: YES. THEM: NO

One important principle of Coarse Entertaining is encountered at an early age—namely, the principle of
Reciprocal Hospitality. This is a phrase which you soon
discover has one meaning for you, who are a Coarse Host,
and another for your mother, who is a conventional or
Gracious Hostess.

The point of Our hospitality is that everybody should
feel good. With Their hospitality this cannot be guaranteed, because too often it is practised in order to repay,
or be repaid, a social debt of honour. In one case the
inspiration is Love, in the other it is Duty; and Duty
is yet another threat to that most precious of all freedoms:
the freedom to choose one's guests.

The conflict between Us and Them over this freedom
begins early in life, a duel between the child representing
Us and the mother representing Them.

The contest is usually fought most intensely around
Christmas time, when the question of parties is disputed.
The child sees no point in reciprocal hospitality for
its own sake. He knows perfectly well that there are no
hosts without guests, and that he and his fellow guests are
as essential to the host as an audience to an actor. He is
doing his host a favour, and feels under no obligation
to do more than say thank you for having him.

Mother, on the other hand, doesn't see things this way.
Every time her little jewel is asked to a party it means his
host must be invited back. This involves her in the considerable expense of providing at Christmas time not only
a present for her child to take to the host of each party
he is invited to but also a present for every one of the
guests who come to *his* party.

The fact that so many guests come to his party, and have to be given presents, is almost entirely due to his mother's dutiful observance of the conventions of her class. If you are asked out, she says, you must ask them back, whether you like them or not.

This, as the child recognises instinctively, is entirely contrary to the spirit of Coarse Entertaining. You ask people to your house because you like them, not because owing to some technicality you are considered to owe them a meal. Any pressure by his parents to do what they consider is Done, though he may be forced to submit, inevitably strengthens the child's determination to follow the precepts of *his* code of hospitality for life.

Literal, textbook reciprocal hospitality—an ice for an ice, a mousse for a mousse—is unacceptable because it can involve host and guest in boredom and unnecessary expense. The child may not care too much about the expense; it isn't his money. But he cares about boredom just as passionately as the man he is father to.

The worst hazards of reciprocal hospitality are encountered when (at any age) you move to another town or go to live in the country.

From out of nowhere well-meaning people will appear to importune you, not to come to tea (an inconvenient but harmless convention), but to be exhibited at a dinner party where you will meet a selection of guests assembled by your hosts, who trapped you into all this when you made what you thought was the non-committal, one-no-trump reply: 'We'd love to come sometime, perhaps later on—when we're settled in.'

The invitation proves inescapable, of course, and you find yourself dining most reluctantly in the company of people with whom (your hosts among them) you have nothing in common except that you now pay rates to the same rural district council as they do.

You meet the local doctor and the local solicitor, and immediately vow to yourself to keep in the best of health and to have no legal problems. There is a stock-broker who commutes—one imagines to escape from the shrill piercing voice of his wife. They are all enormously richer than you are and don't seem to be interested in anything you are, like cats, shrub roses and early Louis Armstrong.

Their children, you are not surprised to learn later, have all dropped out in a spectacular manner; their daughters have married West Indian bus conductors, and their sons are either in jail for pushing reefers or play in pop groups. And, having met their parents, it is understandable. The children needed a change.

The prospect of reciprocating hospitality of this kind is very depressing. The question of being able to give them as good a dinner as they gave you is no problem. Coarse Entertaining is not based on Coarse Cookery; as a general rule it should offer the best food not that the host, but his wife, can cook.

Reciprocal catering is easy. Unfortunately, food is not everything, and whether you could keep up the sort of conversation you heard at the original dinner party that let you in for all this is another matter. The only way to do that, surely, would be to ask all your fellow guests at that party *en bloc*, but they are the last people you want to see again.

You could, of course, leaven the occasion with some of your own friends, whose congenial company would at least entertain you, if not your other guests, but this would be an unfair act and unforgivably contrary to Our standards of behaviour. These standards forbid any rash experiments in incompatibility likely to lead to a breach of the peace which it is our right as hosts and guests to enjoy undisturbed.

The easiest way out is to get your wife to write and thank your hostess for an enjoyable evening spent in such charming company, and end her letter with 'You must come and have dinner with us as soon as my husband has finished the book he's writing—which, please God, will not be long now.'

Even if her husband has never put pen to paper, except to mark a race card and write out a cheque for the book-maker, a wife can safely defer reciprocal hospitality indefinitely by this means. Her husband is, of course, writing His Novel. Everybody knows that everybody has at least one novel in them, and this explains everything.

As it is unlikely that you will ever be asked too obviously after the book's progress (which would make the enquirers look a little over-eager for that return invitation) the whole matter can be forgotten. The fact that The Novel looks like being three times as long as *War and Peace* is none of their damn business. You are not asking their critical opinion, only for their understanding of the sufferings of literary genius.

A reluctantly accepted invitation, in short, carries no obligation to reciprocate. It is enough to plead incompatibility of temperament and reflect that divorces have been granted for far less.


*ENTERTAINING BEGINS AT HOME*

The principle of refusing to reciprocate unwelcome hospitality is, of course, one of the less important items in the Code, but like most of the others it is founded on

Help yourself and pass it round

self-interest. Thus every host and guest is inclined to evolve a few principles of his own, some of which may well conflict with those adopted by other bona-fide practitioners.

High up among my own most important principles, for instance, I rate that of the host's enjoyment and well-being. This, rather surprisingly, can lead to considerable family dispute one way and another.

My own preference for a dinner party is a total of four people—us, and two guests, who can be a married couple, two girls, two men, a cohabiting unmarried couple; the status and combination is unimportant so long as there are only four of us altogether.

The reason for this preference is that with a party of six or eight people it is not only difficult to get more than a couple of words in edgeways, but you don't get

enough to eat. The delicious new French beans out of the
garden get marooned up the other end of the table, and
your polite requests that please would somebody pass
them down to you are drowned in the noisy polyphony of
conversational *tuttis*. Attempts to fill up your glass are
equally hopeless. 'Help yourself and pass it round—do',
you said, and by the time the bottle gets back to you it
is nothing but dregs.

It is only when your guests have gone and you are
helping with the washing-up that you get a chance to
finish your dinner properly. The beans are cold by now,
but no less appetising for that; the cheese board that never
reached your end of the table apparently had Stilton
on it at one time. However, the undistinguished low-fat
Dutch cheese that's left is better than nothing, and is
healthier for you anyway.

A book of advice to hostesses informs me that it is
better to have four dinner parties with six guests than one
party with twenty-four. My experience tells me that it is
best to have twelve dinner parties with two guests only,
if I am to get the nutritional inpour that I need to survive.

Another thing in favour of limiting a dinner party to
four is that once that number of guests is exceeded there
is a risk of their being incompatible. Perhaps this happens
only to us. I know when I was young I constantly found
myself in a pub between two intimate friends, one of
whom talked to me only of cricket and racing, the other
only about twelve-note music. An affection for me and for
alcohol were the only things my two friends had in
common; until Dylan Thomas joined us, when we all
had him and a lot more alcohol in common.

*HISTORICAL NOTE*

Co-operation has always been a powerful principle of
Coarse Entertaining, not just in matters of washing up or
helping to get a drunken guest into a taxi, but in one
of the most typical of all its forms: the bottle party.

With the passing of time the host tends to prosper enough
to give parties where he, and not his guests, provide the
bottles; but the tradition of the bottle party never dies;
it is carried on by each new generation during its hard-
pushed teens and twenties. The gifts of the bottle-party
magi may vary a little between one epoch and another
according to drinking fashions of the time, but the spirit
and purpose of the occasion remain the same, and the
host, by getting each guest to be a host, still stands to
do well out of it. This aspect of the bottle party, however,
will be discussed later.

As an institution the bottle party is probably as old as
the bottle itself. Its history does not seem to be well
documented, however. Little seems to be known about
it until the 1920s, when its practice flourished and the
very term 'bottle party' became synonymous with un-
speakable drunken orgies, attacked by bishops as 'worse
than Ancient Rome'.

In fact, the bottle party could not have been a more
harmless institution, and it was enormously welcome to
those who could not afford to entertain their friends.
Just like today, of course.

In the 1930s the idea of the bottle party was adapted
to combat the idiocy of the English licensing laws. Un-
licensed London night clubs, wearying of police raids,
hit on the idea of describing themselves as 'bottle parties'.
The procedure was simple. The customer would present

... worse than Ancient Rome ...

himself at the entrance of the club, where the secretary would ask if he had an invitation to the bottle party. No? Then would he please sign a form which read:

I, the undersigned, hereby declare that I have lost my invitation to the Bottle Party at the Buck House Club and offer to pay five shillings towards expenses.

What the expenses were was never explained, but having paid his five bob the customer was asked whether he had ordered a bottle. No. They hadn't let him in yet.

The bottle had to be ordered from the wine merchant, they explained—from the Buck House Vintage Company, who had absolutely *nothing* to do with the Buck House

Club. It merely happened to be the name of the wine merchant the guests ordered their liquor from when they decided to hold a bottle party at the club.

However, you didn't have to go to this wine merchant and buy your bottle and drink it at the club. You got your bottle through the waiter, who sent your order round to the wine merchant twenty yards down the Mews, who sent the bottle to you by a boy on a bicycle. Liquor could always be delivered to a customer at any hour, but taken away by the customer only during permitted hours.

It only added to the confusion to be told that since the club had no license the waiter was not a waiter selling drinks, but the wine merchant's agent.

In short, if you told the wine merchant's agent that you'd lost your invitation to the bottle party, and that you wanted a bottle to show that you had been going to order a bottle, if you hadn't lost the invitation you'd never had, then everything would be all right.

The only real advantage of this form of bottle party was that, though you paid through the nose for your bottle, you could at least keep it all to yourself. All your 'host' got out of it was the money, and you didn't have to thank him for anything.

## CHÉRISSEZ LA FEMME

The equality of women ranks high among the principles of Coarse Entertaining. The hostess not only has equal rights: she is encouraged by all men to assert them. For without her skill and experience the standard of cooking would be very low.

I know that the greatest cooks, the Escoffiers and the

Carêmes, were men and that Haute Cuisine is a male preserve, but I for one have absolutely no masculinist feelings about this. The suppression of women cooks would be disastrous, for we would then have to resort to Coarse Cookery, which would be most out of place.

Thus the misogynist has no place in our society. For the benefit of those whose English does not run to Greek, a misogynist is a man who blames women for the lipstick he finds on his glass in a pub, instead of blaming the barman who is supposed to have washed it up.

It is a matter of solid sociological fact, rarely acknowledged, that the invention of lipstick has done more for public hygiene than anything since the invention of the water closet. It makes Them wash up glasses—or at least provides evidence that they *haven't* been washed up.

In the end, perhaps Coarse Entertaining and Haute Entertaining differ only in the means, not the end. Brillat-Savarin might have been writing in praise of Coarse Entertaining when he defined the joys of *gourmandisme* as 'an impassioned, reasoned, and habitual preference for everything that gratifies the organ of taste—good food and drink'.

We could not have put it better ourselves.

# 2  Organisation

I am indebted to the *Radio Times* for bringing to the public notice a full-time occupation of great but shamefully underestimated importance. A broadcaster was billed in the Third Programme as being 'himself a painter, poet, musician and organiser of events'.

Few of us concerned with the Coarse Arts may be painters or poets or musicians, but, by God, there isn't a one of us that isn't an Organiser of Events. And it is about time this was recognised, too, for it is a serious business, requiring skill, imagination and ingenuity.

Think of the events we have to organise and how it has to be done. And when—because we must remember that ours is an amateur pursuit, and there is no compensation for 'broken time'. We have no secretaries to send out invitations, no smiling, comfortably bosomed cook downstairs with whom the lady of the house can discuss, and decide on, her menu 'at least' (says the classic manual of the late Mrs Sarah Tyson Rorer, of Philadelphia) 'four days before the dinner party'.

It is a pity about the invitations, but the telephone is a chummier, quicker and more reliable means of communication, and can include more detailed information (such as who has been invited, and does Mary drink red or only white wine).

The written invitation may sometimes have to be resorted to, in confirmation, when your guests are making their first visit and you have to tell them how to get there. These instructions should be given with great care. Directions like 'turn R' or 'turn L' are usually understood, but it's no good saying that your house is the white weather-boarded farmhouse with the pitched flint walls on the south side of the road going west past the Green Man.

Few people outside the county know a pitched flint wall from a bull's foot, and even fewer can tell which is the south side of a road. On the other hand, they can hardly fail to recognise the Green Man, if they happen to pass it on their way to you. But if they're not going to pass it, or don't know the Green Man already, they won't know to find you on the right-hand side of the road 150 yards before they get to it.

The answer ought to be a thumbnail map, of course. But how many people can read a map? Or make one that tallies with the instructions, come to that?

The R.A.C. recently gave me a Paris route which told me to 'proceed on the Quai de Bercy (river on left)'. Fortunately, I had read somebody else's map first. Anybody who proceeds on the Quai de Bercy with the river on his left can only be doing it for his life-insurance money, for he is driving the wrong way along one of the most ferocious one-way race tracks in the world.

The thumbnail map that went with this route card showed the Quai de Bercy quite correctly to be a west-to-east *sens unique* with the Seine on the right. The printed instructions contradicted the map flatly: river on the left. Obviously the Styx.

Of course, in the country, none of your instructions, either oral or written, is any use except for daylight travelling. You just don't invite anybody to dinner in the winter who hasn't already been to dinner or drinks in the summer.

Equally, the metropolitan guest has his problems after dark—the impossibility of distinguishing street-names in unfamiliar districts, of being confronted by 'No Entry' signs at the bottom of streets you always want to get to the top of.

But at least these problems can be solved by taking a taxi. Public transport is all very well but—contrary to the belief of politicians who would like us to use nothing else—it rarely offers a door-to-door service, and even more rarely does it wait up to bring you home. Besides, it is such an unsafe way of taking your contribution to a bottle party.

## THE BOTTLE PARTY

> Oh Thou, who didst with Pitfall and with Gin
> Beset the Road I was to wander in
>                                OMAR KHAYYÁM

As we have seen, your first experiences as a Coarse Host are likely to have been paid for by somebody else— children's parties, your coming-of-age. And so, later on, are bottle parties.

The difference is that where your mother may have insisted on introducing unwelcome elements to tour children's parties, and your parents are bound to have invited a lot of their own contemporaries to your coming-of-age, the bottle party is an exercise in the organisation of hospitality that is your own responsibility. You can ask whom you like, but as you are not paying for it, you can't be sure that you'll be able to drink what you like, unless you contribute it yourself.

You have your obligations, of course, such as providing soft drinks for mixing with hard liquor; and things to eat, so that at least some of your guests can drive home safely. But even though you can make sure of getting your own favourite drink at your own expense, the rest of the fare is a complete gamble. However well you may think you know your guests, you can't be sure what they're likely to bring.

A certain amount can be done towards planning a balanced collection if the host suggests to his friends when he invites them that it would be useful if they could lay hands on a bottle of some particular drink. As part host and part guest in your own home, in organising a bottle party you must do what you can to ensure that your gift horses are all of different colours or the occasion can be exceedingly drab.

It must be hinted as gently but as clearly as possible that you will welcome guests' friends with more widely open arms if they pay their entrance fee, too. It is not economic sense if some decorative and beddable floozy arrives empty-handed and proceeds to drink your Scotch before staggering off with some guest who wasn't her original escort. This creates a poor impression all round.

To anybody who has ever been to an English boarding school, either for boys or girls, the principle of the bottle party will be familiar, for it is firmly rooted in the traditional dormitory feast. Although, as you will recall, the emphasis in the Dorm Feed was entirely on food, of course, it was still essentially a co-operative, communal venture.

The successful bottle party offers guests a choice of drinks such as they will find in a Paris café, and a lot more (unless they're lucky) they won't; and it leaves you as host with a legacy of half-finished, sometimes not even opened, bottles on which you can subsist for days afterwards. You will also inherit a number of retunable quart beer bottles which you can cash in to help swell the holiday fund.

The bottle party is a great revealer of personality and taste. There are guests who bring what they want to drink themselves; there are those who bring what they don't want to drink themselves, because they hope somebody else will have brought what they do want to drink; and there are others who bring quantity in preference to quality (no great fault, this, as there comes a time in the evening when this is just what is needed).

There are the eccentrics who will bring bottles of unlikely exotic spirits distilled from ground-nuts and tobacco seed, or a bagful of a dozen miniature bottles of liqueurs which have no immediate use at a bottle party, but will come in useful—if nobody touches them—for your *pamplemousse Suzette* later on.

Never heard of it? Well, prepare half a grapefruit in the ordinary way; remove the core. Cover the top of the fruit with brown sugar and put it under the grill until the sugar is melted and the flesh of the grapefruit is browned.

Pour a teaspoonful of Benedictine (or brandy, or both, or any other liqueur) into the hole left by the core, and serve as a first course, a last course, or for breakfast.

The amount of liqueur used is, of course, entirely a matter of taste. I merely said a teaspoonful because it looks more modest. You can pour a whole miniature bottle into the hole, if you want to. In fact, that's about the best thing you can do with a miniature bottle. The liqueur will overflow, but you will naturally have placed the grapefruit in a saucer from which you can drink the ullage.

The inventory of the typical bottle party of twenty-five people or so may—as I suggested earlier—change in detail between one generation and another, but its fundamental character does not vary. It is essentially a

The amount of liqueur used is of course entirely
a matter of taste

youthful Bohemian gathering presided over by a young
Bohemian host who though he is flat broke, like most of
his friends, nevertheless also has a few friends who are
not. It is these who put the gilt on the gingerbread and
explain how, among such familiar items as quart bottles
of beer, flasks of Chianti, bottles of plonk, and the odd
bottle of 65 proof gin, there appear such luxuries as good
brandy, rum, Irish whiskey, Benedictine, Curaçao, Coin-
treau, Strega, Grand Marnier, grappa, slivovitz, marc
de Bourgogne, three or four bottles of Vichy and some
Cyprus sherry.

The inclusion of Vichy and Cyprus sherry as 'luxuries'
is not a bizzarerie. Only the affluent have enough money
to bring soft drinks as well as hard liquor. Vichy water
can be very welcome during the evening as a kind of sorbet
between main drinks, and next morning to soften the
host's hangover. And a cheap sherry added to tomato
juice makes a surprisingly tolerable long drink out of
two uninspiring ingredients. A tolerable long drink is
essential at any bottle party, if only as a means of deferring
the moment when it turns into the orgy everybody is
expecting.

After having kindly lent the hall and provided soft
drinks there remains the host's final contribution: the
provision of food for his guests. This is achieved by being
married to, or living in blissful sin with, a cook who can
run up something good and filling to eat like outsize
quiches, or nourishing risottos and other rice dishes.

But apart from the drink, one of the most noble features
of any bottle party is its egalitarian spirit, a shining example to politicians of what fair shares for all really means.

## A FEW PEOPLE IN FOR DRINKS

> Drink! for you know not whence you came, nor why:
> Drink! for you know not why you go, nor where.
>
> OMAR KHAYYÁM

The organisation of 'a few' people to come in for drinks brings the host up against the impossible ambiguity and imprecision of the English language.

How many is a few? Not many, is the dictionary's answer. A good few, on the other hand, is a fair number. Unless you know how few not many is, and how many a fair number is, you aren't any the wiser.

Experience suggests, however, that 'a few' is always roughly twice as many as you bargain for—except before lunch on Sundays in metropolitan surroundings, where nearly always fewer people turn up than you expect. This is usually because it is all the city dweller can do to get up and struggle round to his local pub for cigarettes before it shuts.

In the country Saturday nights are less exhausting, and those who say they'll come round usually do.

The Sunday-morning assembly is important as a testing ground. It is when you can ask people you don't know very well and want to see if you'd like them to come to dinner, or to one of those evening gatherings where a fair number of friends come in for a good few drinks.

On a Sunday morning people usually arrange that their lunch at home is ready about two o'clock, give or take five or ten minutes or drinks. Even if your guests aren't going to lunch at home, the English Sunday ensures that they'll have to keep an eye on the clock if they are going to lunch out.

Although a Sunday twelve-till-two session interrupts one's reading of the Sunday papers, the occasion has an informal, relaxing quality that is peculiarly enjoyable—largely, I believe, because its traditions and limitations are unaffected by the habits and customs of individual guests, which can seriously disturb the smooth path of entertaining at other times of day.

In the country one quickly discovers that it is not differences of education, accent, money or social standing that create barriers, but the rudimentary and insoluble question of when you eat your evening meal.

We learnt about this when we first moved to the country and asked our neighbouring farmer and his wife in for drinks. They came, as invited, at half past six. By 8.45 we were getting a little restive and they showed no signs of moving. They left at ten o'clock and their starving hosts were then able to have their dinner.

Perhaps they might have seen the light if we had invited them to stay to dinner, but if by some chance they had accepted we would have been sunk. All the food in the house was a couple of chops intended for the dinner we were waiting for.

When they had gone we realised that our guests had had some form of meal at 5.30 and had come over to us to spend the evening, expecting sandwiches and sausage rolls at the end of it.

One might imagine that this evening routine was the result of a life lived according to the demands of television. This is not the case at all; it is television which lives according to the demands of this evening routine. Which is why we have no television. Not only would an aerial spoil the look of a seventeenth-century central chimney, but we already have so many satisfactory ways of wasting time free of charge that to introduce another which inter-

fered with dinner, as well as needing a licence, would be
pure folly.

After our experience with our farmer we were never
caught again. Thereafter anybody whose eating habits
we were doubtful about was asked for Sunday-morning
drinks, when we knew that they would leave as soon as
*their* empty stomachs started rumbling for the hot Sunday-
midday dinner waiting for them at home.

Even the exclusion of Tea Folk from the company of a
few people in for drinks before dinner does not, unfortunately, guarantee that you will get your dinner as punct-
ually as you hoped. There are some right stickers among
Dinner Folk, though we don't suffer from them quite
so much as big-town hosts do. In London you are lucky
to get your guests out before 9.30. This is because they all
seem to eat only in restaurants where it is unheard of to
arrive before 9.30, and even less heard of to leave before
2.30 a.m., or the last dog-tired waiter has collapsed, which-
ever is the later.

(Many of these restaurants charge you handsomely
for your surroundings and the food you eat, both of
which are sometimes worth the *détour*. But what you're
really paying for is the ground rent for your exclusive
occupation of a furnished table on a five hour
lease.)

Faced with a crowd of plastered stickers in London,
there is nothing for it but to resign yourself to dining
late too and organise things accordingly—either on or
off the premises.

In the country laggards usually have to be invited to
stay on to dinner. The invitation may embarrass them
into going, or they may accept it. (You will, of course,
have previously organised a non-troublesome meal for
just such an emergency.) Either way it enables the host

B

to stop propping up the mantelpiece and sit down with his drink.

Once you get to know your regular laggers it is sometimes a good idea to send them a card, not to remind them of the date (which you told them when you invited them by telephone), but to draw attention quietly to the hours of play. So that it doesn't look too pointedly personal, it is advisable to have this gentle admonition printed, as though you sent it to everybody.

But the cards must not be printed in the pseudo-copperplate lettering still favoured by Gracious Hostesses. It sets a bad example to children, who are being taught to write decoratively for the first time since the eighteenth century.

Better to make imaginative use of the vast range of typefaces now available, particularly the more hideous ones which will catch the eye:

---

## CAN'T

### REMEMBER

### *IF YOU SAID*

### 𝔜𝔢𝔰 𝔬𝔯 𝔑𝔬

### *but if you can*

### **DRINKS 6 to 8**

### *at the Hugheses's*

---

The day and date are filled in by hand

As the sending out of these cards must not be overdone, a large stock of them is not needed. They can be effective, however, for where a telephoned invitation will tell the guest when proceedings are to start, only a written invitation ever mentions the time you hope to God proceedings will stop.

Guests are divided into three classes: those who know when to go, those who know when to stay, and those who don't know when to do either. It is the last class that have to be taught not to keep you up nights.

## PEOPLE FOR DINNER

'A long course dinner', says Mrs Rorer, of Philadelphia, in a chapter headed 'The Course Dinner', 'must never be undertaken by those who keep only one or two servants.'

Allowing for the all-too-familiar misspelling of 'Coarse', Mrs Rorer's words are only too true. In fact, one should never undertake a long Coarse Dinner at any time, no matter how many servants one can lay hands on (which seems to be the right phrase for the *au pair* age).

'Where only one servant is kept', continues Mrs Rorer, 'a small three-course dinner is most satisfactory.'

I suppose we can't really count our obliging young daily as 'keeping only one servant', but at least (crossing our fingers) we've kept her quite a time now. As servant-less hosts, however, we have none the less found the small three-course dinner most satisfactory.

Now, while those who practise Coarse Entertaining are open to suggestions from all quarters, even Gracious Hostesses, we have to draw the line somewhere.

Mrs Rorer goes on: 'In fact, a crust of bread and a cup

of tea daintily and handsomely served is much more hospitable than an elaborate dinner party served in an ill-heated and ill-lighted room.'

Maybe. But the question is: if you have the genius to be able to serve a crust of bread 'handsomely', why cannot you devote some of that genius to well-heating and well-lighting a room *and* running up an elaborate dinner party? Certainly none of the rest of us who had Mrs Rorer's gifts would have any trouble doing all this. And she has servants, too.

The organisation of the simple three-course dinner is largely a question of argument between host and hostess about the number of guests. To the hostess a table for four or six people makes little or no difference so far as the cooking is concerned. To the host, who is responsible for the wine (as well as being roped in to help with a lot of washing up), numbers are everything.

A dinner party of four will inevitably get given better wine than a party of six. It is a matter of more than simple arithmetic; if a party of four means two bottles of good wine, six means three bottles. Which means that a dozen bottles of good wine will last six dinners *à quatre*, but only four *à six*.

It is most important that this should be looked at from the host's point of view. He does not personally drink more when entertaining two guests, or any less when he's entertaining six. It is just that he likes an excuse to drink his good wine more often.

Once it has been decided whether the small dinner party is going to be for four (where the wine will be good), or for six (when, the host having lost the argument, the wine will probably be less good), the organisation of what everybody is going to eat is left to the lady of the house who, instead of handing her cook the bill of fare at least four days in advance, will plan the whole thing herself in an afternoon.

Meanwhile, let me quote Alexandre Dumas' definition of dinner:

> A daily and essential act which can be worthily performed only by people of wit and intelligence, since at dinner it is not enough to eat; one must talk with a discreet and serene gaiety.
>
> Conversation should shine with the rubies of the red wines of the *entremets*, assume a delicious smoothness with the sweetmeats of the dessert, and acquire a true depth with the coffee.

The author of *The Three Musketeers* was too busy getting on with the story to over-write, as a rule, but like any glossy-magazine wine correspondent, once he dipped his pen in a glass of wine he couldn't resist it.

## TAKING THEM OUT

Most of the headaches of arranging the small dinner party can be avoided, of course, by taking your guests out to a restaurant and lavishing hospitality on them there.

Organisation in this case consists of reserving a table in a restaurant you know, or at least you know from a reliable informant is still all right, even though it has changed hands several times since you were last there, and instructing your stockbroker to sell enough shares to provide extra capital to cover the cost of drinking, at four times its true value, the same wine that you drink at home.

Any really sensible host would do a few sums before setting out on a jaunt like this. He would realise that it would be cheaper to hire a professional cook to come in for the evening and produce a good meal—an expense more than offset by the cost of drinking wine from his own cellar.

The introduction of professional help on this scale, however, is entirely contrary to the principles of Coarse Entertaining. You already have a resident and professional cook at home; in fact, you're married to her, and it would be altogether unethical to pay a visiting professional more than the pittance she gets from you. You certainly wouldn't get anyone else for less.

In any case, even if trades union ethics didn't enter into it, the whole idea of taking your guests out to dinner is to give your wife a night off. She would hardly get that if there was a hired deputy messing about in her kitchen.

This is one of the great differences between Us and Them. The Gracious Hostess never gets a night off, but that's because she never has a night on.


## WEEKENDS

The best time for having people for the weekend is between Tuesday and Friday.

This is because it is still not generally realised in England (or, if it is, nobody does a damn thing about it) that by coming to stay with you from Friday to Monday your guests are choosing the worst days of the week, as you are absolutely on your own without daily help of any kind.

. . . you already have a professional cook at home . . .

Of course, the midweek weekend may cause a slight disruption in the working lives of your guests, but there is nothing that cannot be put right by a little ingenuity, and once the unfamiliar routine is accepted it will be found most enjoyable by guests and hosts. Many of our lotus-eating friends, indeed, find the midweek visit most convenient; it enables them to spend Friday to Monday with somebody else, and so enjoy two weekends in one week.

The first great advantage of the midweek visitor is the hostess's knowledge that her daily will be coming in the morning and so make it easier for her to organise a slightly messier series of meals than the conventional Friday-to-Monday weekend allows.

The amount of washing-up guests have to do after meals on Fridays, Saturdays and Sundays is something they are almost entirely spared by staying midweek. On the other hand, comparative freedom from major washing-up operations does not exempt them from a certain amount of do-it-yourself amusement, such as being sent out for a walk on the Downs (which is much pleasanter midweek). The obstinately inactive guest, of course, will be encouraged to put his feet up and read a book after lunch, while his hosts have their afternoon kip.

The town-rooted reader about to stay in the country for the first time should be warned that there is a world of difference between a country house and a house in the country.

A country house is what advertising agencies photograph Bentleys, and the glossies photograph Gracious Hosts, their children, horses and labradors in front of. It is also, one knows from personal experience, very likely to have blazing log fires in the winter, which heat the chimney wonderfully—but nothing else.

A house in the country is where Coarse Entertaining is found; there are no blazing log fires in the winter because the hosts had the sense to prefer personal comfort to perishing picturesqueness. They put in central heating and turned the inglenook into a wine cupboard. Mind you, they probably lowered the value of the house by thousands of pounds, scrapping the inglenook. Apparently England is full of middle-aged dreamers who live only for the day when they can retire to the country and have their very own inglenook, to scorch their faces, foster their chilblains, and stoke up their bronchitis at—all exactly as shown on American telly by the British Travel Ass.

The organisation of summer and winter board and lodging varies considerably. In summer the guest from London asks—or at any rate is offered—little more than the opportunity to relax, sniff at the flowers, read in the shade and enjoy the pure air and quiet of the countryside. He will not, of course, feel a total stranger, for we can provide him with all the jet planes, helicopters, lorries, motor bikes, buses, petrol fumes, and minis with sawn-off silencers going about their daily business that he needs to make him feel it is a home from home.

In the winter the Coarse Hostess has extra responsibilities towards her guest. His bed has to be aired, a water bottle put in it, his bedroom warmed, his window wedged to prevent rattling and penetration by wind, rain and snow. (The window has to be wedged in summer, too, in our house, to keep out the din of the morning village rush-hour, as well as wind, rain and snow.)

True, winter spares the hostess the organisation of summer diversions like picnics at Sissinghurst (no barbecues; they are things you are guests at, not hosts). But it is a season when the hostess is no longer helped out by nature. There is no sunshine to enjoy, no flowers to sniff and admire, no shady spot to curl up with a good book to fall asleep over in.

Where the summer guest may be left to wallow in the beauty of the countryside, the winter guest has to have his attention diverted from the gales, the frosts, the fog, and from the bitter east wind with drizzle in it (weather which, as our gardener says, 'aint very sweating —damping a little bit, too'), from the driving rain and thunderstorms and all the glories of nature he is offered in exchange for the security of his sheltered London home.

One item entails organisation all the year round and that is the provision of newspapers. This is considered most important by those ladies whose books on gracious living are so invaluable in enabling the Joneses to keep out in front.

'Nothing is more annoying,' says one of them, 'than for a guest to find, on coming downstairs, that everyone is talking about a crisis in the newspapers and to know nothing about it.'

Hosts, too, consider the matter important, though not for the same reasons. They never talk about any crisis in the newspapers. Crises have been ten-an-old-penny for the past twenty years and have long had no discussion value at any breakfast table. Or does the lady mean literally 'a crisis in the newspapers'? Non-publication of the papers owing to some footling union sulks in Fleet Street certainly gets plenty of comment, if not discussion, at our breakfast table all right.

In a two-paper household like ours there is no problem about a paper for midweek guests. They get mine, and I have to amuse myself as best I can over my morning tea with last Sunday's coloureds or old copies of the *New Yorker*.

On the rare occasions when we have guests on Saturdays and Sundays I do better. They still get my daily paper on Saturday, but I have a copy of the *Financial Times* that day. This is because many years ago my wife owned a couple of obscure American shares whose progress could be watched only in the Saturday issue of the *Financial Times*. The shares were eventually sold, but the paper was not cancelled because we had got to like the gardening feature.

Sundays, of course, is the easiest day of all. We have three 'quality'—that is the most costly—papers. One of these is in three sections, another—which can be shared by a married couple—is in two. For myself, I always begin with the third, the indivisible *Sunday Telegraph*, to learn from its enterprising, up-to-the-minute local correspondent how the officers—the *officers*, s.v.p.— on the French boats of the Newhaven–Dieppe route we aim to travel by next week are on getting on with their strikes.

When we have asked our guests whether they would perhaps prefer a copy of the daily paper they have at home, it is surprising how often their choice is the old red-flag-waving rabble-rouser of our youth, the *Daily Express*.

# 3  Practice Makes <u>What?</u>

One thing that is contrary to all the principles of Coarse Entertaining is any attempt to get away with anything.

At least, not when it matters. You will never hear of any of us doing what much richer, grander, but extremely naive hosts constantly boast they do—namely, give their guests cheap, sweet colonial-type sherry out of a decanter, with the excuse that 'they won't know the difference, anyway'.

How does he know? Does he really expect his guests to tell him to his face that his drink is revolting?

This sort of host does not entertain many Coarse Guests, which is lucky for him, because they would not only certainly notice the difference but would be very likely to tell him so. If he had been honest and apologised for his sherry from the start—he'd run out of his good stuff, and this was all the village post office had left— nobody would mind, so long as they didn't have to drink a second glass of it.

But to say nothing and to try to fool us by pouring it out of an expensive decanter . . .

The question of sherry is a very important one. It is probably the most expensive drink one can have in England. A good bottle, poured out by the generous glassful its quality demands, lasts no time at all—perhaps just long enough for four people on two aperitive occasions.

Apart from anything else, once the bottle is opened it is likely to go off if it isn't finished up, hooray. So if you haven't got people coming in soon for a meal, you can look after the finishing-up process yourself.

The provision of drinks for a few people demands of the host an altruism that is rarely needed in other forms of Coarse Entertaining. There is a good sporting chance that he will enjoy the food offered to his guests at dinner (he better had . . .), but there is none that he will be able to stomach a drop of anything he keeps for his drinking guests.

For them he has to keep medium sweet sherry (which he dislikes and whose quality he therefore cannot possibly judge objectively), a variety of vermouths, Dubonnet, coca-cola in case children have to be dragged along for Sunday drinks too. There were summertimes when it was possible to mix one of the sweet drinks I never minded sharing with guests. This was a long and very refreshing drink consisting of one-third red vermouth, one-third lemon squash, and one-third soda-water.

Owing to the apparently complete disappearance of straightforward manufactured lemon squash with bits of lemon actually floating about in it, it is no longer possible to make this drink properly. Nothing calling itself 'lemon drink with permitted sweeteners' is any use at all.

If only a couple of people come round for a drink things can be different, and the host can afford to make a good and aggressive dry martini to share with his guests, but in larger company he probably makes do with gin and tonic, wondering why it came to be such a class-associated drink that certain districts are known contemptuously as the 'gin-and-tonic belt'.

When we were younger, gin and tonic was the staple midday drink of some of the most gifted musicians and painters who ever died of alcohol in this country. Their steady evening drink was whisky. This drinking pattern was common—and fatal—to all of them.

A few people in for evening drinks is usually rather less straightforward than the Sunday-morning session. On Sundays the guest who can find nothing he fancies in your repertoire can often be satisfied—or at least, appeased—with a Guinness, a lager, or even a glass of plonk. But in the evenings one must be prepared for the guests with a known idiosyncrasy, and get in a bottle of the only thing that seems to make him happy. This is usually something pretty odd, like Fernet Branca and lime, or cherry brandy which he drinks with soda. With any luck he may leave enough for the next time he comes to see you.

Occasions like bottle parties and people in for drinks, whether before lunch on Sunday or in the evening, present comparatively elementary problems. At least, I do not remember being particularly put out, when I was a very young host at a bottle party, being asked for 'a little wait wain off the ace'. My guest was a dance-band leader's waif, and when I had puzzled out exactly what she wanted she was given *plonque du jour* like everyone else.

Most emergencies—such as a teetotal guest or one on the wagon for medical reasons—can be dealt with easily enough in any house lived in or visited by children. The prospect of invasion of our house by nephews and nieces below drinking age always leads to our stocking up a wide variety of non-alcoholical, highly carbonical drinks, among which there may be one that can be kept down by an adult.

The temporary teetotaller, the guest on the wagon, often solves his problem in a most interesting manner, choosing something not normally associated with alcohol, like ribena or apple juice. He leaves lime, bitter lemon, tonic, soda, ginger ale and tomato juice very severely alone.

Perhaps there is a psychological cure for dipsomania in this?

## CONVERSATION PEACE

Modern etiquette and match-the-Joneses books are full of the rules to be observed if your drinks party is to be altogether *comme il faut*. These concern the clothes you must wear, the canapés you must offer your guests, the way you must introduce your guests to each other, the drinks you must give the men, the non-drinks you must give the women.

Without having to look once at these rules, the givers and takers of Coarse Entertaining instinctively do just the opposite. Certainly, little black cocktail ensembles with pearls are worn, but by the men, not the women.

Introductions tend to be a little haphazard, and in the end people often leave without knowing the names of those they have been talking to. One thing never happens in our company, and that is the breaking-up of a sympathetic conversation by the hostess, who takes you away from the person you like talking to, to introduce you to somebody you obviously won't.

Such hostesses never rescue you from a bore. They are only too pleased that the bore is fully occupied, and does not need to be passed on to somebody else. I knew somebody who suffered this from a mother-in-law he once had. It became such an intolerable feature of his social life that he changed his mother-in-law by marrying somebody else's daughter.

... interrupted by the introduction of a third person

Almost as bad as being dragged away from a sympathetic companion to meet somebody else is, to have your conversation with them interrupted by the introduction by the hostess of a third person. All continuity of thought and relationship is hopelessly shattered. If you're not careful, or even if you are, you will find that your earlier chum rats on you; they catch sight of a friend across the room and walk away, leaving you stranded with the newcomer.

These are incidents which occur regularly in classy company. With Us the bores are not invited in the first place, though this doesn't mean that some otherwise welcome guest will not bring a boring house guest.

The drinks you offer the men are the drinks they want. The drinks you offer the women are the drinks they want,

not the drinks too many men and etiquette-book writers
think they ought to want. If a woman would like a
brandy and soda, Scotch or vodka on the rocks, she gets it.
In short, equal drinks for the more than equal work a
woman puts in one way and another at any party, in
any capacity.

If at any time you are a guest where there appears to
be only a fruit cup consisting mainly of soda and Yugoslav
Yquem, a quiet word in the host's ear that you suffer
from an unnatural craving for sugar called hyper-
saccheromania and are therefore on a strict no-sugar
diet, often produces a real drink. But remember to
be consistent: don't ask for a brandy and ginger ale or a
gin and Dubonnet.


## WOT LAYS BEFORE US

> Little do we know wot lays before us
> DICKENS

The same books which tell you how to give a successful
drinks party naturally have even more to say on the way
you should arrange a dinner party that will earn you an
enviable reputation for *soigné*, even *recherché*, entertaining.

Mrs Rorer, of Philadelphia, in her chapter 'Table
Waiting—or How to Train the Waitress', with its famous
section headed 'A Course Dinner' (who *does* correct
her proofs for her?) suggests that the minimum staff
seen above stairs includes a butler and a waitress or
dining-room maid (*anglice*: parlourmaid).

Books written quite a time after the Second World
War still surprisingly tell you how butlers and parlour-
maids should behave, though not—which I would have
thought no less important—how you should behave

towards them. But these books also set out codes of behaviour for those who, though they have no servants,
would still like to do the right thing graciously.

You and I, for our part, soon learn to our surprise
that we have been doing a butler's job all our married
lives, and quite a lot of a parlourmaid's too. I don't know
about you, but personally I have always had one essential
qualification for a butler: I am clean-shaven. According
to the highest authorities, butlers and footmen do not
wear moustaches. I have, however, no physical distinguishing marks that qualify me for the part of parlourmaid, unless she's pregnant.

A butler's activities include polishing the silver, laying
the table, cleaning boots and shoes, decanting and
serving the wine, bringing in a tray of drinks before
lunch, before dinner, after dinner, before bedtime,
visiting the village pub to put on bets with the local
bookie's runner, answering the door, taking guests'
coats, announcing their names, and eventually that
dinner is served, madam, and then serving at it.

Any househusband (Why not? It's the masculine form
of housewife, and a dreadful name *that* is for anybody)—
any househusband will recognise among the butler's
duties his own everyday chores. Unfortunately, unlike
the butler, he not only doesn't get paid for it, but he gets
none of the perks either.

An hour or so before the dinner party you lay the table
(six of everything, because you have given way to your
wife and there are four guests instead of the two you hoped
for), decant three bottles of your second-best wine (because you have given way to your wife, etc.), set out the
drinks on a tray, which is too small to hold all six glasses
(needed because you have, etc., etc.).

Laying the table, as everyone knows, is principally a

matter of putting the right implements in the right sequence at each guest's place. This is not very difficult
—once you have learnt to reckon how many spoons make
six, and that instead of laying the frayed old napkins
you and your wife are 'using up' when alone, you must
use something a little more elegant.

What is not so easy is to ensure that, as host, you have
the French mustard at least within stretching distance,
and not placed out of reach so that you have to shout
in vain for it over the company's chatter. (This is another
familiar hazard of the four-guests-to-dinner extravaganza.)

As I have said, it is not difficult to lay out the silver
in the right order; what is almost impossible is to get
people to use it in the right order. The more animated the
conversation at dinner, the more likely it is that knives,
forks and spoons are used out of sequence, starting
with the accidental use of a serving spoon for the soup
and ending up with a fish knife to eat strawberries with.

Then there are those who, following your lead (either
because they don't want you to feel conspicuously non-U
or because they think it's a good idea) use their pudding
spoon to get as much off their plates of the sauce your
wife has gone to so much trouble to make. This inevitably
leaves half the guests without the spoon they need for
the pudding.

And that means that as you have only six of the posh
silver spoons (all in use because, etc., etc.), a lot of plate
oddments in various stages of excoriation have to be
routed and rattled out of the back of the kitchen drawer.

## TO THE CLOAKS

In households where there is a butler or parlourmaid the reception of guests is of no concern to the host. The bell rings, the door is opened, the ladies are asked if they would care to take their wraps off upstairs. The guests are then announced and are received by the host and hostess.

In a household where the househusband has to do all this the difficulties start when you open the door and are confronted with a couple of guests whose names you have suddenly forgotten. All you can remember is that the woman is called either Rosalind or Rosamund.

The question of what to do about their wraps is something no etiquette book tells you. As a butler-less househusband, who answers doors, you are faced nowadays with married couples who both apparently wear wraps. Perhaps you should suggest that they both leave their wraps upstairs? But this would mean sending the man up into your wife's bedroom to take his clothes off.

Even in our liberal age this hardly seems quite correct. Better to be on the safe side and suggest that everybody should hang their coats in the hall. You regret this as soon as you have spoken. Room has to be made on the hall stand already overburdened with gardening hats, town hats, jackets, old mackintoshes, and an Italian straw hat with a gaudy MCC ribbon on it and a label inside marked 'IL PREFERITO'. Most of the family clothes fall on the floor, but after a series of intricate and slapstick operations a peg is eventually found.

In a normal household the next most important duty performed by the butler is the announcement that dinner is served.

Now, while the social advice books are on fairly safe

The question of what to do with their wraps is something
no etiquette book tells you

ground when you have a butler or parlourmaid, they
are not always very reliable when you haven't. This is
because their authorettes have no experience of what real
deprivation means.

They counsel the Have-Not hostess to slip away un-
obtrusively to the kitchen, where her daily will be waiting
to serve up the dinner she—the hostess, that is—has
already cooked earlier in the day. The hostess tells her
daily she is ready to start, and returns to the sitting room
to finish her drink in a correctly gracious manner.

This may do for some Have-Nots. For the rest of us,
the underprivileged Have-less-than-Nothings, this talk
of a daily being in the kitchen to serve up dinner is pure
let-'em-eat-cake stuff.

'The daily will be waiting' indeed! The word 'daily' may mean every day in a dictionary, but dictionaries don't need domestic help. Otherwise they'd know that a daily comes for two hours three mornings a week, if you're lucky.

The chances of getting her out at night to serve up anybody's dinner are very slim, most of all on a Saturday night, when she has left at noon on Friday and will not be back till Monday morning—unless, that is, you have a daily whose husband has left her. In that case, she'll come to you for company as much as anything.

Such treasures are rare, however. Like blue Cheshire cheese, the situation cannot be manufactured. It is an accident and it is no good going round trying to bribe husbands to leave their wives, just to make your housework easier.

Punctuality in serving dinner is observed more as a means of satisfying appetites than—if the hostess is clever —of preventing the food being spoiled. Nevertheless, as in the high Philadelphia society where Mrs Rorer moves, 'a few minutes' grace is allowed to professional men, as physicians'.

In our more modest social circles a few minutes' grace has to be allowed not only to Dr Godot, but to journalists, actors, stage managers, painters, flute players, vets and a host of other friends who, if they know they have a next meal coming, don't know at all when they're going to get it.

Without butler or parlourmaid, the hostess shouts loudly from the kitchen (to make herself heard over the boozy chatter of her inattentive guests) that dinner is ready. If, as one of our sympathetic counsellors imagines, the host is going to pass round the *hors-d'œuvre* on a big dish, the hostess knows better. There is one sure way of starving her guests to death—by enlisting her husband's 'help'.

But before we get to dishing out—I mean up—the dinner we must consider what should be on the menu.

Without staff we are advised that three courses are enough. Not for our guests they aren't. They are Coarse Guests, and, like their hosts, have healthy appetites. A dinner party of eight or ten people given by our authorette with a butler and parlourmaid, offers fish or soup, meat or game, *an exciting pudding*, savoury, dessert, coffee.

Personally, I can't see any other reason why a party of four or six shouldn't eat exactly the same as one of eight or ten. Why less to eat for fewer people? It is the number of guests that needs the help of a butler and parlourmaid, not the food they eat. There is nothing in that bill of fare that cannot be found in any Coarse Dinner of the most unambitious nature.

Except, of course, *an exciting pudding*. Lady social writers, on the topic of food, sprinkle adjectives around like pigeon feed, producing gems like (cross my heart) 'a prawn cocktail can be a dramatic surprise', and 'this jellied tomato salad has a glamorous air'. One is therefore unlikely to be excited by anything called 'exciting'—least of all a *pudding* (as though it were a pair of socks or a grand piano).

## THE ORDER OF SERVICE

Feed and regard him not
SHAKESPEARE

As every hostess has been told by Philadelphia's Mrs Rorer, 'serving dinner without a maid is, of course, a difficult task, but it can be done if thought is given to the first arrangements'.

The first arrangement thought must be given to is to get your guests to do it themselves. The idea of the host taking a big dish of *hors-d'œuvre* round the table is the sort of ridiculous luxury only our social betters could think of. At this stage of the evening, as host you are far too occupied in more essential tasks such as pouring the wine.

When eventually you sit down and are able to anticipate the enjoyment of a meal which, in spite of all the bother and attention it entails is a pleasant change from the stews and omelettes and grilled chops you have to eat the rest of the week, you instinctively take the *pâté* or *hors-d'œuvre* passed to you by the lady on your right, and pass it on to the lady on your left. From her the dish continues on its clockwise journey, and unless you can make frantic signals which will be understood by your wife at the other end of the table, where the dish has stopped, that is the last you are likely to see of it.

When this happens all you can do is chew olives until it's time for the next course. You may well ask why, since you are among friends, you do not simply ask loudly for somebody to pass you what you want. The answer is that you are among very cheerful, talkative friends and can't make yourself heard.

It's not that you are too polite to interrupt; you are just not very good at it.

If there happens to be soup instead of *hors-d'œuvre*, or anything else the guests can help themselves to, you stand a better chance. If you are forgotten this time it will not be for long. Your wife will find herself with an extra plate in front of her, when she thinks she has finished serving. This may give her a clue.

The second course, of meat or game, will involve carving. This will be done at a side-table and is known as serving dinner *à la Russe*, a custom which in the best society has now supplanted the form known as the English style, where the joints are carved on the table. Carving at a side-table is (the authorities tell us) 'for good reason, as the host cannot well fulfil his social part if he has to do the carving'.

In our household that is not the reason the host doesn't carve: he can't. In the words of another social commentator, 'bad carving tortures the heart of the smiling [?] hostess and leaves the dish unsightly'.

This same commentator suggests that 'should the carving be done in the old English fashion at table, an opportunity is presented for one of the gentlemen flanking the hostess to offer his services. This should never be done by an inefficient carver, nor should a carver ever stand up to perform his task, however difficult.'

To enlist the help of a guest as carver, even one so skilled as to be able to sit down at his work, is an original idea, but carries the principle of audience-participation a little far. A guest-carver is likely to make the portions unnecessarily small because he is carving somebody else's joint, or unnecessarily large, for the same reason.

The non-carving host is not such a rarity as you might suppose, although in some households the fact takes some time to sink in. At least, that is all I can think from reading Mrs Rorer: 'If the host does not carve, he simply, by motion, makes this known, and the turkey is lifted, carried to the side-table, and there carved, then placed in front of the host to serve.'

Unless this is the first dinner party of your married life, and at the crucial moment you decide you can't face the carving, it seems a bit quaint that before you make your

The non-carving host is not such a rarity

disability known by a simple motion, such as a shake of thy gory locks, the parlourmaid should have gone to the trouble of bringing in the turkey and actually placing it in front of you, only to have to take it all away again.

But then this is the sort of muddle they all tend to get into, the Haves. The rest of us leave the carving to the hostess, who rightly spurns the offers of help from any gentlemen flanking her. In any case she has known the joint or bird intimately since it was raw.

In most cases, however, there will be no question of carving at all. Even such a stickler for the proprieties as Mrs Emily Post tells us to have no fear of giving our guests *bœuf bourguignonne* again, merely because they had it last time, if it is the *spécialité* of your *maison*. One likes to think that even if one's guests have been eating it in other people's houses every night for the past week, they won't have had it so good as they get it with you.

However, the chances are (you hope) that the last time they ate the dish was at your house months ago and that they have been looking forward to eating it again ever since. Indeed, in a county like ours, which seems to dine eternally off pheasant and broiler chicken, we like to think that our *spécialité* provides a welcome change which is worth *le détour* or even *le voyage*.

It is possible, of course, that some of your guests won't like what you offer them anyway. Here Mrs Emily Post comes to your rescue again. Well-brought-up guests will have learned from her that they are expected to eat what is put in front of them, and look as though they were enjoying it.

A stern admonition, this, which makes one suspect that Mrs Post put notices in her spare bedrooms telling her guests to leave the key with the reception desk and evacuate the room before noon.

One may notice, however, that a particular guest nevertheless leaves olives uneaten on her plate. You remember next time and give her none, only to find that suddenly she has learnt to love olives and now complains if she doesn't get her share.

If you can't win, at least it all happens in a world of hospitality where guests' complaints are welcome and constructive—or, at any rate, an everyday occurrence.


## SERVICE OUT OF ORDER

The conventions of the order in which guests are served vary between one household and another. In my family, the host is served last but one—if at all. The hostess serves herself last.

In parts of America, on the other hand, it is the custom of the hostess to be served first. This is not, as you might imagine, a way of trying it out on the bitch, as it were, to reassure the guests that what the hostess is eating is safe.

The object of the custom is to spare the guests embarrassment by quietly demonstrating to those who might not know which knife and fork or spoon to use for the course being served. The hostess places the correct instruments on her plate, as though she were going to start eating; but she doesn't. She is just silently 'communicating' and putting people at their ease; she eats only when she sees everybody else is served and properly equipped.

In other parts of the world the host is served first. We have English friends who live in Italy and the master of the house is always served first. The dishes are then taken by the maids clockwise round the table—the hostess being served halfway through the journey— and the last person to get their dinner is the guest of honour, the lady on the host's right.

For a moment I thought that the master of the house was testing the food for possible poison (the Borgias used to live not far away), but obviously this would have been carrying altruism and conscientious hospitality too far. In the end I could only suppose that as the host was always served first when *en famille,* to arrange to serve him last, and his principal guest first, when he had company, would be too much of a strain on his Italian servants' medieval insistence that a woman's place is at the end of the queue.

Private habits, like the one I have just mentioned, do not as a rule affect the basic conventions of general entertaining. There are times, it is true, when we have a certain air of Disgracious Living about us—for instance, when you eat in the kitchen and everything is served straight from the saucepans off the stove (which keeps things hotter and saves washing up). And when guests are asked to keep their knives and forks from one course to the next, in the French bistro manner (which also saves washing up).

The washing-up saved by these dodges is the washing-up that has to be done after the small dinner party guests have left—that is, the guests of a small dinner party, whose kind offers of help have been declined with thanks.

On those occasions, however, when some pagan festival or other like Boxing Day is celebrated, and the number of guests approaches double figures, then the guests are encouraged to help—particularly by the host who, with any luck, can avoid a lot of hard work when it's long past his bedtime.


## BLACK? WHITE? SIT TIGHT

One of the more comforting and sensible features of the good Coarse Dinner party is the custom of serving coffee at the table. The disrupting habit of breaking up the company before the meal is properly finished may have been all very well and thoughtful in the days when it enabled the staff to clear the dining room and get off to bed. Unfortunately, we staffless many cannot get off to bed, and having coffee in the drawing room isn't going to get us there any earlier. There is, therefore, no excuse for disturbing conversation and digestion by not ending a meal where you began it.

And why migrate only for coffee? You're not a cripple, are you? Pursued to its logical conclusion in the home the practice could lead to having each course in a different room, ending with pudding in the attic.

One very important reason for having coffee and liqueurs at the dining table is that it does away with the barbarous habit of banishing women from the table before the meal is over.

If women want to go and powder their noses, they can do so without all the ridiculous ritual of leaving the men over their cigars and port to discuss matters which are too schoolboyish or boring (usually both) for feminine ears.

Nowadays, thank goodness, no holds or topics are barred in general conversation at the dinner table, and there is nothing the men could possibly talk about (except their operations) that they could not equally discuss with women.

Worst of all, the deplorable habit of segregating the guests with the coffee interrupts the flow of conversation three times: first, when the women leave the room, then when the men are interrupted by having to join the ladies, who are then interrupted in *their* conversation.

In houses where this barbarous custom still prevails the men seem to enjoy having banned the women from their company so much that it becomes virtually impossible to shift them from their gossiping. Instead of 'Shall we join the ladies?' it is usually a matter of an impatient hostess coming in to tell them for God's sake break it up.

Ban-the-Women households are also households where the men who stay behind are offered brandy or port by their host, and the women who are sent out are offered by their hostess nothing but a selection of those sickly liqueurs which most men and all waiters seem to think women always drink. Not in our house, they aren't. Drinks like that are considered fit only for *crêpes Suzette*.

When, on the occasions that a Ban-the-Women couple

are asked back to dine with us, they never seem to notice that while Benedictine is eagerly accepted by the visiting wife, my own very conspicuously drinks armagnac. But it makes no impression. Next time we go there it is sticky liqueurs all over again and no choice for the unliberated women.

Alexandre Dumas thought very little of the system altogether, pointing out—in the course of an historical study of gastronomic customs and standards—that 'quite contrary to the English, who send their women out with the dessert, it was with the dessert that the ancient Greeks ceremoniously brought in their beautiful courtesans: Aspasia, Läis, Phryne'.

However, as a host I don't really want to emulate the Greeks in this. I mean, I don't want a lot of beautiful *poules de luxe* brought in with the dessert. I just want the ones I've already got round the table to stay until after the coffee.

## OBSERVANCES AT TABLE

In all sports and pastimes, whether cricket, rugby, travel, gardening, bridge, cookery or entertaining, it is essential to know the official rules of the game thoroughly. Otherwise, how can you enjoy the breaking—or, at least, the bending and ignoring of them?

The rules of etiquette of dinner parties given in Society in the early 1900s are still oddly valid today as a guide to what we may observe or omit, according to our temperaments.

My particular source in this case is a massive volume which aims to serve as *Everybody's Everyday Reference Book*.

This perhaps explains the solecism in a work which includes a big section on 'Aids to the Study of English', of calling a napkin a 'serviette'—on the grounds, one supposes, that a French word is somehow daintier than an English one, especially one confusable in the dim English mind with babies' nappies.

It must be stressed, of course, that the mere breaking of rules does not automatically result in Coarse Entertaining; it may, indeed, lead to coarse behaviour, which is to be deplored at all times.

However, the non-observance of some of 'the usual observances at table' (hints on which are offered, with masterly tact and cunning, 'to the very few who may need them') can break some pretty ridiculous conventions. For instance: 'The guests unfold their serviettes and place them across the knee, not like foreigners who fix them inside their collar'.

In our corner of society this is one of the first rules to be ignored. We do not suffer from old-fashioned xenophobic quirks of this kind; we have established plenty of good brand-new-fashioned ones of our own.

Besides, since we also ignore the rule 'Never take two helpings of soup, even if asked', guests are expected to tuck their napkins into their collars and diamond chokers as anti-splash guards in showing their enjoyment of our soup, which their hostess will be most hurt if they don't have at least two helpings of.

Other taboos include a second helping of fish and 'a large quantity of sauce'. The first we accept; any observant guest will see that there would never be any fish left for a second helping. The second is up to the eater: if the sauce is good we hope he will take as much as he wants, and what's more, use a spoon to finish it properly up with.

The hint that in helping yourself to dishes handed round, you should 'act quickly, and have regard to the wants of others, neither taking a microscopic portion nor a huge one', can be half-accepted. Huge portions are not encouraged. But if you want to take a microscopic portion nobody will think any the worse of you—least of all your host, the Forgotten Man at the end of the table.

He will think very highly of you—particularly if it is one of the vegetables that always get finished up before he can protest that he hasn't had any.

Apart from advising us to eat oysters with a fish knife and fork (what do you do with the knife, for heaven's sake? Cut the oyster into nibble-sized fragments?), the very few who may need the hints in table deportment are finally besought to

Aim at noiselessness both as regards eating, drinking, breathing, and every other possible source of disagreeable sound.

Do not speak or drink with food in the mouth. Keep the moustache free from traces of soup, and use only the serviette in wiping the mouth.

Keeping the moustache free from traces of soup is nowadays the least of life's problems. The greatest is to keep the beard out of the soup, to say nothing of your hair.

The great object of conversation is not to gain information or to display it, but to give mutual pleasure. Keeping this end clearly in view we may lay down a few principles and rules which minister to its attainment.

c

With these words my Social Guide of 1908 begins its section on the Art of Conversation.

One of the dictionary definitions of conversation is sexual intercourse, though that is hardly what the Social Guide can have meant by the term, I imagine. However, substitution of this less familiar meaning for the more usual one gives a certain colour to the 'few principles' set out by the author of the study, to which we have added our own comments.

### GENERAL CONVERSATION

1. By its very nature conversation implies reciprocity.
   *Agreed, but difficult. As everybody talks at once, reciprocity is simultaneous.*

2. This reciprocal quality does not imply that conversation can be measured off into equal portions for each of the parties.
   *Agreed.*

3. Undue spaces of silence are apt to give those who are contributing to the conversation the feeling that the taciturnity is owing either to want of sympathy or interest.
   *Not to worry. Undue—or even due—spaces of silence are unknown. Unfortunately.*

4. Conversation should never be reduced to a catechism . . . We have known amiable people delude themselves with the idea that to ask a multitude of questions will be interpreted as interest on their part in the affairs of their friends.
   *To try to reduce conversation to a catechism would be pointless anyway. Nobody listens to any answers to any questions.*

5. Conversation should not be disputatious.

*Conversation without disputatiousness is not conversation.*
*It is speech-making.*

6. It is always best to avoid religious and political
   subjects in general society.
   *Agreed, but not in case of hurting anybody's feelings;*
   *just to avoid general boredom.*

7. Contradiction requires great management if it
   is not to be rude, browbeating or insolent . . .
   Irascible old gentlemen are entitled to some consideration, even from the youngest and most
   self-confident striplings in the room.
   *Unless the statement of incontrovertible facts is considered*
   *rude, brow-beating and insolent, no management of contra-*
   *diction is required. Contradiction is continuous, spontaneous*
   *and confined to the one phrase 'Nonsense!' As an irascible*

Conversation without disputations is not conversation . . .

*old gentleman myself I am entirely in agreement with the principle that I am entitled to some consideration, particularly from the youngest and most self-confident striplings in the room.*

8. Quotations in those degenerate days should be limited to English and French languages.

*We would go even further: not only should quotations in any language be barred altogether, but also the casual use of any foreign language in the course of conversation, whether a quotation or not, unless you are absolutely certain that everybody in the room understands what you're saying.*

*If somebody clearly doesn't understand, then it is only polite to interrupt the flow of your virtuoso polyglot display —that is, stop showing off—and translate parenthetically for their benefit.*

## NOTES FOR WOMEN

Love and scandal are the best sweeteners of tea
                                              FIELDING

My social Guide of 1908 considers there are two kinds of conversation: General Conversation and Ladies' Social Conversation.

The prejudice implicit in this distinction is not by any means unknown today, consisting, as it does, of a firm belief that no woman is to be trusted when she entertains other women.

Mind you, as a hostess she had a lot to live up to: 'Nothing in the shape of brilliant conversation can ever atone for the want in a hostess of a sunny manner, a frank and hearty reception, spotless cleanliness of person, and unimpeachable neatness of attitude.'

This is only the beginning, however. She must possess
the cardinal virtue of Tact, and 'a great variety of topics,
like the angler with a great assortment of flies', such as a
new drama, a new novel, a new volume of poems, or
the current exhibition of pictures. She must be able to
comment on (not repeat) what was in the morning papers,
and 'in handling such diversified matters, the touch
will be light, and the stay upon each brief, and quickly
succeeded by flying to another flower'.

There then follows as patronising a suggestion as ever
I heard: 'Even in country villages ['Even'? *Particularly*]
there is always something to discuss of general interest,
be it the coming ball, yesterday's hunt, the parish tea-
party, the curate's engagement, the squire's new motor
car, or the opening of the cottage hospital.'

I don't know what sort of village the author of Ladies'
Social Conversation ever went to, but today we have
everything she mentions, and lots more. Like the burglary of the county's chief constable's house, no less, the
secondary school wind band's tour of Germany, the milk
lady's annually new executive car, the latest rape enjoyed
by the village nympho.

Or the laying of new drains which was to take eighteen
months and still isn't finished after nearly three years. Or
the Authorities' belief that everybody in the country
has a car, so that the population of a neighbouring
village no longer needs a bus or train service of any kind,
and is almost entirely immobilised. Or another lot of
Authorities' conviction that a road in our village known
for centuries as Church Lane sounds more genteel if called
'Vicarage Way'.

'Even in a country village', quoth'a!

An oddly topical caution—topical, that is, for us—is
included among the hints to a hostess which is really more

a solid nudge in the ribs for her guests than for herself. It is a caution against dogmatism in 'such high matters as the Fine Arts include'.

Nothing is more irritating, the caution runs, than the assured way in which girls in their teens, who have begun to handle the brush or the chisel, will deliver their preferences for 'impressionism', 'realism', 'genre', etc., and the contempt for all who are not of their school of criticism.

'Great artists', the author adds reproachfully, 'are generally generous in their appreciation of the work of their fellow-labourers. They know the difficulties to be overcome and the triumphs that have been won in a work in which the amateur or the tyro sees nothing to praise.'

Talk about *plus ça change* . . . Only the jargon has changed.

Having been warned of the annoyances to expect, the Edwardian hostess is reminded that even conversation palls, so it is good to vary her 'At Home' by music, recitations and conjuring tricks—a remedy, one imagines, guaranteed to restore general conversation. In modern society, of course, music, recitations and conjuring tricks are recognisable elements in ordinary conversation, and entirely indistinguishable from it—whether At Home or Away.

Finally, the Social Guide becomes 'a little didactic though not homiletic', and sets down three golden rules for conversation which, owing to the changes in social habits and moral values since the guide was published, have to be updated for modern consumption.

The process is simple; the principles are merely reversed.

1. Draw the conversation as much as you can away

from ill-natured tattle and injurious talk. *For 'away from' read 'towards'.*

2. Never exaggerate evil reports for the sake of creating an effect. *For 'never' read 'always'.*

3. Do not encourage scandal. *Delete 'Do not'.*

The only thing about these three axioms is that where, with the 1908 versions, it may have been necessary to draw the attention of some hostesses to them, no present-day host, hostess or guest of any age has any need to consult them in their amended form. They have known it all since birth. I just thought you'd like to see some of the commandments as they were before the stone tablets were broken up for the hard-core on which the treacher-ous path of modern life, etc., is based.

There is, however, an *envoi* to the Guide to Ladies' Social Conversation which contains certain universal truths whose continued validity nobody who practises it would ever question was the very basis of the Art of Coarse Entertaining:

Try to leave upon your guests the impression that they have enjoyed under your roof a really pleasant evening, in which rational discourse has been enlivened by amusement, pleasantries have abounded unmixed with innuendoes or envenomed jibes, and that the bad-inage of lively people has raised the spirits and left no acid or sub-acid feeling in the palates of the most sensitive.

As long as the food and drink are good, there's nothing we can add to that.

## HERE TO STAY, GONE TOMORROW

> Like angels' visits, short and bright;
> Mortality's too weak to bear them long.
> REV. JOHN NORRIS (1657–1711)

When we left London to live in the country our friends were disappointed. Not because we had left London, but because when they came to see us they got house-in-the-country, when they had expected country-house stuff.

The reason for this was mainly that to Londoners anybody who leaves the city to live in the country is rich and retired.

The same belief is held in the country, where anybody who has left London can only be rich and retired. Both beliefs come from the ignorance of how, when and where other people work.

To a Londoner, unless you come to London every day you don't work. To country neighbours, shopkeepers, postmen, electricians, publicans, gas fitters, builders and delivery men, unless you catch a train every morning to a London office, you don't work. It never occurs to anyone that we can't afford to live in London.

How the hell all these people think the books they read, the music they hear or the pictures they see are produced I can't think. But nothing we can do will convince them that we are anything but idle rich.

Perhaps there is one person who suspects we are not, and she is the lady who, when we first came to the country, asked us to support some local Tory hayride. We regretted, but were were Marxists, and had been ever since *Animal Crackers, Duck Soup* and *Horsefeathers*. She drew the right conclusions, I am glad to say, and we have not been bothered since.

I have already explained the difference between a country house and a house in the country. It is obviously something that cannot be stressed too often. Listen to what a quality daily's women's page tells its readers to do in the 'icy, draughty bedrooms' encountered on all winter visits to the country:

> With this long smock nightgown you should be able to sit up and read a chapter or two of the book usually left on bedside tables (wearing a woolly hidden underneath, if necessary). You will look gracious when the household offspring arrive with your morning cup of tea and be adequately, charmingly, covered for corridor marches, sponge bag in hand, in search of the bathroom.

It's a depressing picture, especially that bit about searching for the bathroom. Why isn't the poor girl shown where it is the night before?

In some ways, staying in the country nowadays is a little more carefree that it used to be when people had servants. This may sound a bit paradoxical, but the fact is that when the housemaid unpacked your suitcase you found some pretty odd things laid out on the dressing table.

I know of one man who travelled about a bit and kept—in pre-pill days—a supply of contraceptives in his luggage, just in case. He was a Canadian and was horrified on his first experience of the English country-house weekend to arrive in his bedroom to dress for dinner and find three little packets neatly arranged in a row on his dressing table.

An experience of my own was less mortifying, though it must have puzzled the housemaid much more. In the course of a journey between London and Oxford during the war, I stayed a night with friends near Henley, carrying in my suitcase an old, very sharp ham knife with an eighteen-inch blade, which I was taking from my London home to a temporary home in Oxford, and had forgotten to pack with my other belongings when I first moved there.

When I went to my bedroom I found the knife prominently laid out on the dressing table. I have always wanted to know what the housemaid can have thought I travelled with lethal ham knives for, and particularly why—as far as she she was concerned—I should have brought it for a one-night stay in Henley.

As we have seen already, the modern hostess runs her house quite differently with and without staff. With staff it is one thing; without staff it is quite another. It is her husband, in fact.

As a husband, therefore, you should learn what is expected of you by studying the duties normally performed by those members of the staff whose jobs you are taking over.

Bag-unpacking, dress-pressing, bath-running, up-zipping, and bed-downturning, delicate and time-consuming operations though they may be, are only the final public stages in the process of making a guest comfortable.

For days before the guests' arrival you are busy behind the scenes in a frenzy of backroom activity preparing the spare bedroom—or, if we were being formal, 'the guest room'. Emily Post says it is known only colloquially as the spare room. (This is a misleading term, too. We have a spare bedroom, but no spare room, or room to spare, for anything except in the garden, and not much there.)

Mrs Post is an ever-present help in time of trouble and a comfortable model for all to follow. She it was, you will remember, who said there was no need to avoid giving your dinner guests *bœuf bourguignonne* again, merely because they had had it last time. She is just as reassuring about the spare bedroom. 'It is far from necessary to provide silk sheets', she says. This will come as a relief to the young newly married couple inviting their first weekend guests.

Nevertheless, Emily Post is insistent that 'whether it be in a palace, or in a little but well appointed house, a guest room should be formally exacting', and she gives a list of 'essential requirements'.

The first of these, of course, is a bathroom of its own. This is no longer the luxury it used to be, and its inclusion in the most modest house today is not in any way incompatible with the principles and character of Coarse Entertaining. Any more than having two lavatories is. It is astonishing, though, how many so-called 'family dwellings' built in the last twenty years or less are not properly equipped even in this way.

There is no excuse, however, not to have the next item Mrs Post demands: 'a delightful bed'. On the other hand, allowing for the typical lady social writer's occupational weakness for adjectives, like 'exciting' puddings and 'dramatic' prawn cocktails, whether a bed is 'delightful' or not I would have thought was for the guests to say.

A bed of itself surely cannot be full of any delights unless they are provided by the occupants themselves. The most any hostess can do is give her guests a comfortable arena for their games. It is then up to them.

Care should be taken, however, not to furnish the spare room with any bed that is not properly sprung. This is the sort of bed (called by the late Alexander Woollcott an 'informative double') which if it does not inhibit those who cohabit, can amuse and amaze the rest of the household.

## THE AIR BITES SHREWDLY

The need for plenty of light and air is something Emily Post emphasises, but I think exaggerates. In many houses in the country, old windows may not let in much light, but they always let in a lot of air. For this reason you should warn your guests that the air is always much colder than it is in London, and that where in sunny Chelsea a sash window opened on a summer night can be refreshing, to do the same in the country can lead to pneumonia. In the country, you must tell them, you have to be very careful when and where you let any air into the house.

careful when and where you let any air into the house

Hosts are also advised by the social writers that if windows are loose thin wedges should be made and attached with cords to the window casings.

In our house, wedges have to be more versatile, serving not only to stop windows rattling, but to stop most of the furniture falling flat on its face. Those floors in the bedrooms that do not slope from east to west, slope from north to south. Or vice versa and more so. The main guest room, in fact, slopes from north to south, but with secondary slopes running downwards into the middle of the room from west to east from the west wall, and from east to west from the east wall.

The wedges, I must confess, are not very elegantly carpentered. In fact, they're not carpentered at all; they consist of several layers of small odd rectangles of hardboard piled loosely on top of each other so that they can be removed, or added to, according to the periodic variation in the gradients of the slopes (believed to be about 3 mm a year).

Guests are shown how to manipulate the chest of drawers, using the top drawers as far as possible and holding the chest firmly with the knee when pulling drawers open. If this is not done, the chest will topple forward off its wedges, owing to the floor having what I heard one B.Sc. describe on the radio as 'a high co-efficient of slip'.

With other pieces of furniture, including bookcases, when slightly solider wedges are needed to prop things up, pieces of wood left behind when the house was re-roofed come in useful. In short windows are almost the last thing wedges can be spared for. When the windows rattle we wedge them with bits of newspaper, like anybody else.

Houses in the country tend to have bedroom windows obscured by climbing roses and clematis, but there is no excuse why their darkness shouldn't be properly lightened.

A good light to read by in bed is one of the 'essential requirements'. What is just as essential is a good light on the dressing table, over the basin, to shine into the wardrobe and light the drawers at all times of day, particularly when it's daylight outside through the tangled climbers.

No true host is ever stingy with the wattage. It isn't lights that are expensive, as you know, but immersion heaters, portable oil-filled electric radiators and 1-kilowatt fires.

If, as a guest, you have the misfortune to stay in a badly lit bedroom, remember next time you go there to take a 100-watt bulb with you and fix it into the bedside lamp or wherever. If you are found out, so much the better; you can then explain that you have to travel with a personal bulb on account of your eyes (what else?). It is possible that the penny might drop.

This suggestion is based on the practice of a friend who, whenever he travels in France takes four 60–watt bulbs in his luggage—two of 120 volts, and two of 250 volts; one of each pair of bulbs has a screw fitting, the other a bayonet fitting. He is then equipped to read comfortably in almost any hotel in France, where bedside lights are provided by apprentice glow worms.

### READING, WRITING AND ROMPING

> He shall show you a large upper room furnished
> ST LUKE XXII.12

As for the books for bedside reading, there are no general rules to follow, except that they ought to be of a slightly higher literary standard than those put on the table in the downstairs loo. There you find one old sample copy of *Punch*, last year's *Michelins* for France and Italy and a selection of those annual funnies by Giles, Osbert Lancaster, Hargreaves or Ronald Searle, which people give you at Christmas.

We used to leave the *New Yorker* for visitors, but there were complaints that the articles were always too long to read at one sitting, as it were. So it was withdrawn and put in the guests' bedroom.

On the other hand, there are some houses where the literary quality of the downstairs reading is exceedingly high, and there is no reason why it should not be—but only so long as it provides good random reading. I know a house where the repertoire consisted of the Bible, William Robinson's *English Flower Garden* and *Larousse Gastronomique*—all books divided into short, separate and often unrelated items which can be read quickly.

Magazines are not usually regarded as real bedside reading for guests, but once the *New Yorker* was regularly taken upstairs and left in the bedroom we added *Country Life* in case one of the readers was interested in that sort of thing. There are also copies of *Maison et Jardin, Elle, Oggi*, and the French autumn-collection *Vogue* of 1964.

We do not subscribe to *Country Life*; nor, as some people hint, do we filch our copies from our doctor's waiting room. They are too old even for that. They are the gift of a neighbour who passes them on regularly, six or seven months after he has finished them.

In a house that has never been too big for its books, bookshelves are constantly being added wherever they can be squeezed in—in the kitchen, on the landing and in all spare bedrooms. Inevitably, a lot of books not in everyday use or particularly decorative to look at, get relegated to the spare bedrooms, and while we try to remember to go through the shelves and add one or two more enthralling volumes when guests are due, there is still a preponderance of books in French and German—Molière, Balzac, Goethe—which I have had ever since I was at school. There are also one or two battered, grubby books of fairy-tales which I was given when I first learnt to read, and which I found one of our guests—the mother of two grown-up children—reading intently only the other day.

If you write for a living, however, you take good care that a prominent position in the shelves is given to your own books—especially those that are still in print. Those that aren't, are kept, less conspicuously, on the lower shelves.

Having furnished your guests with a delightful bed, non-silk sheets, bright light, wedges for the windows, and a selection of books carefully chosen with what you hope will prove a profitable ulterior motive, you realise that you have forgotten what is considered by Emily Post a most important feature of any guest room— namely, a writing table.

It is not the table that matters so much as how it must be furnished. Mrs Post expects her guests to find the following items:

> A blotter
> Fresh ink
> Variously assorted pens
> A sharpened pencil
> A scratch-pad
> 'House-stamped paper'
> Envelopes
> A few stamps
> A pair of paper-scissors
> A small bottle of 'mucilage'

It's not the table that matters so much as
how it must be furnished . . .

While all I would add to the above is airmail writing
material, one lady social writer supplies her guests with a
card stating the time the post leaves. This is hardly
helpful any more. The date and time of posting is im-
material. What one really wants to know is not when the
post is collected Here, but roughly what day it is likely
to be delivered There. And no hostess can put that on a
guest's writing table.

Looking at that list of writing-table props, one wonders
what the guest is supposed to do with them. If you are
staying a weekend what on earth do you want to write
letters for? One of the great joys of going away for the
weekend is not having to write letters. Like any other
holiday the most anybody should do is send a you-should-

thank-God-you're-not-here picture postcard of the church and village pump to their friends—unless, that is, your hosts can provide you with coloured postcards of their house and garden, when the same message can be used.

But even if somebody *does* want to write a letter, what on earth are the scissors and paste for? All right, the paste could be useful for re-sealing an envelope you've · stuck down without a letter inside; but that still doesn't explain the scissors. A well-furnished bedroom will contain a sewing box with embroidery scissors, so if you want to sew on a button you have no need of a pair of inevitably de-tempered paper scissors.

But then Emily Post can sometimes be a very puzzling lady. 'If you would have a room in best taste', she says 'do not throw cushions on the floor.' Is she addressing the hosts or the guests? If it is the guests, perhaps they should not be encouraged.

If it is the hosts, again one can agree. But if by 'throw' she means 'strew', then that is another matter. The carefully nonchalant strewing of cushions on the floor in a haphazard manner is an ancient habit—as old as cushions and floors. As a fashion it comes and goes. The Russian Imperial Ballet, the Jazz-and-Orgies era of the 1920s, and now the revival of Art Nouveau, have led to the strewing of cushions on floors comparable only to the strewing of bottles on football pitches.

Mrs Post must have advised her readers during one of the lulls between one cushion rage and another.


*BOIL-IT-YOURSELF KITS*

It is clear, I think, that in the world of Coarse Entertaining defeatism has no part. Every host with guests staying in the house can say truthfully with Queen Victoria, or Tommy Handley, or whoever it was plastered the pubs with the slogan during the last war: 'There is no depression in this house. We are not interested in the possibility of defeat.'

Our motto, indeed, is the immortal phrase used by the late Tyrone Guthrie, who, in moments of crisis, such as total electrical failure and the flooding of the orchestra pit, would come before the curtain and address the audience with the encouraging words: 'Rise above it!'

By 'defeatism' I mean the sort of thing that makes my favourite let-'em-eat-cake social adviser tell us that 'with staff difficulties the custom of giving all guests early-morning tea has gone out of fashion'.

A lady obviously full of social discrimination. By stating that the custom of giving 'all' guests early-morning tea is out of fashion, she implies that *some* of the guests do get it. (She is the same one who gave some of the guests newspapers . . .)

To us staff 'difficulties' of the kind that defeat our helpless gracious hostess are not even a Challenge (which is the modern expression for coping with anything a child could do). They are non-existent. We have no staff: therefore there can be no difficulties. Q.E.D.

In our house *everybody* who wants it has early-morning tea. They make it for themselves with an electric kettle in their bedroom. All they have to do is to pour boiling water into a teapot put on a tray they took up to bed with them the night before.

If there are more guests than electric kettles, then somebody has to do without tea in the bedroom and go down to the kitchen and make it on the stove.

One thing all guests should be aware of is alarm clocks found on the bedside table. When you want the clocks to go, they work only lying on their faces, and die during the night, and you aren't woken. If you don't want them to go, the alarm goes off at 4 a.m.. This doesn't wake you either; you aren't asleep. The clock's deafening tick has seen to that.

Breakfast, like early-morning tea, is another fix-it-yourself occasion. Any guest who thinks that breakfast in the country means kippers and kedgeree, scrambled eggs, boiled eggs, sausages, kidneys and bacon, all in silver entrée dishes keeping warm on a hot plate, with a ham on a side table, must be prepared for a disappointment, and reminded once more that a house in the country is not the same as a country house.

Not only are there no goodies in entrée dishes, but guests do not even conform to the recommended custom in more modest surroundings of eating the same as the host and hostess—and wisely. With a houseful of your guests getting themselves breakfast in the kitchen, and using all the gas rings at the same time, you are lucky if you can make a couple of pieces of toast for yourselves on the toaster, let alone stand a chance in hell of boiling an egg.

That, at least, is how things are on weekdays, when life in country households is dominated by the early arrival— soon after 7 a.m.—of the post lady. Attempts to lie in a little later Mons. thru Sats. are regularly thwarted by the delivery of mail that won't go through the letter box and so leads to impatient knocking and ringing heavy enough to bring down the house and the host from his lair in the morning.

Sundays are another matter. The countryside is quiet, and this wakes guests unused to silence and sends them down to the kitchen to make their breakfast long before you appear.

Well-behaved guests naturally wash up their own breakfast things. If they are town-dwellers you may well wish they wouldn't, when you live in the country. This is because visitors from London are entirely unable to distinguish between organic and inorganic waste. There are two waste bins under the sink, one of which, you tell your guests, is the pig-bucket.

This information is greeted with surprise and excitement. Adults didn't know you kept pigs; their children ask excitedly can they see them.

You don't keep pigs, you explain. The bin is called the pig-bucket because during the war waste food was kept separately and collected to feed pigs with to win the war.

There is a pause. 'Why did pigs win the war?' asks one of the children.

'Everybody had to win the war.'

'Why?' asks another.

'To build a new world,' you reply, 'and ensure colour television for all.'

You go on to explain that the pig-bucket is for putting organic matter in—potato peel, banana skins, scraps of bread, tea leaves—that sort of thing.

'Oh,' say the children, 'we put all ours in the dustbin.'

Yes, you say. You did that too, when you lived in London; but in the country the dustmen come only once a fortnight. So you use all the organic waste for compost.

The word 'compost' is met with blank incomprehension all round. You set about explaining the nature and purpose of compost, its derivation from organic matter (reading them the definition of 'organic' in the *Oxford Dictionary*) and its value in the garden. This all takes some time, and enlightens nobody.

'It's to keep the useful from the useless waste that you

... a mass of unattractive, but highly nutritious, *pourriture*

have two bins under the sink', you add.

The other bin, you elaborate, is for tins, cellophane wrappings, milk-bottle tops, undisposable bottles and in-destructible plastic bottles—anything, in fact, that won't 'break down'.

The phrase 'break down' means nothing to your audience, or, at any rate, not the way you use it.

Inevitably, when you come to empty the pig-bucket on to the compost heap you have to pick out milk-bottle tops and cigarette-packet wrappings from a mass of unattractive, but highly nutritious, *pourriture*.

However, perhaps one should not expect too much of the visitors from London. After all, even though they may not know why or how things happen in a garden, they're always very appreciative of the fresh veg and herbs and flowers you load them with when they go home. Even in deepest winter you can usually find them some fresh mint to take back, or brussels sprouts, or celariac, or leeks.

One thing is absolutely certain: whatever they may have learnt about the compost heap they have always forgotten all about it the next time they come to stay. Like the French telephone. By the time you've learnt the meaning of all the bleeps, buzzings and pippings first on one note then an octave higher, it's time to come back home, and when you get back next year you have to start all over again.

# 4  Oh, Hell! Nowell? Oh, Well . . .

All has now turned to jollity and game,
To luxury and riot, feast and dance
MILTON

With those few well-chosen words Milton described the climax of the Coarse Entertaining year: Christmas.

As all adults gratefully observe, the concentration of those elements listed by Milton comes but once a year. That is true. What is equally true, however, is that the older you get the quicker the occasion comes round and the greater the number of people who invade your house expecting game (or at any rate, poultry), luxury and feast, and bringing in exchange jollity, riot and dance.

To be fair, your guests often bring welcome luxury in the form of liquor and delicious bath soap and decorative nonsense from the modern King's Road equivalents of the olde gifte shoppes.

It is only when you move to the country that you realise the sort of problems you must have raised when you lived in London, and were always going away for Christmas yourselves.

If you had any family living in the country you went and stayed with them. If you hadn't, you went and stayed with somebody else's family. Either way you went away for Christmas, the Family Festival with all the delights and horrors the term implies.

As hosts living in the country the custom, applied in

reverse, means that you now stay firmly put in your own home for the festive season; your family comes and stays with you.

If you haven't any family (at least, for once in a way, no family descending on you like starlings), then you get members of other people's families. Either way, there is no escape from guests of one kind or another.

Even when, on rare occasions, we ourselves have had neither family nor old friends coming to stay, we still don't have an empty house. News gets around that we are having what is cynically called a Quiet Christmas, and for four days we serve as a doss house for a couple of guests of one of our village neighbours, whose hospitality knows no bounds (as the saying too truthfully goes), and who regularly invites more people to stay at Christmas than he has beds or floor space for. As a reward for our co-operation we are given those copies of *Country Life* I spoke about.

As doss-house keepers go, our responsibilities are negligible. The customers make their own beds, have breakfast with their host down the road, and let themselves in when they come back at night.

A calm quiet interchange of sentiments
SAMUEL JOHNSON

There is, of course, no such thing as a Quiet Christmas, except possibly in a Trappist monastery in Siberia; and even then somebody is likely to belch on account of the food in those parts.

There are just Christmases, a very few of which are a scarcely perceptible shade less noisy than others.

The noise does not come so much from the jollity and

game, the rioting, feasting and dancing, as from a house-ful of people of widely differing ages all talking at once. The stranger who comes in for an evening over Christmas and has no experience of English family life in the round (themselves being an only child, perhaps, or foreign) is quite appalled by what is less the thrust and parry of debate, than the cuff and swipe of friendly family dis-cussion.

The stranger is amazed at the heat generated by a friendly *conversazione* on a number of innocuous topics in which all can join, such as education, black people, white people, the Monarchy, the Germans, the French, white people, black people, abortion, education, religion, the French, the Germans, the Americans, the inability of *The Times* to get its Arts feature in the same part of the paper two days running, the BBC, the BBC, the BBC, and the respective merits of Arsenal and Chelsea.

The company meeting, or rather clashing, in the dis-cussion of this typical agenda is a resident team which politely permits, but firmly ignores, any participation by a non-resident audience who may have come in for the evening. ('Residents' include blood-relations who may in fact live, or be sleeping over Christmas, in another part of the county.)

To accommodate more people than you have beds for is not such a problem as it may sound. The resources of friends and relations within a 20-mile radius are drawn on to provide sleeping bags and camp beds, for which you somehow find floor-space in unexpected places, such as the sitting room and the landing.

When we borrowed a camp bed last Christmas we were interested to be offered one of our own, which we had lent to a neighbour in *her* hour of need six years previously.

Sleeping bags and camp beds are strictly for children.

They have an air of adventure about them which is exciting and irresistible; children never mind discomfort so long as it is different from the discomfort they suffer at home. This is why they will pitch tents in the garden and sleep out on cold summer nights on cold rubber ground sheets on cold hard grass; and why they prefer baked beans out of tins and bananas dipped in condensed milk to home cooking, however appetising.

The solution of accommodation problems is largely a matter of improvisation. A far bigger Christmas problem is the provision of enough food to last anything up to seven days, and this has to be solved by organisation.

The seven days of Christmas occur when Christmas Eve falls on a Thursday. The following day is Christmas Day; Saturday is not Boxing Day, but the day after Christmas (and, in the case of one of our nieces, also her birthday). Sunday is Sunday; Monday is Boxing Day; on Tuesday nobody works because it is the day after Boxing Day and the food shops are shut; Wednesday is spent in a state of exhaustion caused by the inactivity of the past few days and the food shops are still shut. (Many of the world's workers decide that it is hardly worth going back to London on the Thursday to do one day's work on Friday, so they rest over the weekend and start again on the Monday. Nice non-work if you can get it.)

The actual feast of Christmas Day is a minor event in your catering programme, but its celebration can involve a lot of scouting around the neighbourhood in search of the right sort of heavy, expensive poultry. In the country you ignore the poulterer and go direct to the farmer, or, better still, to the small breeder who somehow manages to rear a thousand turkeys or more in a couple of sheds on a plot the size of a tennis court.

The small breeder usually lives at the end of a narrow muddy lane that you can drive down forwards but have to drive up backwards, as there is nowhere to turn.

The advantage of personal contact with a breeder is that you can go to him some time before Christmas, and at your leisure choose the unfortunate bird you fancy on the claw (or whatever the equivalent term is for 'on the hoof').

As Christmas approaches, you and the breeder pray for cold weather to keep the turkey from going off, once it has been plucked and drawn. As cold weather in the days before Christmas is extremely unseasonable, you fetch the turkey on Christmas Eve, give it a good wash and a par-poaching in a prophylactic white wine, to get rid of the pong and prevent it tasting like well-hung game. It will then, with luck, keep long enough to roast the following day and be tolerably palatable.

The typical mild weather of a southern English Christmas is a recurrent hazard in the dispensation of hospitality, and there are occasions when a guest brings as a present a brace of pheasants which are nothing less than an embarrassment.

Usually the birds had been pretty high when the donor was given them (which is why he was given them). By the time they reach you they have to be hung up in the garage, in the hope that a good antiseptic frost will halt what is obviously a galloping rate of decomposition.

Fogs in March are said to mean frosts in May; unfortunately, any hope that it will freeze in December as it froze in May is in vain. By the time Christmas is over, and you are able to have the pheasants plucked professionally, no plucking is needed, or indeed possible, and the corpses are buried at the bottom of the garden.

Nowadays, when so many of one's friends have deep freezes, the likelihood of pheasants for Christmas, is very remote. They keep them for themselves, so that when you *do* get cold Christmas weather you have no pheasants for it to do any good to. All that happens then is that the snow leaves you with a lot of stranded, hungry guests.

The unannounced gift of pheasants on Christmas Eve (which is when—if you are going to get any—you usually get them) does little to help with the catering. Even in the pink of condition, unless they are ready for the oven they cannot be used to vary or augment the menus you have laboriously arranged to see you, your guests and any passing trade through the festive season.

The actual stock-piling (if that is the term) of food to last over Christmas involves considerable calculation, particularly in gauging the extent of everybody's appetite, deciding how much bread to get in, and keeping it at all edible for several days. This is a small problem, however, compared with the difficulty of ensuring some sort of variety of diet.

Too much cold meat, salad and baked potato soon gets to be humdrum, so for days before Christmas your kitchen is filled with a series of delicious smells created by your wife's peeling and chopping vegetables for soups, her making of *pâtés*, flans, puddings and pies to ensure that everybody's custom of over-eating is spiced with infinite variety.

During this period you yourself are not so idle either. You are out digging vegetables in the garden, lifting heavy casseroles and pans on to the stove and off it, taking the lids off and expressing your admiration, acting as official taster, and, most important of all, providing the cook with the right drink at the right moment and helping with the non-stop washing-up.

The eventual distribution of all this has to be done by a system of permutation and computation which, if applied to the football pools, would win you a fortune every week.

By the fourth day you're usually too exhausted to put the food on the table, so you throw the kitchen open as a free-for-all and encourage everybody to help themselves from the fridge, cut what they want from the cold turkey or beef, and have as much soup and nourishing rice as will immobilise them, or send them out after lunch for a healthy walk in the rain.


*FIELDS OF PLAY*

One indispensable item in any Christmas household entertaining nieces and nephews who have brought their parents with them is some sort of improvised playroom.

This is necessary because in addition to the presents *you* give them, children also get presents from their parents which, unlike yours, are usually expensive and nearly always the sort that needs floor-space to be enjoyed. The playroom must also be out of earshot, for in addition to the dartboards, clockwork toys, plastic speedway tracks and all the uproar that goes with them, you must provide a gramophone to play particularly noisy Christmas-present records on.

One of the many consolations of married life is the favourable economic consequence of being able to give people presents from both of you to both of them. This isn't very good for trade, but at least it usually leads to presents being useful, like a good bottle of wine or a lot of plants for the garden. And anyway it keeps the balance of payments steady. If one recipient gets one present, whether from one or two donors, he reciprocates with one present, and that is the end of trading for another year.

With children, on the other hand, there is none of this. They may give both of you a single present between you (chosen and paid for by their parents who understandably play the one-couple, one-present convention), but they expect one present from each aunt and uncle, whether they are married or not.

This is not just good business, but sound logic. How, children want to know, can two people give one present? Which of them gives what part of it? If you're given a book, are half the pages given by you and the other half by your wife? And, if so, which half? The first or the second?

You soon learn to avoid the two-donor gift. It is almost as unpopular as a present to be shared between two children.

In between all the eating, drinking and sleeping in your house, Christmas can involve you and your guests in the unavoidable Christmas merry-go-round of visiting friends in the neighbourhood. This is not peculiar to the country; it occurs just as much in any city village community.

How long the merry-go-round goes on depends on how long Christmas lasts. Or, rather, on the speed of the merry-go-round. A short Christmas means twice-daily visits; a seven-day Christmas means daily morning *or* evening visits, but not both on the same day.

As the guests are always the same on each occasion (only the hosts and the venues are different), the first gathering gives you a good idea of whether you will want to attend any of the others. In an intense, four-day series of matches you can meet exactly the same people twice in every twenty-four hours. The guests are not only the same every time: they are the same every year. It is only the guests spending Christmas with the *invités*, and are brought along too, who vary at all.

This annual ritual is in fact a model of good Coarse Entertaining. None of the incompatible crashers you get caught up with during the rest of the year is ever likely to be your host or a fellow guest on the merry-go-round.

Now and then you meet somebody new whom you find entertaining and sympathetic, and provided you meet them early on in the series it is comforting to know that there will be several more opportunities of meeting them again before everybody breaks up for the peace of *après-Noël*. Some unexpected and pleasing friendships are often struck up in this way.

A first gathering gives a good idea of whether you'll
want to attend any of the others

The custom of organised jollity and games at Christmas seems to have died out. At least, in the home. At nursery schools, and whatever kindergartens are called nowadays, traditional singing games are still performed—and rightly, because it ensures that the children don't grow up totally ignorant of the tunes and dances and rituals of what we are told, but in the circumstances can hardly believe, is a Children's Festival. If only it were. . . .

Jollity and game are, of course, more often found at children's parties than in the domestic surroundings of a family Christmas, where luxury, riot, feast and pop music prevail, and so do not concern you as host to visiting children. They get their parties when they get back to their own neck of the woods.

Nevertheless, there are still seasonal traditions to be observed, and every one of them affected by inflation. Chief of these is the money to put into the Christmas pudding. Not only will the silver sixpence now no longer buy even a newspaper, but thanks to an idiotic decimal system unlike anybody else's in history, the sixpence, so far from being levelled down, has been levelled up so much that it has been levelled out of sight. So we have to use the shilling or nickel, as pudding money—a classic case of 100 per cent inflation in the course of twelve short months between the last £ s d Christmas of 1970 and the first decimal Christmas of 1971. And you can't buy much of a newspaper for a shilling either, come to that.

Christmas crackers are another traditional item that has suffered from such regular and unbelievable inflation that you are forced to buy the smallest ones you can, and ensure their not being pulled by using them as table decoration only—scattered in such a way among the fruit and chocolates and boxes of dates, Carlsbad and

Elvas plums and Chinese figs, that they do not attract the children's attention.

The older Christmas hostess may consider it foolishly extravagant to display Carlsbad and Elvas plums and Chinese figs on the table, with children present, but curiously enough they seem to regard them as part of the decoration too. This is because these plums and figs are now so expensive and rarely seen, that they do not recognise them as something you can eat. So, all the more for us.

It is just possible, of course, that one of the children may taste one out of curiosity. In that case, it serves you right for putting them on the table in the first place. You should keep them out of sight, and bring them out only when the children have gone to bed; or, if you're really greedy, when everybody has left for home.

If you want to make sure of diverting any child's attention from the edible Christmas luxuries you really buy for yourselves, the production of fresh raspberries from the deep freeze works wonders.

## LET NOTHING YOU DISMAY

The ritual of setting the Christmas pudding alight with brandy is obligatory and easily maintained. It delights the children who are pyrophiles, if not actually pyromaniacs, by nature, and reassures the adults that the ghastly stodge they are expected to eat as a pagan rite will at least taste of alcohol. Some adults may feel that the brandy would be better drunk out of a glass than poured over a pudding. Not if they drank the brandy we use, they wouldn't.

The smooth working of the preparation, organisation

It delights the children

and mustering of material during the period immediately before Christmas is often interrupted by carol singing. Or, at least, by village children who come to the door at night in pairs, or even singly, and ask threateningly 'Want me to *sing*?'

As nobody has the time or inclination just at that moment to stand at the door and listen to the rather limited repertoire you are likely to be offered, hush money is willingly paid, willingly accepted and the incident is closed.

If you live on the outskirts of a village, as we do, the freebooting carol singers who threaten you (rarely, you are relieved to discover, in bands of more than three) make no pretence of singing for any good cause but their own. Charity begins at home and is supported entirely by your involuntary subscription.

Nearer the centres of villages, on the other hand, you are vulnerable to the attacks of massed choirs from which there is no protection, whom no hush money will silence. They do not ask you if you want them to sing; they don't even ask you if you want to listen. They just sing; and when they have finished the gentry are expected to ask them in—all twenty or thirty of them—for refreshment.

This, I am told, can lead to trouble, but not to the sort you would necessarily expect.

I know of an Essex village where just this sort of thing happened when, a few years ago, the choir performed outside the manor house, the last call before finishing their tour at the vicarage a few yards further on.

At the end of their performance the squire invited the singers in; they were given a wassail of sherry, and since their host was in the wine trade there was plenty of it and more where that came from.

In due course the carollers wassailed off to their last appointment, full of goodwill and oloroso, to serenade the vicar. They sang to him with heart and soul and voice and an increasingly deteriorating intonation and diction.

The vicar, who didn't have much of an ear for music, anyway, was perturbed less by the standard of the performance than by the obvious physical well-being and contentment of the performers. He addressed a few polite words of acknowledgment and retired into his vicarage, his dudgeon as high as his church.

The next morning the squire received by hand a letter from the vicar, who apologised icily for the behaviour of his choir when they had visited the manor house. A most regrettable happening. He did not know how to apologise. And only trusted that the squire would be good enough to forgive the appalling lapse of manners. Please believe him to be, etc., etc., etc.

The squire replied at once. The choir might be the vicar's, he said, but when they came to his house they were *his* guests and he would thank the vicar not only to confine his preaching to the pulpit but to refrain from criticising the behaviour of those who were guests in other people's houses.

The vicar, I hear, is now a bishop. It is believed he had a lot on the Prime Minister of the time.

Whether or not you are plagued with a chorus, instead of a group, of carol singers is largely a matter of luck. (We also have waits in our village; but they work up their vigorous brass-band thirst over at the Hall.) One thing is always certain about Christmas, however: that you find yourself stocking up right until the last moment before the shops shut, no matter how many months earlier you may have started.

What with the Special Xmas Offers in the cut-price liquor stores, and the old practical presents of a bottle some of your friends may give you, it usually escapes your memory that the children coming to stay with you, though they have no difficulty in eating the same food as adults (and eating all the adults under the table in doing so), nevertheless have peculiar tastes in drink.

We have a nephew and a niece who are half French, and so have no trouble drinking plonk. But between meals they have the now international taste of the modern child for coca-cola as well as for the usual orange, lemon and lime 'drinks'—items which, unlike plonk, are not normally found in one's cellar and so have to be specially got in.

If there is any of this rather alien corn left over after Christmas it is no good thinking of putting it away until next year. It won't keep that long. Nor will you be able to find any alcoholic drink to add to it that will make it palatable enough for you to drink it up yourselves. The only thing to do with it is to put it away until the summer, and, at first sign of a hot spell, bring it out to give to the gardener when it's 'very sweating'.

The exception to this, of course, is coke in tins or bottles. Both will keep without losing their nose and full-bodied fruitiness, though—so connoisseurs say—château-canned coke differs very strongly in character from château-*bottled* coke.

Christmas, it will be seen, remains much the same over the years, though in one respect it has changed radically, and for the worse.

In the comparatively short time we have lived in the country the tradesman's traditional practice of sending his customers a calendar, or some other mark of his gratitude for your esteemed custom, seems to have disappeared completely.

Instead of assuring you always of their best attention and their desire to serve you with as much pleasure in the future as in the past, you are now expected to tip the grocer, the garage, the butcher, the baker and—if you're a woman—the hairdresser. Why?

They used to thank you for buying things from them; now you reward *them* for all the charm and personal service they don't give you as they take your money from you—an unbelievable impertinence in the case of the grocer, with his record-breaking inflationary behaviour (see *The Grocer*, any issue).

All this in addition, of course, to the usual and well-earned Christmas boxes for the milk, the papers, the post and the dust. I wonder how long it will be before we're expected to tip the Income Tax collector.

# 5 Passing Trade

*COMFORT STATION*

There is one form of Coarse Entertaining which is peculiar to those who live in a capital city, whether it is London or New York, Paris or Rome, and that is what one might call entertaining the Passing Trade.

In the country you get none of this. You have to *invite* people to come and stay, give them road routes to follow, time-tables to catch trains with, meet them at the station.

If you live anywhere within three miles of Piccadilly Circus you find you are used like the lounge of the Grosvenor Hotel at Victoria, by friends from France, Italy, Scotland, the States, Haywards Heath and villages near Epping.

Friends, relations and in-laws, up for the day, leave their children with you to feed and amuse; and with this in mind you lay in a store of cake, buns and jam, only to find that what they really like is hot-buttered toast and marmalade.

Husbands and wives use you as a meeting place at the end of the day; you are in constant demand as a clandestine trysting place for your friends and their lovers.

Suitcases are left in the hall early in the morning for one's friends to change out of in the evening for the theatre or the opera or a City dinner.

After any party you go to you are always a stopping

place on the way home. 'Do come in for a moment and
have a drink,' you say. 'There's lots of rough red, if that's
all right for you.'

Rough red is just the thing at that time of night, they
tell you, so the invitation is accepted. You don't buy
your plonk in bottles, but in gallon jars, and a new con-
signment had arrived earlier in the day. Everything is
fine until you get the glasses out, fill them up and find
that the fools have delivered two gallons of red and very
sweet vermouth. There is not a drop of anything else
in the place to drink, not even a dribble of soda-water to
dilute it with or a bit of lemon peel to garnish it with.
As it is nearly 2 a.m. you can't do anything about it.

Newspapers give prizes for the best solution to a
dilemma of this kind. There is, of course, no solution.
You just agree tamely with your wretched, tactful
guests that you'd all of you had enough to drink already
at the party, and rise above it.

So far your home has served as a place for day boarders
to put their feet up in, and meet their friends. There are
times, however, when you cease to be the hotel lounge;
you become the hotel.

This is when friends or relations from abroad or out
of town decide to pay a short visit ('just a couple of days')
to London. You know nothing of their intention until
they have already arrived in London, when they will
ring up and say that there isn't a single hotel room to
be had (any fool would know that, in the middle of June),
and could you possibly put them up. Just for a night.
Honestly.

You agree with as welcoming an air as you can put on
(which isn't much, acting not being really in your line),
and make up your spare bed.

Naturally they have brought you a present from

abroad—a bottle of *eau de toilette* which has duty-free shop stamped on every sniff of it. It is a kind thought, however, even if it is poor compensation for the cost of the laundry, the enormous cooked breakfasts and, above all, the telephone calls you have to pay for.

In addition, you have to answer all their incoming calls, take messages for them when they're out and, because the flat is built that way, listen to their talking on the phone when they're in. The inescapable won't-take-no-for-an-answer, won't-be-any-trouble-at-all marauders who flop down on you are perhaps the only real drawback to living in a metropolis. More than ever, you realise the true horror of having other people at the breakfast table. Breakfast is the most intimate of all meals; it should be eaten in bed, and like bed it mustn't be shared with a third party.

While you live in London you become so accustomed to being used as what is called in Italy an *albergo diurno* ('a "daytime-hotel" providing "wash and brush up", bath, shave, etc.') that when you move to the country you naturally hope your old friends will do the same for you when you come up to town.

But they don't. A wave of mass emigration seems to have set in since you lived there, and you discover that most of your friends have left London to live in the country too.

All you can do then is to visit London less often, or more often for a short period at a time (back home in time for tea). When it comes to staying a night you are really foxed. What Londoner knows which hotel he should stay at? In all his born days only foreigners from Manchester or New York have ever stayed in hotels.

Rich or poor, the only thing to do is stay at the Ritz. It is very central, handy for the Tube, the chicken

. . . and could you possibly put them up . . .

sandwiches are excellent, and the gin and tonics are enormous.

Today we are relieved to find that a new generation of *albergo diurno* friends is coming along—the children of those who used to drop in on us. Among them are nephews who used to pass the time with us between trains from their prep school on one side of London to their home in Sussex. They were always miserable in London during these few hours, fretting to get back to the scent of green fields and baked beans on toast.

Now they are grown up they live in London and have become more typically Londoners than any of the rest of us who were born and bred there.

And thank goodness they have. The Ritz isn't as cheap as it was and without them we would have nowhere to stay the night in London at all.


## ACCORDING TO FREUD

To dumb Forgetfulness a prey
THOMAS GRAY


Whether you read Shakespeare, who talked of the 'parting guest', or Pope, who talked of the going guest, both writers were agreed that their guests should stand not upon the order of their going, but go at once.

Ways and means to speed the going guest who is so long a-parting after closing time in your house have already been suggested. With guests who have been to stay with you pressure has to be put on them to leave, not because your dinner is spoiling in the oven, but because they are likely to miss their train unless you drive them to the station at once.

A recurrent feature of departing guests is the discovery

after they've gone of things they've left behind—the most common being books, combs, toothbrushes and cigarettes. None of these items is much trouble to pack and send on.

The occasional jumper or cardigan left behind because the weather grew warmer is a bit more trouble—at any rate, for your your wife who has to tie it all up into a parcel.

Perhaps the worst of all, though, is the habit of girls leaving behind them pairs of knee-length boots—the sort with zips up the side and very soft flabby tops, which they thoughtfully bring with them to wear while showing their children the cows, or picking primroses.

(They'd like to pick wood anemones to take home with them too, but we can usually dissuade them. It is something generations and generations of Londoners have failed to learn: that wood anemones will be dead and useless by the time they get them home.)

Packing up boots like these to send on is like trying to wrap a pound of tripe for posting in brown paper and string, and expecting it not to slip out of both.

When the boots are really too floppy to make sense as a parcel we send them back in the smallest cardboard box we can find—usually something from the village post office which had originally contained two dozen Brobdingnag packets of wheat crystals.

This involves a lot of string, a lot of brown paper, a lot of cellophane tape, and a journey by car to the post office.

All right, it's a chore. But a pleasing one to anybody who believes Freud's theory that your unconscious leaves things behind in places your unconscious doesn't want to leave because it likes it so much there. And what, you ask yourself as you turn everything upside down in the

. . . like trying to wrap a pound of tripe

toolshed to find a box to post the boots in, could be more gratifying to know than that?

On the other hand, there are guests—not staying guests, but local in-for-a-drink guests—who don't believe in Freud, but know enough about it to leave something behind as an excuse to call in and fetch it. They craftily reckon that you will interpret their 'forgetfulness' in the usual Freudian manner, and so feel flattered that you should be so universally loved.

As you are no fool, when they ring up next morning to ask whether they had left a silk scarf in the hall last night, you say yes they had, and that you'll drop it in during the morning on your way to the station. This prevents them calling in for their lost property in time for a drink in the evening by firmly denying them any chance or need to do so, and implying clearly that you are going to London for the day, and therefore won't be back home by the time they'd like to scrounge another drink, anyway.

There is no surer way of ensuring an undisturbed everyday existence than insisting on fetching and carrying things which, if you didn't, would lead to other people doing it, and dropping in to pinion you with a lot of talk you can do without.

It is particularly important to do this when you have borrowed a book. The owners will always go out of their way to save you the trouble of returning it personally; they would love to come and fetch it. You forestall this by getting in first, and making sure that at the same time you fetch back any books you have lent them.

You are being extremely unfriendly of course, and deliberately so, in self-defence. But by your behaviour and kindness it looks as though you were being most obliging.


## TO FEED WERE BEST AT HOME

From its many manifestations discussed in this book, it will be clear that Coarse Entertaining does not mean primitive entertaining. On the contrary, it has a certain quality of *soigné* extravagance and the spontaneity of the personal touch that put most gracious livers to shame—which is quite likely at that, but what I mean is those who live gracious lives. The wine is often better and more plentiful, mistakes can be immediately rectified as the hostess has direct control over everything that goes on in the kitchen. We do not have to rely on *au pair* girls, or ageing couples from Spain or Sicily for help. The middle man/woman/girl is missed out and everything works more smoothly as a result.

## THANKS FOR THE MEMORY

The harassed etiquette authorities who write in women's magazines on how what somebody in our village has aptly christened The Cut Glass Set should behave as hosts and guests, deplore the modern decline in the bread-and-butter letter. This is hardly surprising. People who have to read about etiquette in order to know how to behave at the dinner table are not very likely to know what a bread-and-butter letter is anyway.

The custom of writing bread-and-butter letters after a pleasant evening or weekend has, fortunately, not died out. Coarse Entertaining, being good entertaining, naturally merits a guest's thanks, and it is not regarded as enough, as it is in some circles, to ask your hosts back the following week and think you've done all you need because, after all, you said thank you for your dinner when you left, didn't you?

The bread-and-butter telephone call is frowned on by some, but it can very often be more satisfying than a letter.

Any good dinner party will lead to guests and their hostess wanting to discuss it the next day. Questions too trivial or complicated to put in a letter can be asked easily on the telephone and receive an immediate and equally trivial or complicated answer.

There are some people, however, who are just temperamentally incapable of writing to say thank you for anything—Christmas presents, a night's lodging, or a book you think you might amuse them.

You are naturally irritated and offended, but on reflection this is probably unfair. It is obviously psychological—as the G.P. says when he doesn't know why you have a temperature of 102 degrees. And like the G.P., I know of no cure.

# 6 Counting Your Blessings

The first of earthly blessings, independence
GIBBON

The outsider, glancing casually through this book, will
probably be surprised at the omission of what, in at
least one sense of the adjective, could be described as the
coarse entertaining of the wedding-eve stag party. Nobody
but an outsider would notice this, for it is an institution
which offends against our most cherished principles
and is therefore outside our orbit.

It is exclusive, anti-feminist and consequently sexually
discriminating. It is also very childish.

From what I hear, however, the stag party is beginning
to die out. This is encouraging, for it means that at least
one of the more imbecile displays of the Anglo-Saxon
schoolboy mentality is being grown out of. It is only
the eternally adolescent male who would organise a kind
of wake to brighten the last hours of 'freedom' of a friend
and fortify him against the living death of marriage, with
all its terrors and seaside-picture-postcard promise of
brawny, bullying wives, waiting up for their husbands
with rolling pins.

While there is always the hope that the Anglo-Saxons
are, in fact, growing up, the stag party's decline may well
be due to the increasing shortage of protagonists who
need commiserating with. No young man today is going
solemnly to leave the girl he has been living with for

months to go out for the evening with the boys on an all male booze-up merely because they're due to get married next day.

Invitations, by all the canons of Coarse Entertaining, are for both members of the household, or they are not accepted.

Which is why we are spared the stag party.

Whatever some may consider its shortcomings, at least Coarse Entertaining does not involve you in the financial and organisational worries you would suffer if you had to follow the rules laid down by Emily Post in her *Blue Book of Social Etiquette*. (The term 'blue' hardly seems the right word to describe a book of quite alarming correctness and purity. Perhaps it was a publisher's trick to catch the eye, like nudes on paperback covers of Jane Austen.)

Even in our modest world it costs the parents of a bride a pretty new penny to lay on the props and pro-vender custom requires. That they are not subject to Mrs Post's social code and standards is a blessing well worth counting.

The Blue Book insists that in addition to the usual engraved invitation cards, the services of a professional secretary, the trousseau, the awnings and decorations for the church and the house, the engagement of choir, soloists and organist at the church (though the choir and soloists—like those silk sheets—are not obligatory, you will be pleased to hear), the boxes of wedding cake, the carriages or motors for the bridal party from house to church and back, the Collation (which sounds highly ecclesiastical, and is in fact a term used in the Catholic Church), and the champagne—in addition to all this, the parents of the bride are responsible for hiring the orchestra at the reception.

The details of this final obligation will intrigue all who are interested in the arts. An orchestra, says Emily Post, 'may mean fifty pieces with two leaders'.

The idea of two leaders for a fifty-piece orchestra is something quite new. All one can think is that some smart orchestra-booker must have talked Mrs Post into believing that by having two leaders she was having twice as good an orchestra as anybody else.

How the division of the two leaders' labour was to be arranged is not explained. Perhaps one of them looked after the strings, while the other looked after the wind and percussion.

Or perhaps the leaders took it in turn to conduct; or perhaps the second leader was there to take over when the first leader got too drunk mingling with the guests to climb back on to the stand. The whole scheme has more than a hint about it of the finale of the Marx Brothers' *Night at the Opera*.

However, as Mrs Post goes on to say, the orchestra need not be a fifty-piece combo; it could also mean a piano, violin and drum, or a violin, harp and guitar.

I cannot see the need for a drum in the first of the two trios, unless it is there to play a roll to introduce the embarrasingly facetious speeches always made on these occasions. (Why a toast to the happy couple can't be proposed and drunk without a speech, I have never understood. Toasts are for drinking, not for listening to.)

The drum has otherwise little musical part to play in the repertoire usually trotted out at wedding receptions— unless, of course, the trio consisted of Teddy Wilson, Stephane Grappelli and Philly Joe Jones.

The second chamber music group, of violin, harp and guitar, seems to me to have endless possibilities. It is a most unusual combination of instruments, with a fascinating range of unusual colour and mood capable of inspiring any composer. And, I would say, entirely wasted on a wedding party.

## BLESSINGS WE COULD DO WITH

It is customary in Society to seat an engaged couple next to each other at every dinner party they go to. Once you are married, however, hostesses the world over make sure that though you may arrive and leave her house together, once you are in it you and your true love will never meet again.

As you never sit next to your spouse at your own dinner parties, when can you sit next to them, if not in other people's homes? Nobody ever answers the question.

Only at intimate parties of not more than four people

Toasts are for drinking, not for listening to

altogether is this enforced separation tolerable, because then conversation is general and so none of you misses anything.

But once there are six or eight at table you lose the chance of your both being able to talk to the same person if you want to, or—most important—to each other if you don't.

The seating at a table for six should be arranged like this when you are guests:

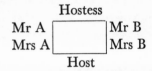

Hostess

Mr A      Mr B
Mrs A     Mrs B

Host

Mr and Mrs A can then both talk to their hostess and their host in turn, and Mr and Mrs B can do the same. This avoids one of the most frustrating things about any other dinner party: being unable as a married couple to share a third person's company, so that when you get home you have to tell your spouse how you wish they had been able to talk to the person you sat next to at dinner on the opposite side of a table.

It may be objected that in this way you, Mr and Mrs A, never get to talk to Mr and Mrs B. True, you don't both of you get to, but the hostess can link Mr A and Mr B, and the host can link Mrs A and Mrs B, so that both of you get to know your opposite numbers.

With eight at table the number of permutations is increased by the introduction of an unmarried couple, Mr C and Miss D.

This will inevitably mean that either host or hostess is going to be flanked by a member of their own sex, and the conventional alternation of M with F can be restored only by having ten people at the table. And that's too

many, just to observe a tidy convention. The seating
for eight, therefore, is:

Hostess

| Mr A | | Mr B |
| Mrs A | | Mrs B |
| Mr C | | Miss D |

Host

In this way the hostess can talk to both Mr A and Mr B
and their wives as before; Mr and Mrs A can talk to
Mr C; Mr and Mrs B can talk to Miss D; the host can
talk to Mrs A and Mr C, to Mrs B and Miss D; and to
Mr C and Miss D.

This may be disturbing to those brought up to the
custom of breaking up married couples merely because
it is a custom, but to the slightly shy in company that
may include people they are meeting for the first time
(this happens even in the practice of Coarse Entertaining),
to be spared the almost choreographic ritual of small-
talking first to your neighbour on one side, then to your
neighbour on the other, is a great relief.

Of course, the system I propose can often result in either
host or hostess or both having nobody to talk to when the
married couples go into huddles, or turn their attention
(at the eightsome meal) to Mr C and Miss D, but who's
going to complain of that?

As a host I find a period as dummy enables me to get
down to serious eating and drinking. There are altogether
too many interruptions of a host's, and a hostess's,
enjoyment of their own food and wine at most dinner
parties.

# 7 Dilemmas, Crises and Other Situations

Informality in all things, while it is one of our most sacred principles, and enjoyed by both hosts and guests, can nevertheless lead to a number of perils and hazards for the host, and occasionally for the guest.

Everybody must know the feeling of standing on the doorstep of somebody's house, and suddenly wondering in a panic if it is the right day. It nearly always is. But one day it isn't: you are a week too early. This situation, affecting both host and guest, is the result either of lack of co-ordination, failure of communication, or plain aberration—usually all three. It nearly always happens when the invitation, given over the telephone, is for lunch on a Sunday. 'Next Sunday' nearly always turns out to have been Sunday week.

Usually it is the host who feels worst about it; he is upset because he knows how his guests must feel, and he is even sorrier that there is absolutely nothing in the house to run up a makeshift meal with. The guests for their part are less disappointed by not getting the lunch they hoped for (after all, they'll be coming the following Sunday for it), than upset because they know how their host must feel.

Once every two years or so, when you've invited a few people in for Sunday drinks on the day summertime ends, a couple asked for 12.30 (when else?) will turn up at 11.30, having forgotten that they should have put their clocks back.

You have only just finished your leisurely, paper-reading breakfast, nobody has washed up, and the last thing you want is a drink before even the pubs are open.

All you can do is pour a drink for your visitors (whom you don't know very well, anyway), concoct some near-soft drink which is likely to make you sick so soon after your breakfast coffee, and at the first opportunity nip up to the bedroom and telephone the rest of the people you've invited to come over as soon as possible. One of the people you've asked can't be reached, and when she eventually arrives at 12.45 GMT she is embarrassed because she's convinced she's late: everybody has obviously been drinking for hours.

Guests who arrive for lunch on the wrong day and guests who arrive at the wrong time for drinks on a Sunday are nothing, however, compared to those who arrive for the wrong meal.

If you've expected them for dinner and they arrive for lunch they can be sent away to come back later. But if you've invited them for lunch and they come for dinner there's nothing to be done.

Telephone them when you've waited lunch for an hour? There is no reply. Perhaps they're on their way. They aren't, as you begin to suspect after waiting for another half an hour; '12.45 for 2.30' wasn't how you had put it, exactly. They've gone out for the day, and have planned to be back at just the right time to come to dinner.

And come to dinner, they do. You have to improvise; which means pasta and omelettes, and serve them right.

There are two kinds of unexpected guests: those who are expected, but come at an unexpected time, and those who aren't expected at all, ever, but get brought along by somebody you *are* expecting.

The second type happens to you when those you invite suddenly get landed with a house-guest, and you say sure bring them along. You are not obsessed by the symmetry of table plans and the neat alternation of M with F, so you manage to squeeze in the extra guest though you have to sit him on a bathroom chair to do so.

Another problem is the guest, expected or unexpected, who turns out to be a vegetarian, without anybody having warned you.

Vegetarians usually cause more embarrassment than trouble—mainly because you have been unable to make any provision for them; but so far as feeding them goes, they are usually pretty accommodating, and seem to be able to make a hearty meal out of a boiled egg and vegetables.

Acts of God are probably the most powerful source of trouble for any host.

On the grounds that you're nearer God's heart in a garden, than anywhere else on earth, the country dweller gets extra generous personal attention when God's Acts are being distributed.

Thunderstorms, floods, droughts, frosts, and the east winds that bring the farm's dungheap to your very nostrils, are such everyday manifestations of divine action that they are barely noticed.

Now and then, however, God comes out with a real humdinger of an Act—with the accent on the hum. This is the Plague of the Dead Mice.

The mice don't all die at once under the floorboards. They die in a carefully arranged sequence from the middle of December to the middle of March. The sequence is such that whenever one dead mouse has been located and removed, another dead mouse takes its place, and the process of putrefaction is so ordered that the peak of pong is reached whenever you have people coming to stay, or to dine, or to see you about something very important.

Indeed, for many years, as he lived nearby, the editor of a periodical I write for once a year, used to come and fetch my piece towards the end of February, which was his deadline. But I hardly needed him to remind me of the date. Every year, when the deadline approached, there was a dead mouse in full pong under the landing floorboards. It was an Act of God that explained the origin of the term 'deadline' a little too literally.

Dead mice under floorboards can be dealt with eventually. Dead mice behind the panelling of a house with eighteen-inch thick walls of wattle, daub and lambs wool behind a brick exterior, are at the mercy of the Lord who, in his infinite wisdom, will alone decide when the stinking has to stop.

Meanwhile, people come in for drinks on a cold February Sunday morning. The drawing room smells like frying garlic (which makes a change from the landing, where it smells like boiling brussels sprouts).

Your only hope is to open all the windows wide, turn on two electric fires in addition to the welcoming (but not very warming) wood fire in the grate. If they can't smell the mouse your guests will think you unnecessarily eccentric fresh air fiends, especially as you have never really looked healthy fresh-air types at all. If they can smell the mouse, they are unlikely to remark on it, so you never know whether your drastic measures have worked or merely frozen everybody to death.

## QUESTION WITH ANSWER

People seem to smoke less during meals than they used to. There was time when it was a general habit to light up between every course, if not actually between mouthfuls.

Do they now take more interest in their food and wine, or is it that they are better mannered? Or have they at last realised the seriousness of a dangerous habit? It is difficult to say.

One thing deters smoking, we discovered, and that is to keep some very stale filter-tip Gauloises to offer people when they have run out of, or forgotten to bring, their own cigarettes.

We tell them the Gauloises are straight off the Dieppe–Newhaven boat. So they were—eight years ago. In desperation they accept your offer. Nobody ever smokes more than one, and lives to tell the tale.

## QUESTION WITHOUT ANSWER

If you can't argue in your own house with a guest, and a guest can't argue with his host, what are you to do?

Find neutral ground, I suppose.

But where do you find that, late after dinner—unless you both go round to somebody else's place?

Or are challenges issued to 'come outside', perhaps?

It hardly seems worth it, just to dispute the religious aspects of abortion and the Pope's refusal to admonish the MCC.

## QUICK CURTAIN

An embarrassment all too frequently shared by a host and his guest, is when the guest does not know everything he should about another guest he is talking to, and drops a reverberant clanger.

This usually happens when a party is too big and introductions get a little perfunctory as the place fills up.

The most brilliant example I know of a dropped clanger and an inspired recovery bears recording as a model for everybody who may find themselves in a similar situation (and who doesn't?).

That fine actor Ernest Thesiger (himself described by *Debrett* rather reluctantly as 'a member of the dramatic profession') once found himself at a large dinner party, sitting next to a young woman whom he treated to a colourful diatribe on the decadence and depravity of the English aristocracy.

'Take that one over there,' said Thesiger, indicating a woman some way up the table, 'she's typical. Cruel to her children, beastly to her servants, snobbish and vicious.'

'That's my mother,' said the girl.

'Good!' exclaimed Thesiger, slapping the table with delight, 'Then you know *exactly* what I mean!'

## A LITANY FOR HOSTS

From lipstick and make-up on towels;
From refusal to use the kleenex, prominently put there
for them to use instead (or do they all think they're
actors?),
*Good Guests, deliver us*
From cigarettes stubbed out on papier mâché coasters;
From cigarette butts thrown down the loo;
From cigarette butts thrown into the fireplace in
summer, and on the lawn at any season;
From cigarettes smoked in bed,
*Good Guests, deliver us*
From dogs brought to stay without warning, that
widdle on the grass and kill it, and interrupt con-
versation as no cat is ever bad-mannered enough
to do;
From the habit of using every one of the 5 towels on
glorious display in the guest bathroom for *one*
person to choose from,
*Good Guests, deliver us*
From randy husbands, shrill-voiced wives, broken
glasses, broken springs, and soda-water on the
furniture,
*Good Guests, deliver us*
From outstayed welcomes, and drinking us out of
house and home,
*Good Guests, deliver us*

## A LITANY FOR GUESTS

From bedrooms without curtains, waste paper baskets
or ash trays;
From dim bedside lights;
From basins without mirrors over them, and no chairs
to put your clothes on;
From boiled bread and wet lettuce,

*Good Hosts, deliver us*

From pillows stuffed with old goloshes;
From eiderdowns that slip off on to the floor;
From double beds with troughs down the middles,
cold bathwater, blunt knives and bottled mayonnaise,

*Good Hosts, deliver us*

From the idea that if they *do* have curtains in the bedrooms they're any use unless they are interlined and
proof against the summer dawn's early light and
the din from the birds that goes with it;
From warm drinks and fruit cup, damp beds, sweet
sherry and too-hot curries,

*Good Hosts, deliver us*

From breakfasts with starch-reduced bread, instant
coffee, sweet jellied marmalade, hot hard-boiled
eggs, unspreadable hard-frozen butter straight from
the fridge,

*Good Hosts, deliver us*

## A LITANY FOR US ALL

From frozen taps and smoking chimneys, death watch
beetle and rising damp;
From power cuts, squeaking floor boards, and over-
flowing lavatory cisterns;
From jackdaws that fall down the chimney and beams
you hit your head on;

From over-polished parquet and sliding rugs, cheap towels that don't absorb water and raincoats that do;

From window cleaners who arrive when you're in your bath;

From neighbours who spray their weeds and kill your roses;

From unbidden guests, who (said Shakespeare, and he was no fool) are often welcomest when they are gone;

From other people's newspapers delivered in error;

And from all other Acts of God and civil commotion, disposable bottles, over-chlorinated water, beer in tins, another dead mouse under the close-carpeted bedroom floor, *Good Lord, deliver us and God Bless Our Home*

**ENVOI**

If all be true that I do think,
There are five reasons we should drink;
Good wine—a friend—or being dry—
Or lest we should be by and by
Or any other reason why.

HENRY ALDRICH (1648–1710)
*Dean of Christ Church*

*Ringmer,*
*Sussex*